INTRODUCTION BY R.L. STINE

Dear Readers:

When I was a kid back in Ohio, our lives pretty much revolved around comic books. My friends and I carried big stacks of them everywhere. We read them over and over, we traded them, we talked about them incessantly.

Of course, my favorites were the EC horror comics, such as *Tales from the Crypt* and *The Vault of Horror*. Those comics were big influences on me. They gave me the enthralling idea of combining horror with humor.

Back then, I never dreamed I would get a chance to write a comic book series. So the Man-Thing series has been a dream come true for me. Taking that massive garbage heap of a character and making him come alive was a wonderful challenge for me.

Thank you, Marvel. And thank you, especially, Germán Peralta and Rachelle Rosenberg for making my first-ever comic book story look so GOOD!

R.L. STINE

May 2017

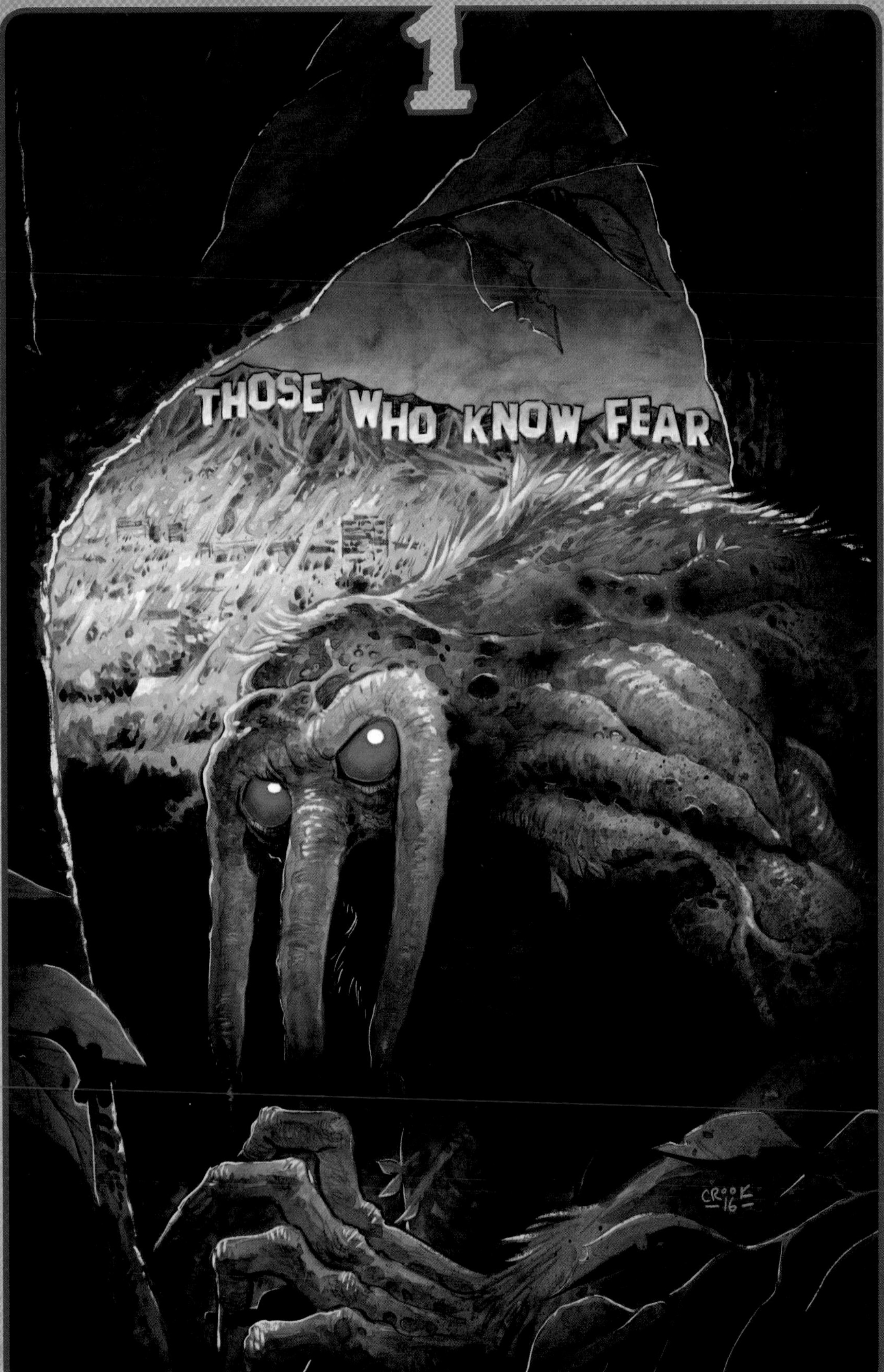
1
THOSE WHO KNOW FEAR
CROOK 16

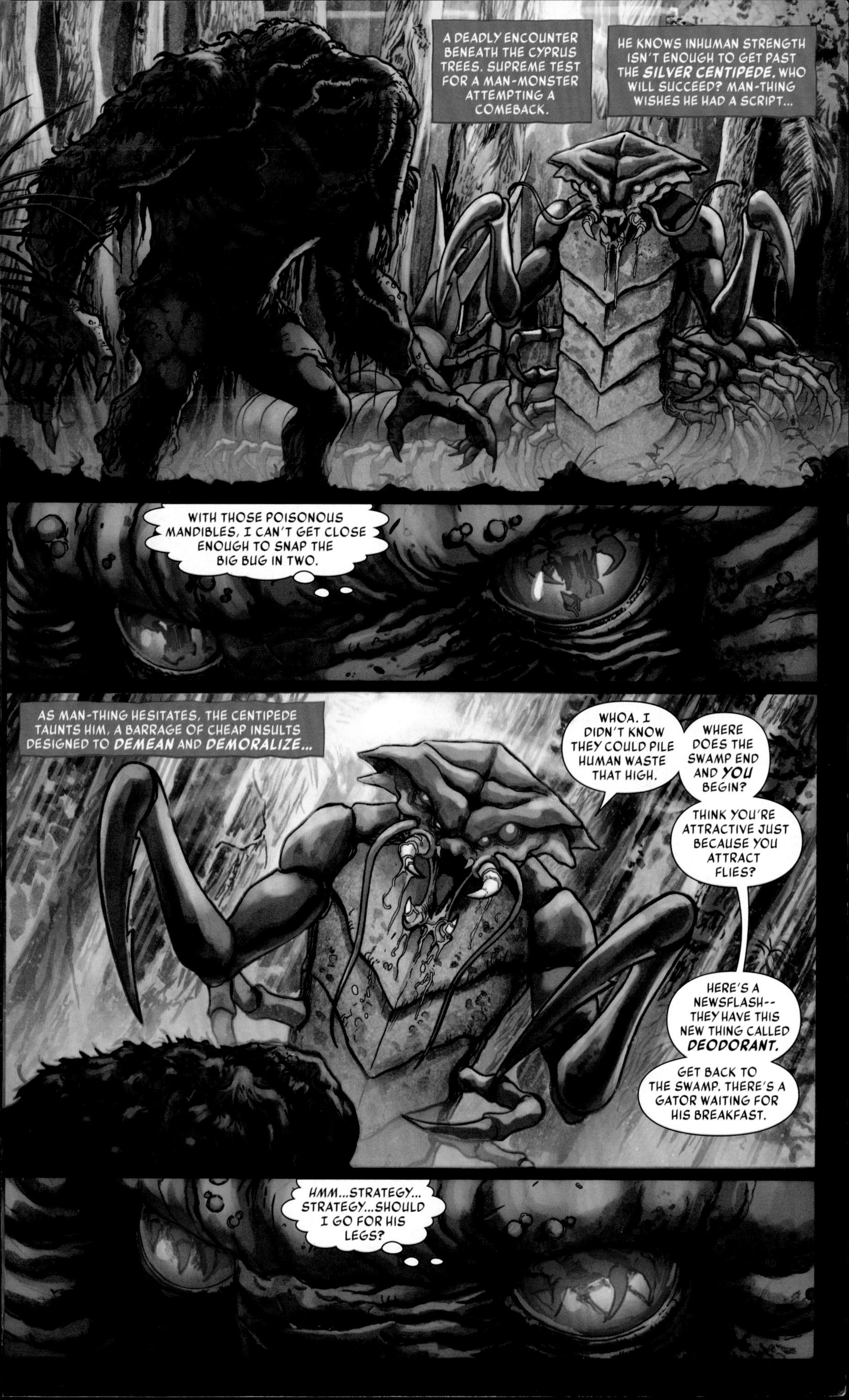
A DEADLY ENCOUNTER BENEATH THE CYPRUS TREES. SUPREME TEST FOR A MAN-MONSTER ATTEMPTING A COMEBACK.
HE KNOWS INHUMAN STRENGTH ISN'T ENOUGH TO GET PAST THE SILVER CENTIPEDE. WHO WILL SUCCEED? MAN-THING WISHES HE HAD A SCRIPT...
WITH THOSE POISONOUS MANDIBLES, I CAN'T GET CLOSE ENOUGH TO SNAP THE BIG BUG IN TWO.
AS MAN-THING HESITATES, THE CENTIPEDE TAUNTS HIM, A BARRAGE OF CHEAP INSULTS DESIGNED TO DEMEAN AND DEMORALIZE...
WHOA. I DIDN'T KNOW THEY COULD PILE HUMAN WASTE THAT HIGH.
WHERE DOES THE SWAMP END AND YOU BEGIN?
THINK YOU'RE ATTRACTIVE JUST BECAUSE YOU ATTRACT FLIES?
HERE'S A NEWSFLASH-- THEY HAVE THIS NEW THING CALLED DEODORANT.
GET BACK TO THE SWAMP. THERE'S A GATOR WAITING FOR HIS BREAKFAST.
HMM...STRATEGY... STRATEGY...SHOULD I GO FOR HIS LEGS?

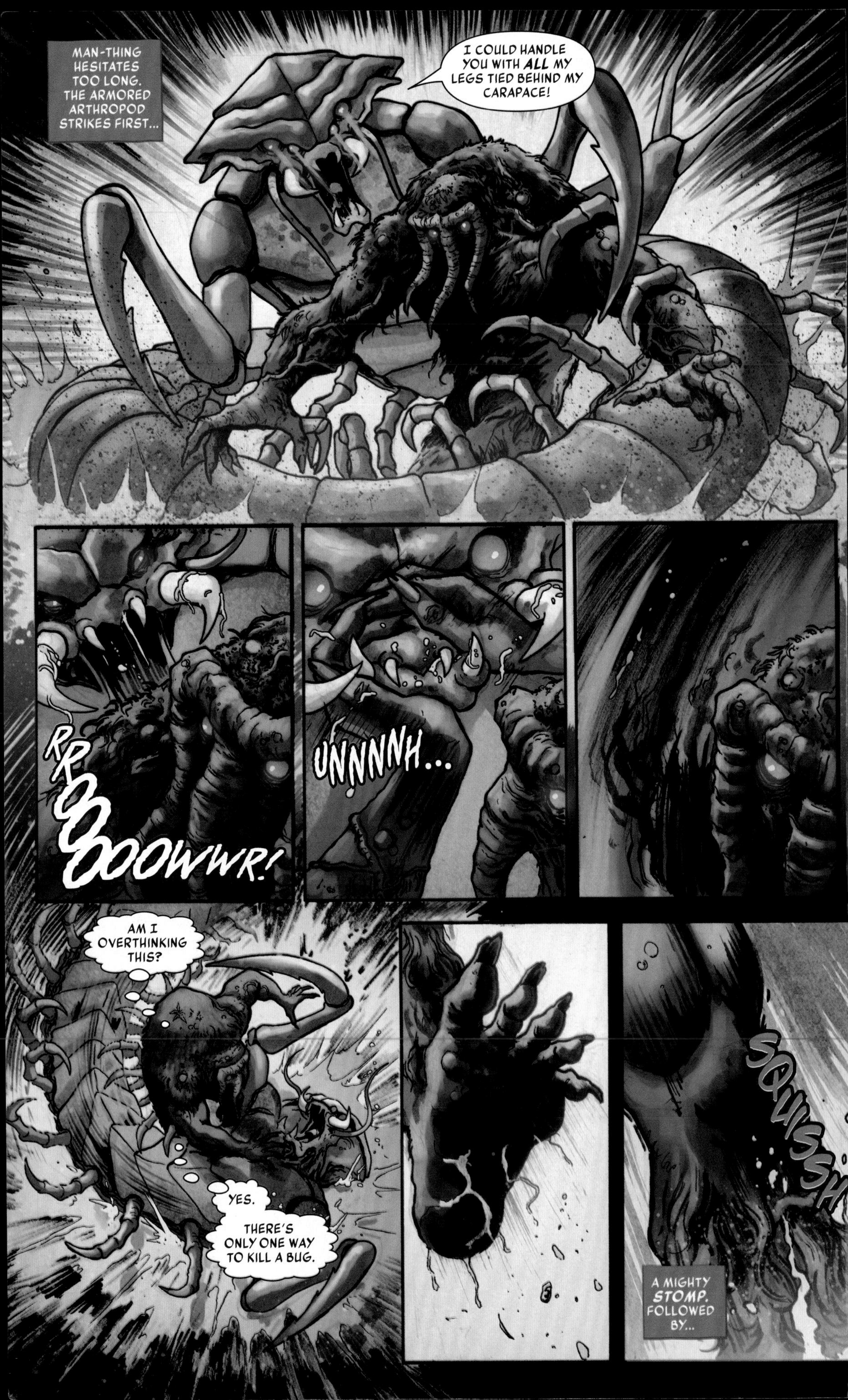
MAN-THING HESITATES TOO LONG. THE ARMORED ARTHROPOD STRIKES FIRST...
I COULD HANDLE YOU WITH ALL MY LEGS TIED BEHIND MY CARAPACE!
RROOOOOWWR!
UNNNNH...
AM I OVERTHINKING THIS?
YES.
THERE'S ONLY ONE WAY TO KILL A BUG.
SQUISSH
A MIGHTY STOMP. FOLLOWED BY...

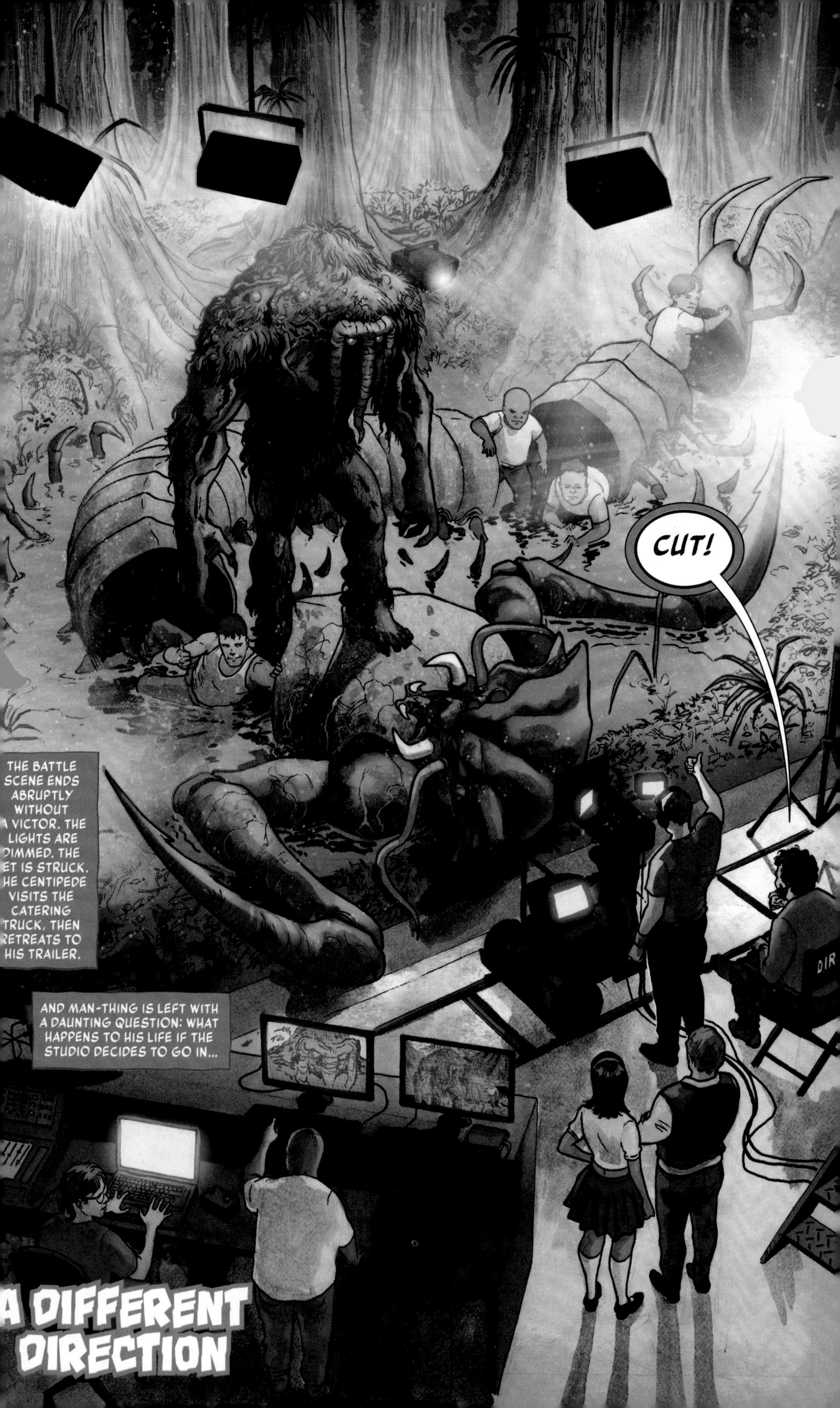
CUT!
THE BATTLE SCENE ENDS ABRUPTLY WITHOUT A VICTOR. THE LIGHTS ARE DIMMED. THE ET IS STRUCK. HE CENTIPEDE VISITS THE CATERING TRUCK, THEN RETREATS TO HIS TRAILER.
AND MAN-THING IS LEFT WITH A DAUNTING QUESTION: WHAT HAPPENS TO HIS LIFE IF THE STUDIO DECIDES TO GO IN...
A DIFFERENT DIRECTION
DIR

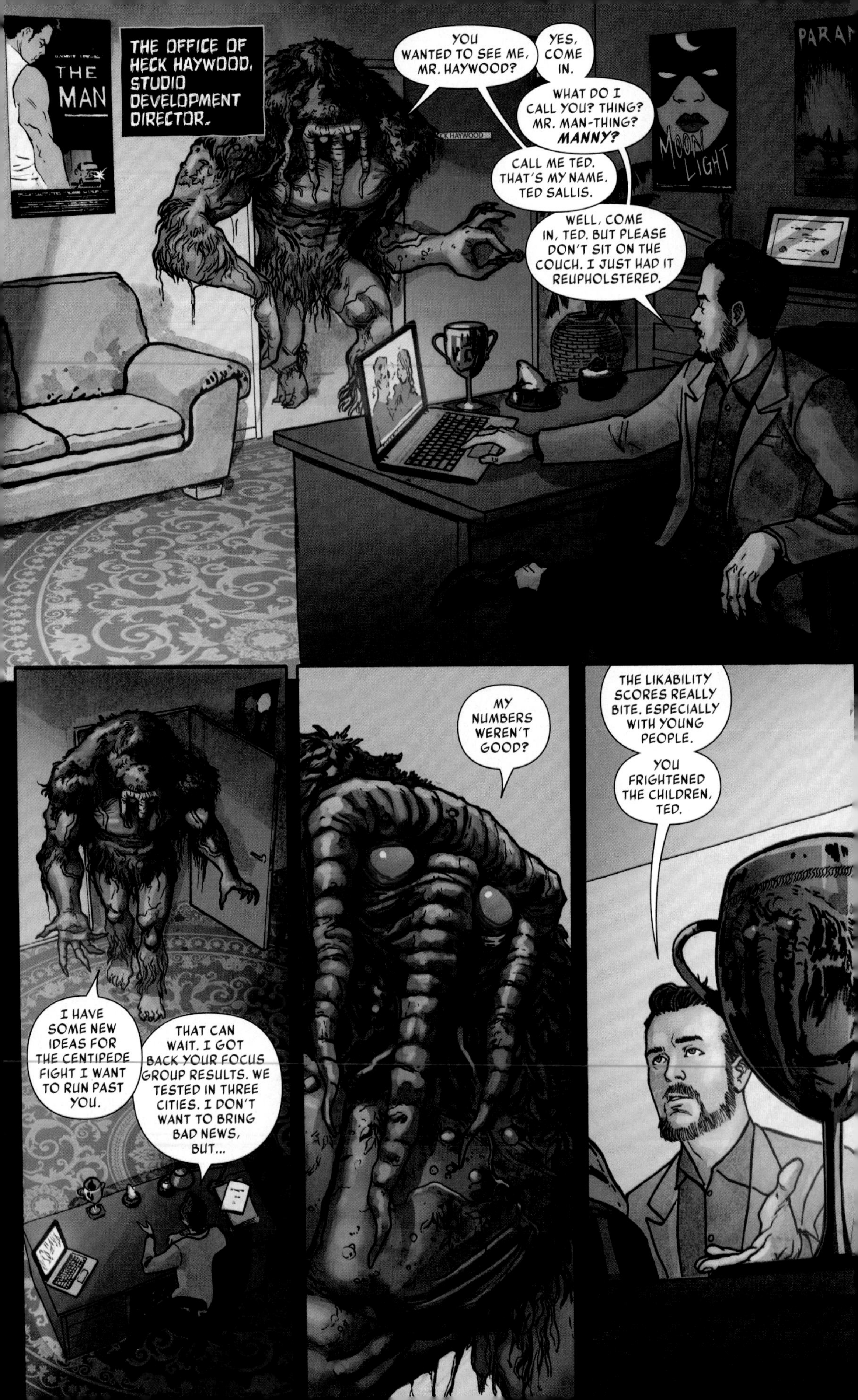

THE MAN
THE OFFICE OF HECK HAYWOOD, STUDIO DEVELOPMENT DIRECTOR.
YOU WANTED TO SEE ME, MR. HAYWOOD?
YES, COME IN.
WHAT DO I CALL YOU? THING? MR. MAN-THING? MANNY?
CALL ME TED. THAT'S MY NAME. TED SALLIS.
WELL, COME IN, TED. BUT PLEASE DON'T SIT ON THE COUCH. I JUST HAD IT REUPHOLSTERED.
MOON LIGHT
I HAVE SOME NEW IDEAS FOR THE CENTIPEDE FIGHT I WANT TO RUN PAST YOU.
THAT CAN WAIT. I GOT BACK YOUR FOCUS GROUP RESULTS. WE TESTED IN THREE CITIES. I DON'T WANT TO BRING BAD NEWS, BUT...
MY NUMBERS WEREN'T GOOD?
THE LIKABILITY SCORES REALLY BITE. ESPECIALLY WITH YOUNG PEOPLE.
YOU FRIGHTENED THE CHILDREN, TED.

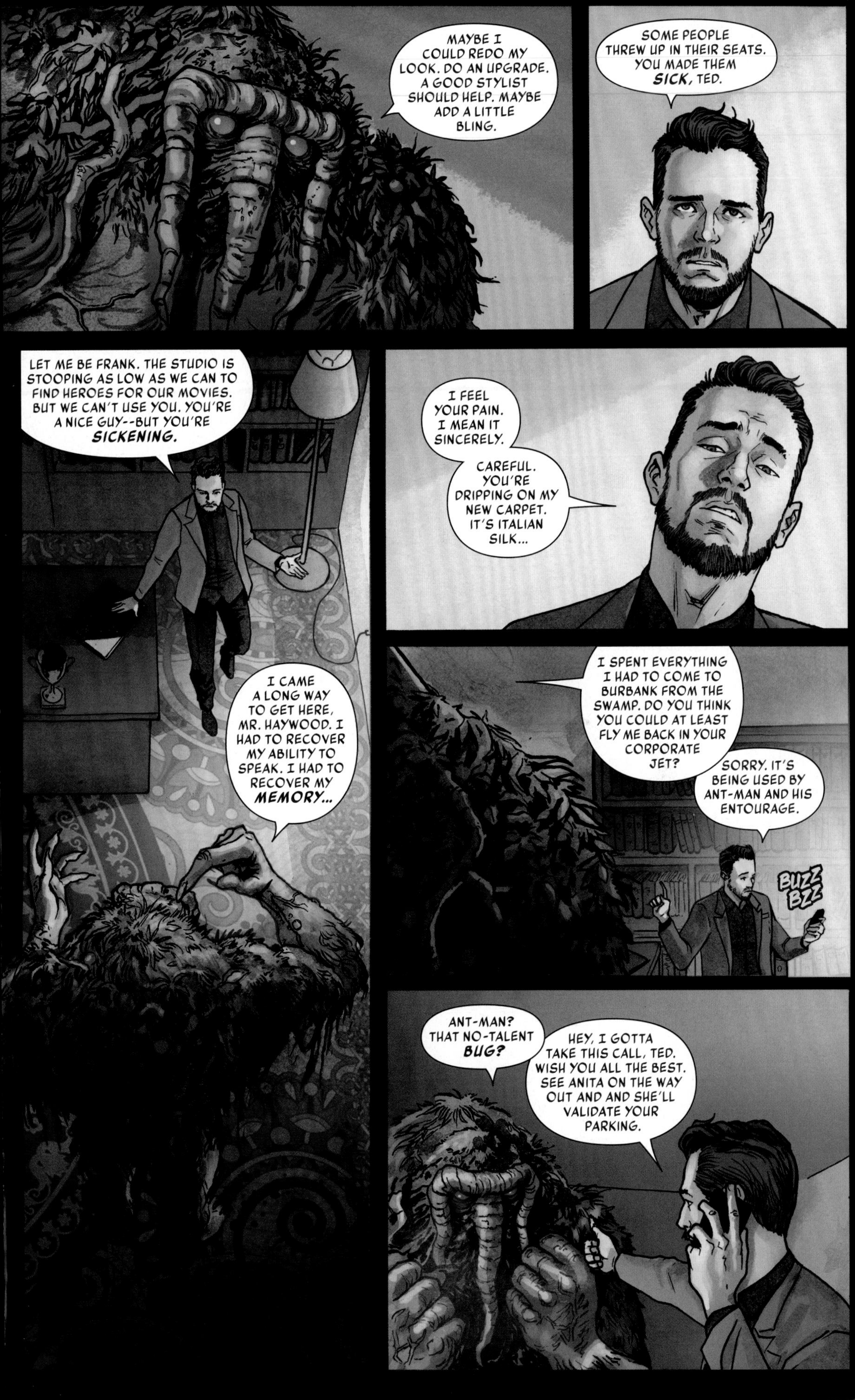
MAYBE I COULD REDO MY LOOK. DO AN UPGRADE. A GOOD STYLIST SHOULD HELP. MAYBE ADD A LITTLE BLING.
SOME PEOPLE THREW UP IN THEIR SEATS. YOU MADE THEM SICK, TED.
LET ME BE FRANK. THE STUDIO IS STOOPING AS LOW AS WE CAN TO FIND HEROES FOR OUR MOVIES. BUT WE CAN'T USE YOU. YOU'RE A NICE GUY--BUT YOU'RE SICKENING.
I CAME A LONG WAY TO GET HERE, MR. HAYWOOD. I HAD TO RECOVER MY ABILITY TO SPEAK. I HAD TO RECOVER MY MEMORY...
I FEEL YOUR PAIN. I MEAN IT SINCERELY.
CAREFUL. YOU'RE DRIPPING ON MY NEW CARPET. IT'S ITALIAN SILK...
I SPENT EVERYTHING I HAD TO COME TO BURBANK FROM THE SWAMP. DO YOU THINK YOU COULD AT LEAST FLY ME BACK IN YOUR CORPORATE JET?
SORRY. IT'S BEING USED BY ANT-MAN AND HIS ENTOURAGE.
BUZZ BZZ
ANT-MAN? THAT NO-TALENT BUG?
HEY, I GOTTA TAKE THIS CALL, TED. WISH YOU ALL THE BEST. SEE ANITA ON THE WAY OUT AND AND SHE'LL VALIDATE YOUR PARKING.

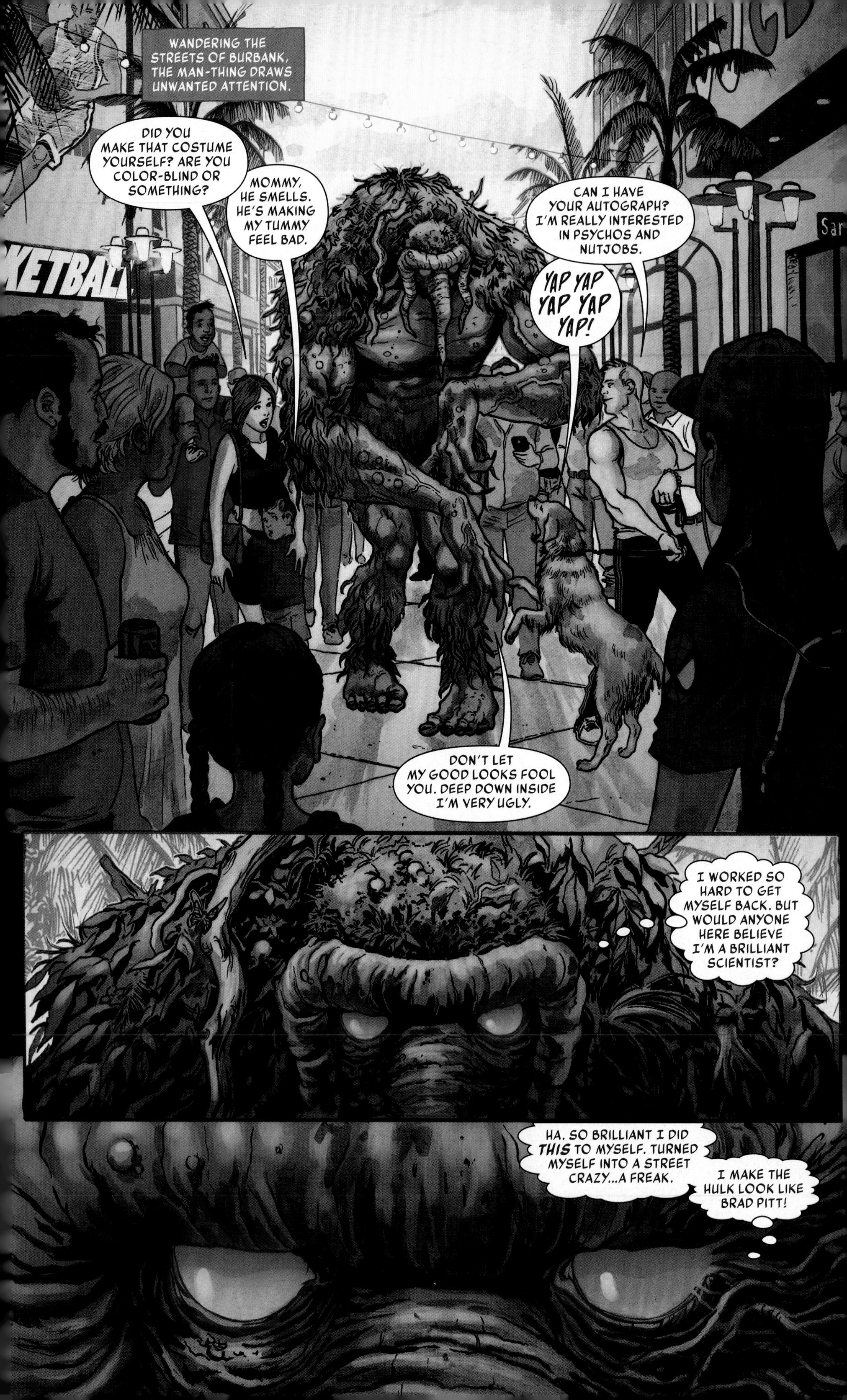
WANDERING THE STREETS OF BURBANK, THE MAN-THING DRAWS UNWANTED ATTENTION.
DID YOU MAKE THAT COSTUME YOURSELF? ARE YOU COLOR-BLIND OR SOMETHING?
MOMMY, HE SMELLS. HE'S MAKING MY TUMMY FEEL BAD.
CAN I HAVE YOUR AUTOGRAPH? I'M REALLY INTERESTED IN PSYCHOS AND NUTJOBS.
YAP YAP YAP YAP YAP!
DON'T LET MY GOOD LOOKS FOOL YOU. DEEP DOWN INSIDE I'M VERY UGLY.
I WORKED SO HARD TO GET MYSELF BACK. BUT WOULD ANYONE HERE BELIEVE I'M A BRILLIANT SCIENTIST?
HA. SO BRILLIANT I DID *THIS* TO MYSELF. TURNED MYSELF INTO A STREET CRAZY...A FREAK.
I MAKE THE HULK LOOK LIKE BRAD PITT!

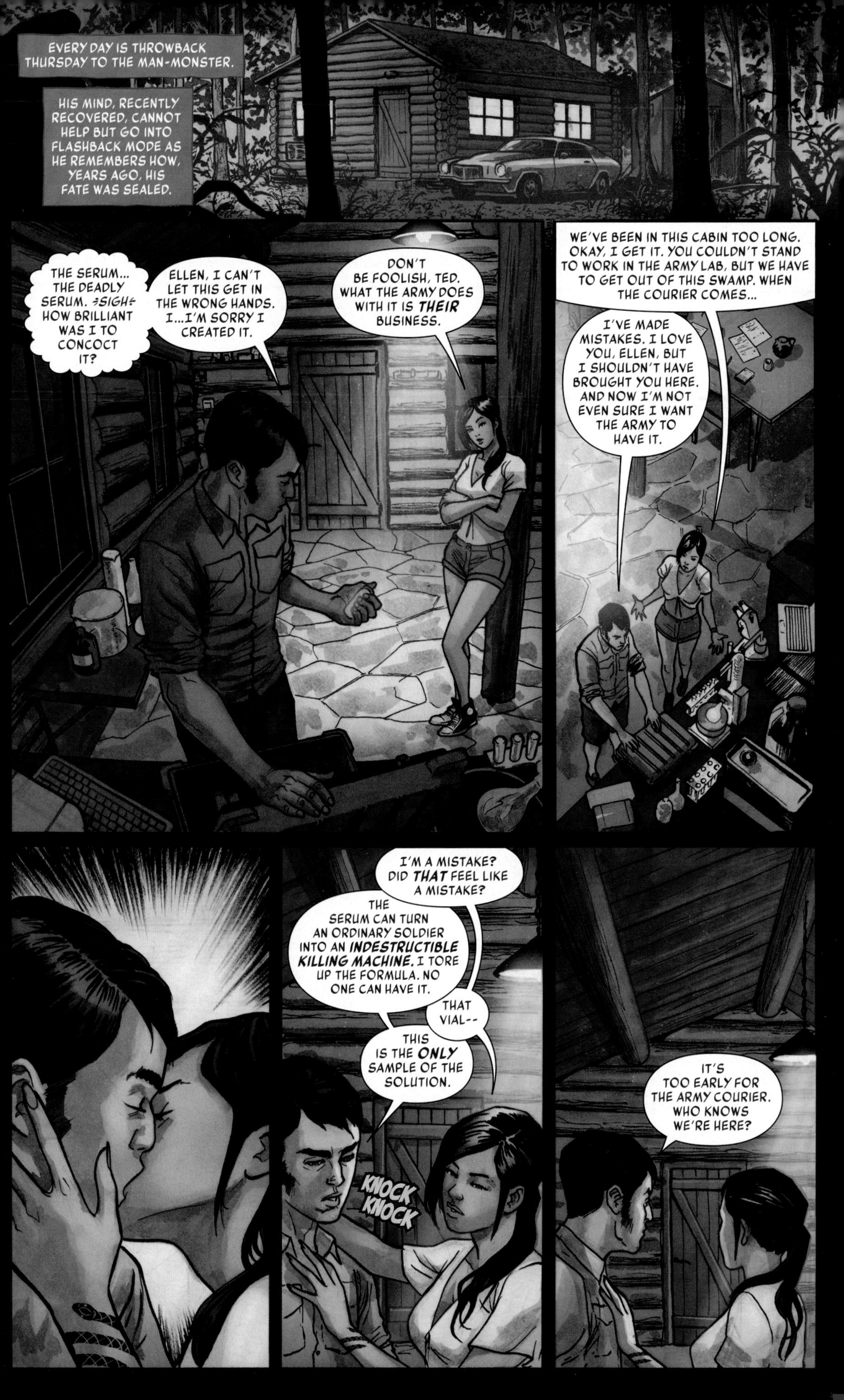
EVERY DAY IS THROWBACK THURSDAY TO THE MAN-MONSTER.
HIS MIND, RECENTLY RECOVERED, CANNOT HELP BUT GO INTO FLASHBACK MODE AS HE REMEMBERS HOW, YEARS AGO, HIS FATE WAS SEALED.
THE SERUM... THE DEADLY SERUM. ≠SIGH≠ HOW BRILLIANT WAS I TO CONCOCT IT?
ELLEN, I CAN'T LET THIS GET IN THE WRONG HANDS. I...I'M SORRY I CREATED IT.
DON'T BE FOOLISH, TED. WHAT THE ARMY DOES WITH IT IS THEIR BUSINESS.
WE'VE BEEN IN THIS CABIN TOO LONG. OKAY, I GET IT. YOU COULDN'T STAND TO WORK IN THE ARMY LAB, BUT WE HAVE TO GET OUT OF THIS SWAMP. WHEN THE COURIER COMES...
I'VE MADE MISTAKES. I LOVE YOU, ELLEN, BUT I SHOULDN'T HAVE BROUGHT YOU HERE. AND NOW I'M NOT EVEN SURE I WANT THE ARMY TO HAVE IT.
I'M A MISTAKE? DID THAT FEEL LIKE A MISTAKE?
THE SERUM CAN TURN AN ORDINARY SOLDIER INTO AN INDESTRUCTIBLE KILLING MACHINE. I TORE UP THE FORMULA. NO ONE CAN HAVE IT.
THAT VIAL--
THIS IS THE ONLY SAMPLE OF THE SOLUTION.
KNOCK KNOCK
IT'S TOO EARLY FOR THE ARMY COURIER. WHO KNOWS WE'RE HERE?

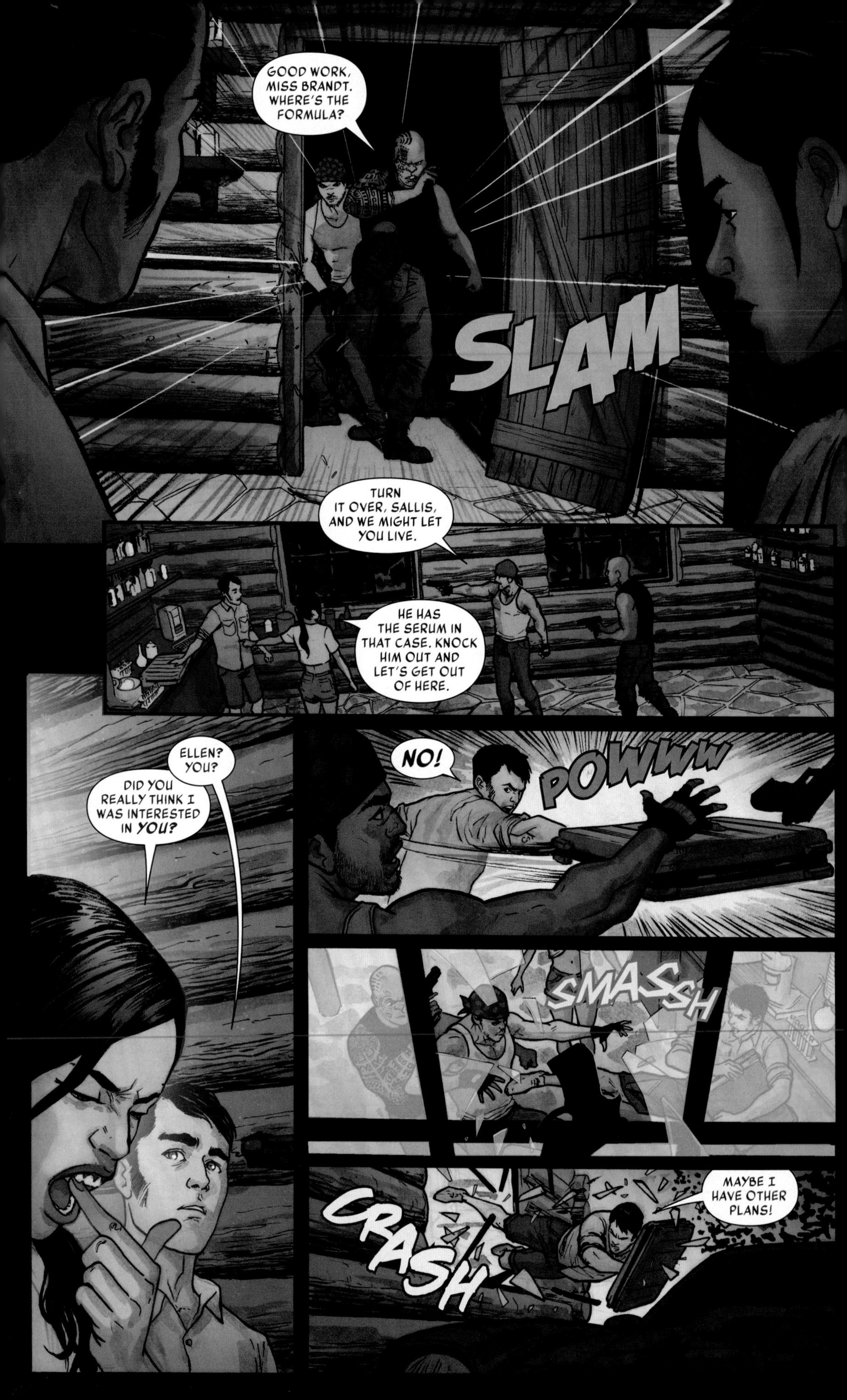
GOOD WORK, MISS BRANDT. WHERE'S THE FORMULA?
SLAM
TURN IT OVER, SALLIS, AND WE MIGHT LET YOU LIVE.
HE HAS THE SERUM IN THAT CASE. KNOCK HIM OUT AND LET'S GET OUT OF HERE.
ELLEN? YOU?
DID YOU REALLY THINK I WAS INTERESTED IN *YOU?*
NO!
POWWW
SMASSH
CRASH
MAYBE I HAVE OTHER PLANS!

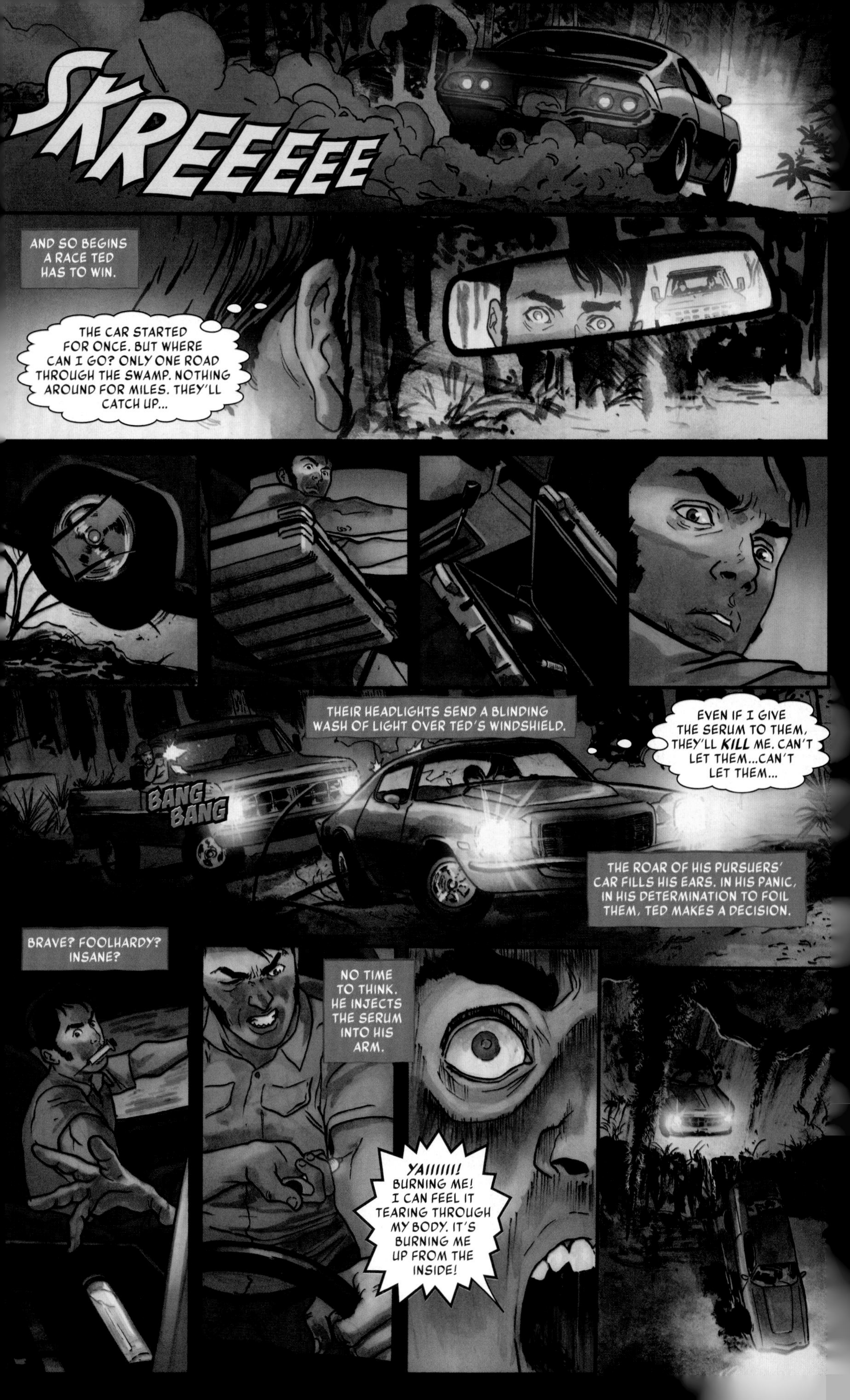
SKREEEEEE
AND SO BEGINS A RACE TED HAS TO WIN.
THE CAR STARTED FOR ONCE. BUT WHERE CAN I GO? ONLY ONE ROAD THROUGH THE SWAMP. NOTHING AROUND FOR MILES. THEY'LL CATCH UP...
THEIR HEADLIGHTS SEND A BLINDING WASH OF LIGHT OVER TED'S WINDSHIELD.
EVEN IF I GIVE THE SERUM TO THEM, THEY'LL **KILL** ME. CAN'T LET THEM...CAN'T LET THEM...
BANG BANG
THE ROAR OF HIS PURSUERS' CAR FILLS HIS EARS. IN HIS PANIC, IN HIS DETERMINATION TO FOIL THEM, TED MAKES A DECISION.
BRAVE? FOOLHARDY? INSANE?
NO TIME TO THINK. HE INJECTS THE SERUM INTO HIS ARM.
YAIIIIII! BURNING ME! I CAN FEEL IT TEARING THROUGH MY BODY. IT'S BURNING ME UP FROM THE INSIDE!

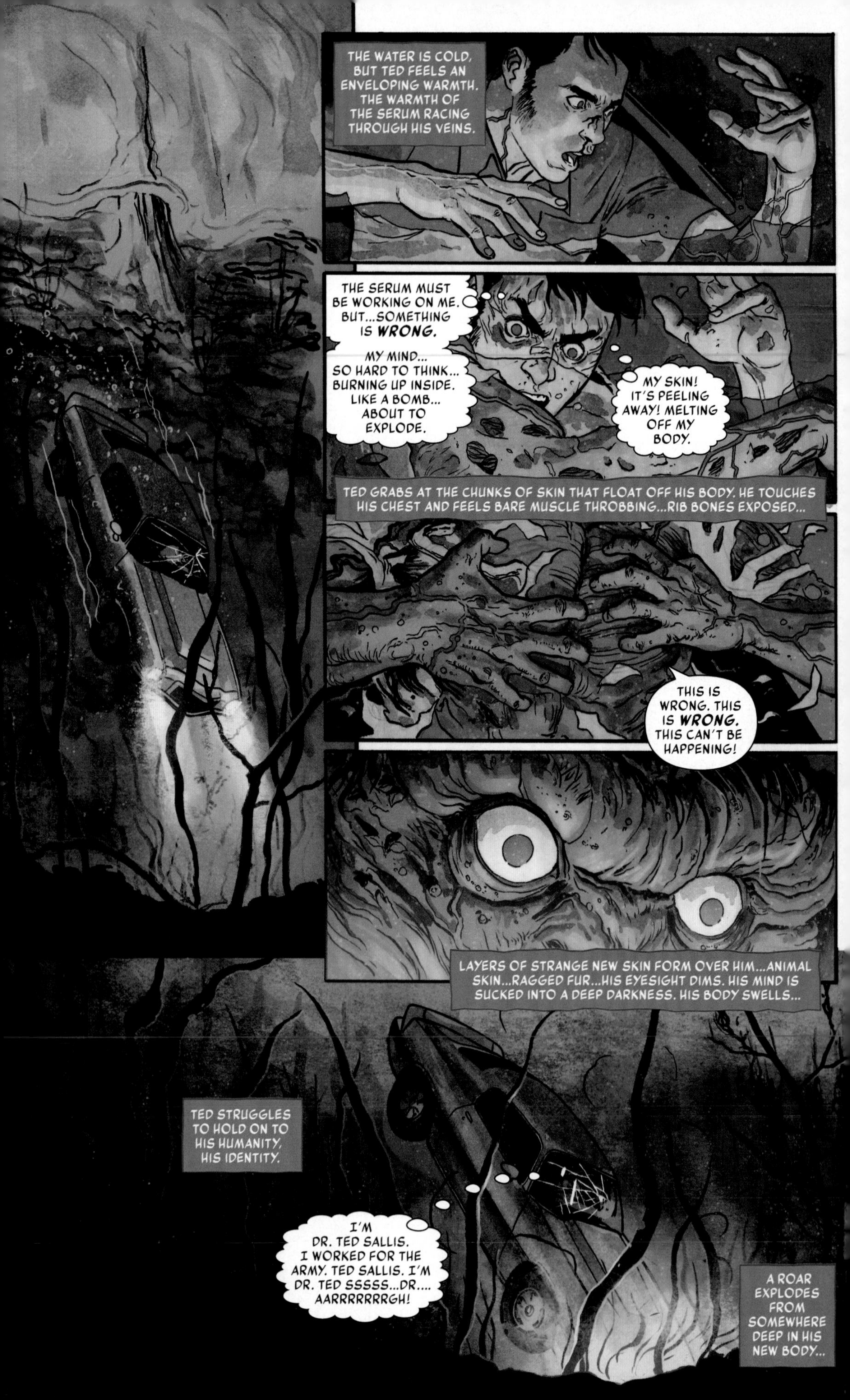
THE WATER IS COLD, BUT TED FEELS AN ENVELOPING WARMTH. THE WARMTH OF THE SERUM RACING THROUGH HIS VEINS.
THE SERUM MUST BE WORKING ON ME. BUT...SOMETHING IS WRONG.
MY MIND... SO HARD TO THINK... BURNING UP INSIDE. LIKE A BOMB... ABOUT TO EXPLODE.
MY SKIN! IT'S PEELING AWAY! MELTING OFF MY BODY.
TED GRABS AT THE CHUNKS OF SKIN THAT FLOAT OFF HIS BODY. HE TOUCHES HIS CHEST AND FEELS BARE MUSCLE THROBBING...RIB BONES EXPOSED...
THIS IS WRONG. THIS IS WRONG. THIS CAN'T BE HAPPENING!
LAYERS OF STRANGE NEW SKIN FORM OVER HIM...ANIMAL SKIN...RAGGED FUR...HIS EYESIGHT DIMS. HIS MIND IS SUCKED INTO A DEEP DARKNESS. HIS BODY SWELLS...
TED STRUGGLES TO HOLD ON TO HIS HUMANITY, HIS IDENTITY.
I'M DR. TED SALLIS. I WORKED FOR THE ARMY. TED SALLIS. I'M DR. TED SSSSS...DR.... AARRRRRRRGH!
A ROAR EXPLODES FROM SOMEWHERE DEEP IN HIS NEW BODY...

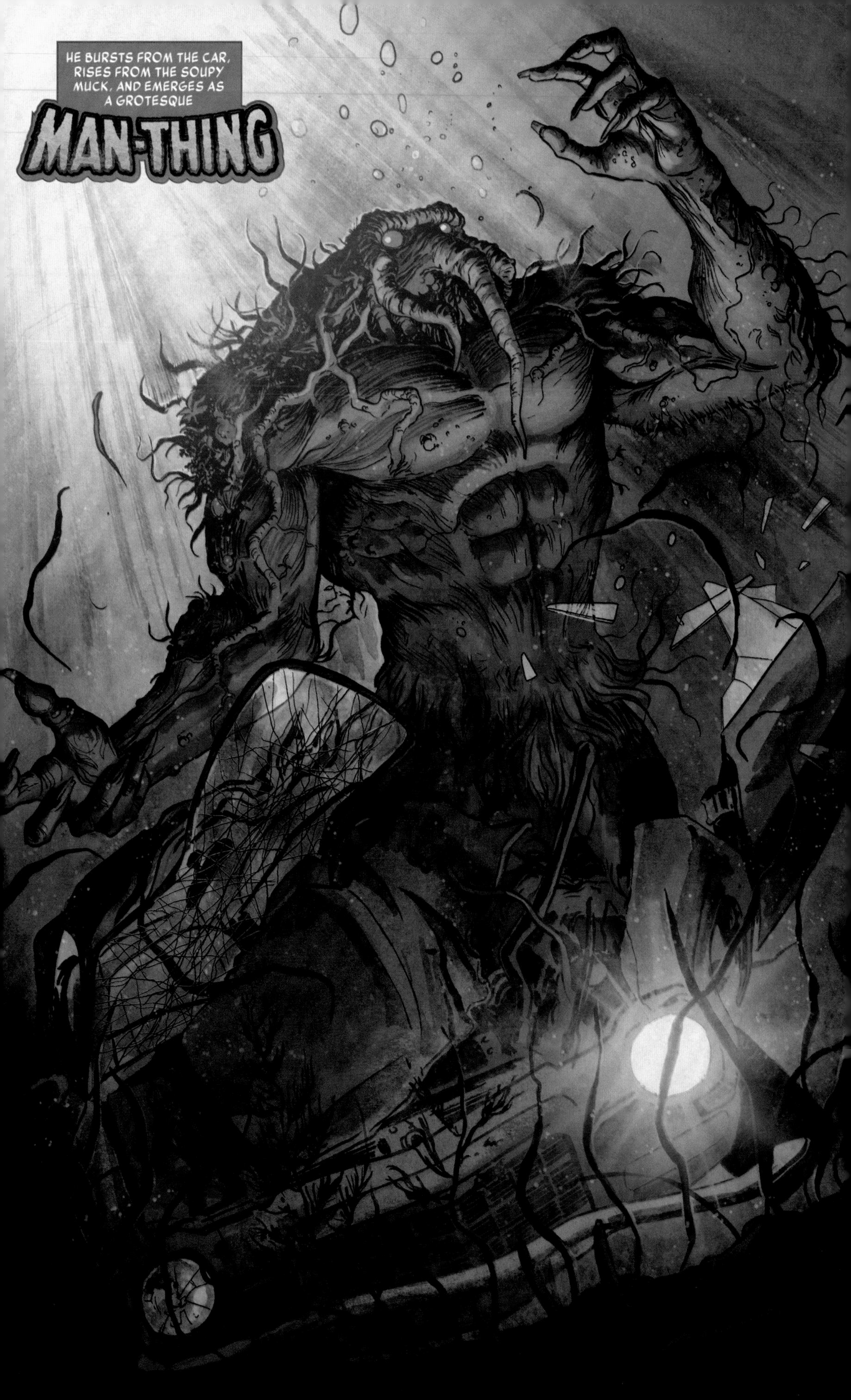
HE BURSTS FROM THE CAR, RISES FROM THE SOUPY MUCK, AND EMERGES AS A GROTESQUE
MAN-THING

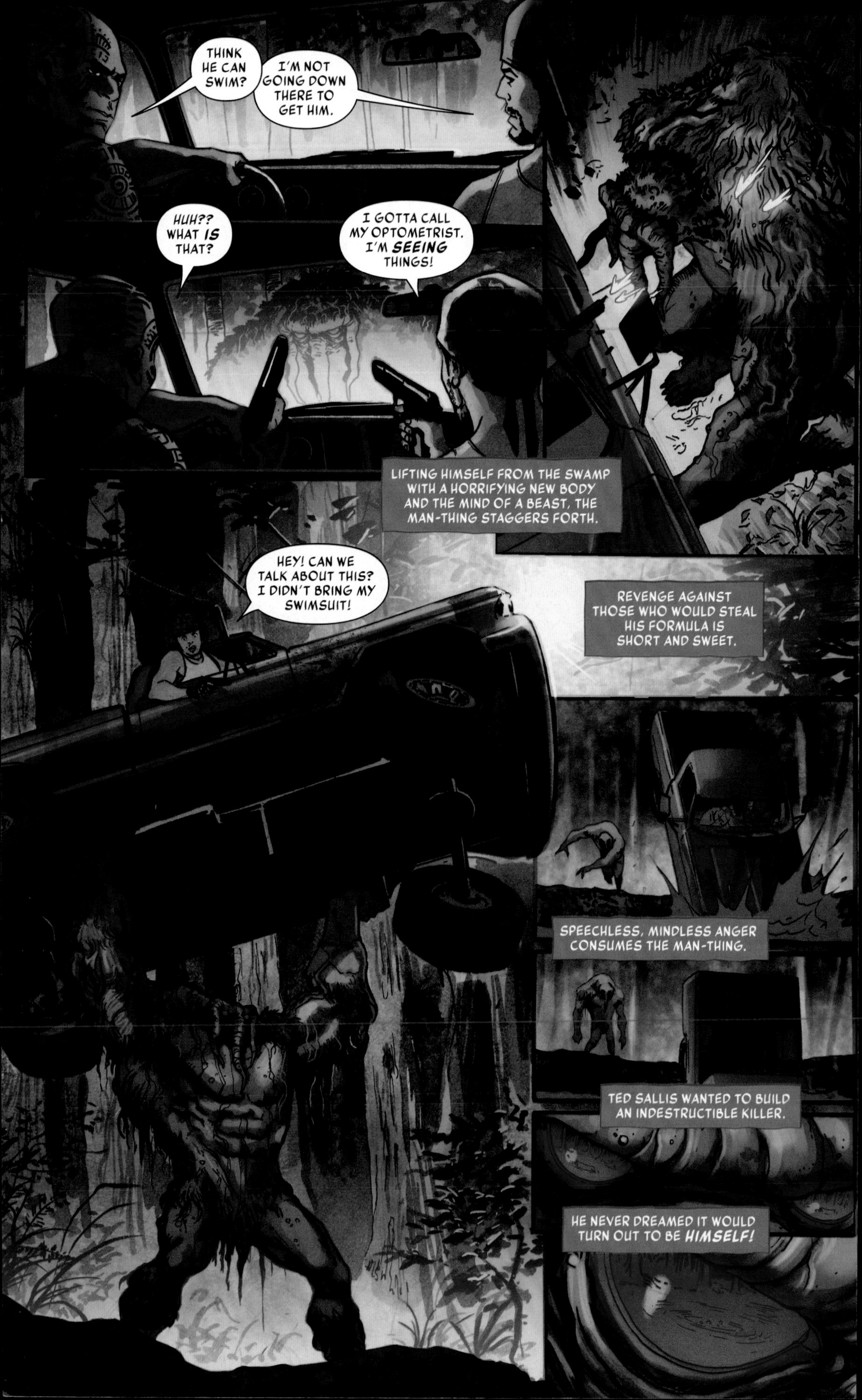
THINK HE CAN SWIM?
I'M NOT GOING DOWN THERE TO GET HIM.
HUH?? WHAT *IS* THAT?
I GOTTA CALL MY OPTOMETRIST. I'M *SEEING* THINGS!
LIFTING HIMSELF FROM THE SWAMP WITH A HORRIFYING NEW BODY AND THE MIND OF A BEAST, THE MAN-THING STAGGERS FORTH.
HEY! CAN WE TALK ABOUT THIS? I DIDN'T BRING MY SWIMSUIT!
REVENGE AGAINST THOSE WHO WOULD STEAL HIS FORMULA IS SHORT AND SWEET.
SPEECHLESS, MINDLESS ANGER CONSUMES THE MAN-THING.
TED SALLIS WANTED TO BUILD AN INDESTRUCTIBLE KILLER.
HE NEVER DREAMED IT WOULD TURN OUT TO BE *HIMSELF!*

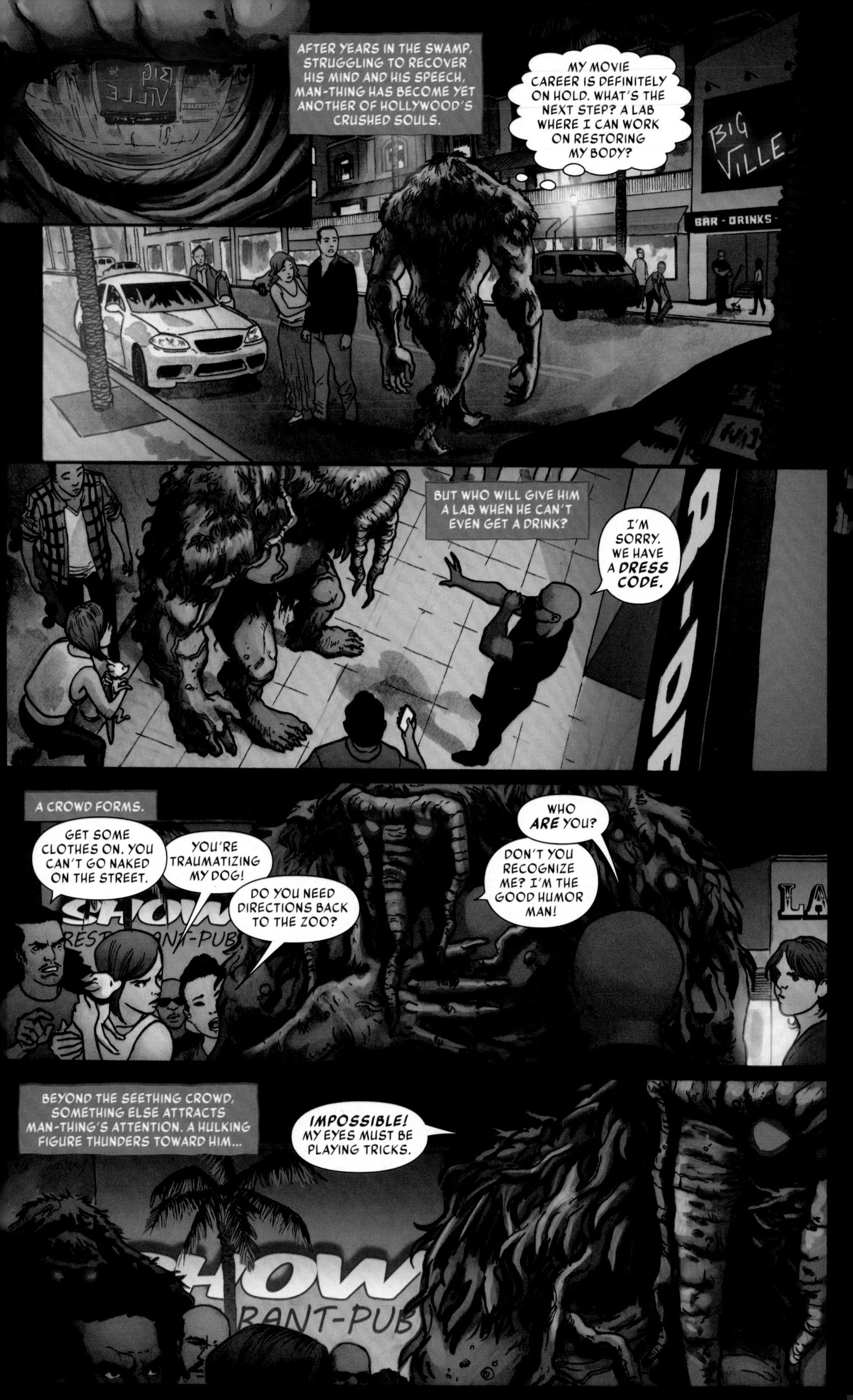
AFTER YEARS IN THE SWAMP, STRUGGLING TO RECOVER HIS MIND AND HIS SPEECH, MAN-THING HAS BECOME YET ANOTHER OF HOLLYWOOD'S CRUSHED SOULS.
MY MOVIE CAREER IS DEFINITELY ON HOLD. WHAT'S THE NEXT STEP? A LAB WHERE I CAN WORK ON RESTORING MY BODY?
BIG VILLE
BAR - DRINKS -
BUT WHO WILL GIVE HIM A LAB WHEN HE CAN'T EVEN GET A DRINK?
I'M SORRY. WE HAVE A **DRESS CODE.**
A CROWD FORMS.
GET SOME CLOTHES ON. YOU CAN'T GO NAKED ON THE STREET.
YOU'RE TRAUMATIZING MY DOG!
DO YOU NEED DIRECTIONS BACK TO THE ZOO?
WHO ***ARE*** YOU?
DON'T YOU RECOGNIZE ME? I'M THE GOOD HUMOR MAN!
BEYOND THE SEETHING CROWD, SOMETHING ELSE ATTRACTS MAN-THING'S ATTENTION. A HULKING FIGURE THUNDERS TOWARD HIM...
IMPOSSIBLE! MY EYES MUST BE PLAYING TRICKS.
RANT-PUB

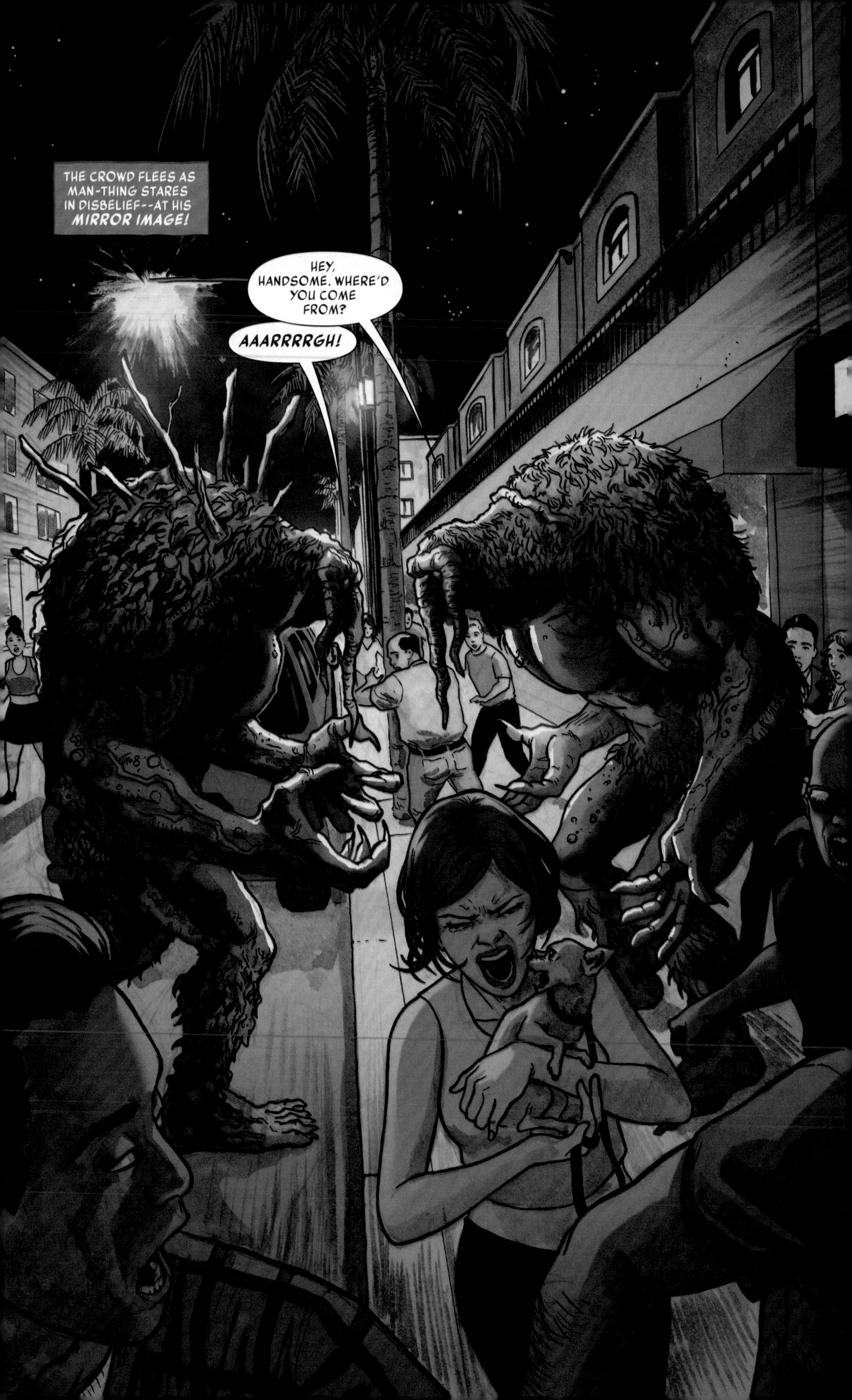
THE CROWD FLEES AS MAN-THING STARES IN DISBELIEF--AT HIS MIRROR IMAGE!
HEY, HANDSOME. WHERE'D YOU COME FROM?
AAARRRRGH!

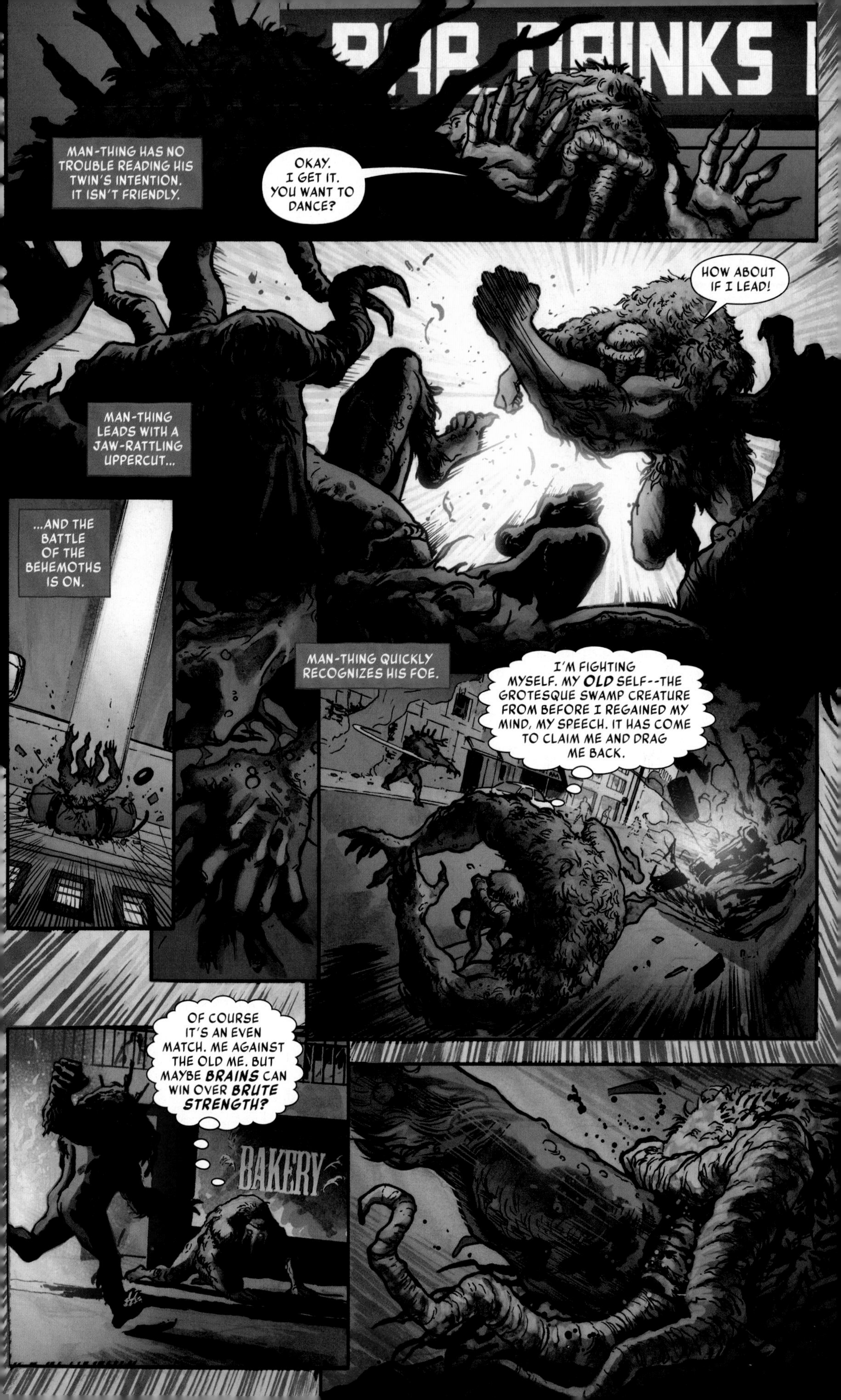
MAN-THING HAS NO TROUBLE READING HIS TWIN'S INTENTION. IT ISN'T FRIENDLY.
OKAY. I GET IT. YOU WANT TO DANCE?
HOW ABOUT IF I LEAD!
MAN-THING LEADS WITH A JAW-RATTLING UPPERCUT...
...AND THE BATTLE OF THE BEHEMOTHS IS ON.
MAN-THING QUICKLY RECOGNIZES HIS FOE.
I'M FIGHTING MYSELF. MY OLD SELF--THE GROTESQUE SWAMP CREATURE FROM BEFORE I REGAINED MY MIND, MY SPEECH. IT HAS COME TO CLAIM ME AND DRAG ME BACK.
OF COURSE IT'S AN EVEN MATCH. ME AGAINST THE OLD ME. BUT MAYBE BRAINS CAN WIN OVER BRUTE STRENGTH?
BAKERY

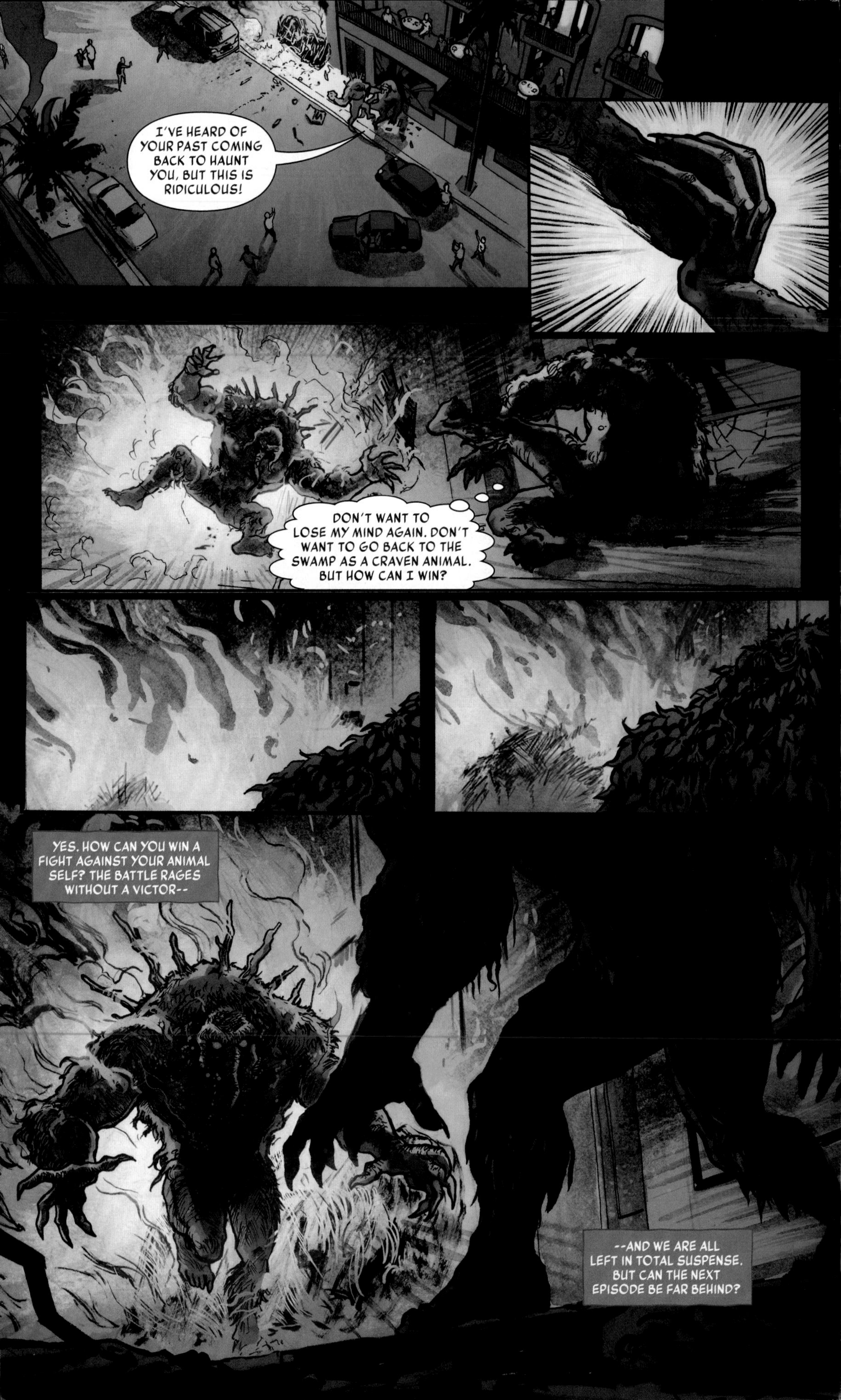
I'VE HEARD OF YOUR PAST COMING BACK TO HAUNT YOU, BUT THIS IS RIDICULOUS!
DON'T WANT TO LOSE MY MIND AGAIN. DON'T WANT TO GO BACK TO THE SWAMP AS A CRAVEN ANIMAL. BUT HOW CAN I WIN?
YES. HOW CAN YOU WIN A FIGHT AGAINST YOUR ANIMAL SELF? THE BATTLE RAGES WITHOUT A VICTOR--
--AND WE ARE ALL LEFT IN TOTAL SUSPENSE. BUT CAN THE NEXT EPISODE BE FAR BEHIND?

2

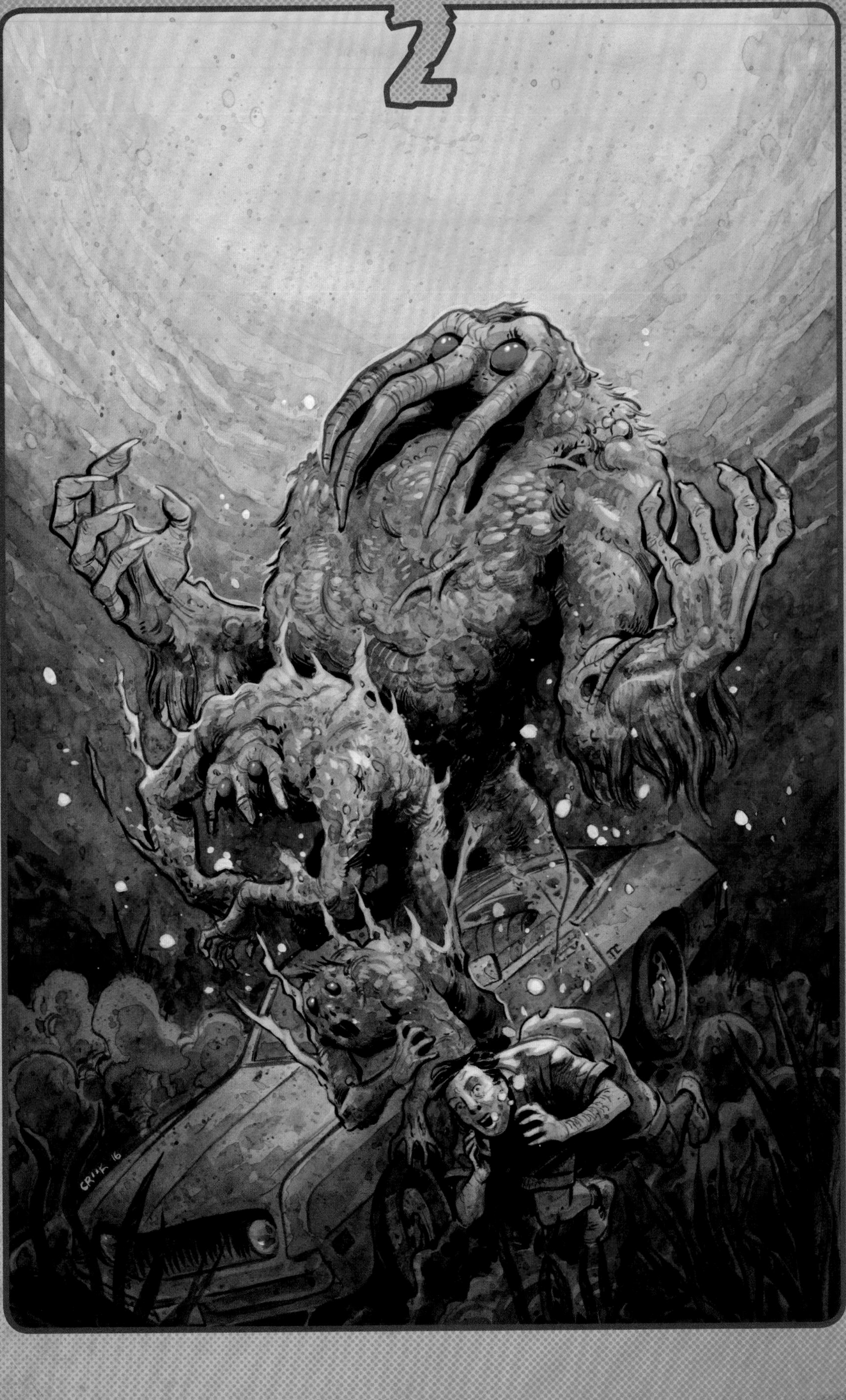

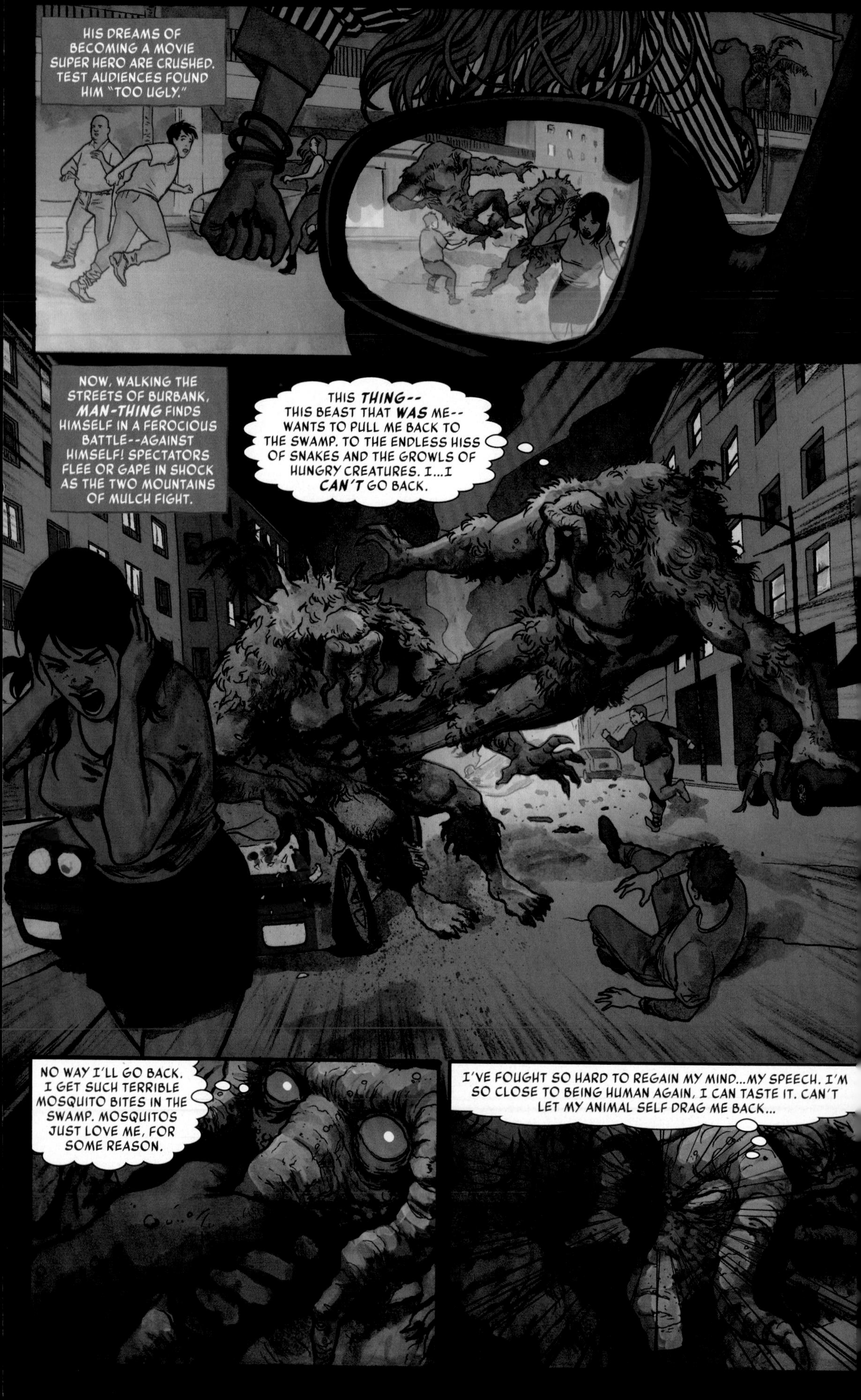
HIS DREAMS OF BECOMING A MOVIE SUPER HERO ARE CRUSHED. TEST AUDIENCES FOUND HIM "TOO UGLY."
NOW, WALKING THE STREETS OF BURBANK, MAN-THING FINDS HIMSELF IN A FEROCIOUS BATTLE--AGAINST HIMSELF! SPECTATORS FLEE OR GAPE IN SHOCK AS THE TWO MOUNTAINS OF MULCH FIGHT.
THIS THING-- THIS BEAST THAT WAS ME-- WANTS TO PULL ME BACK TO THE SWAMP. TO THE ENDLESS HISS OF SNAKES AND THE GROWLS OF HUNGRY CREATURES. I...I CAN'T GO BACK.
NO WAY I'LL GO BACK. I GET SUCH TERRIBLE MOSQUITO BITES IN THE SWAMP. MOSQUITOS JUST LOVE ME, FOR SOME REASON.
I'VE FOUGHT SO HARD TO REGAIN MY MIND...MY SPEECH. I'M SO CLOSE TO BEING HUMAN AGAIN, I CAN TASTE IT. CAN'T LET MY ANIMAL SELF DRAG ME BACK...

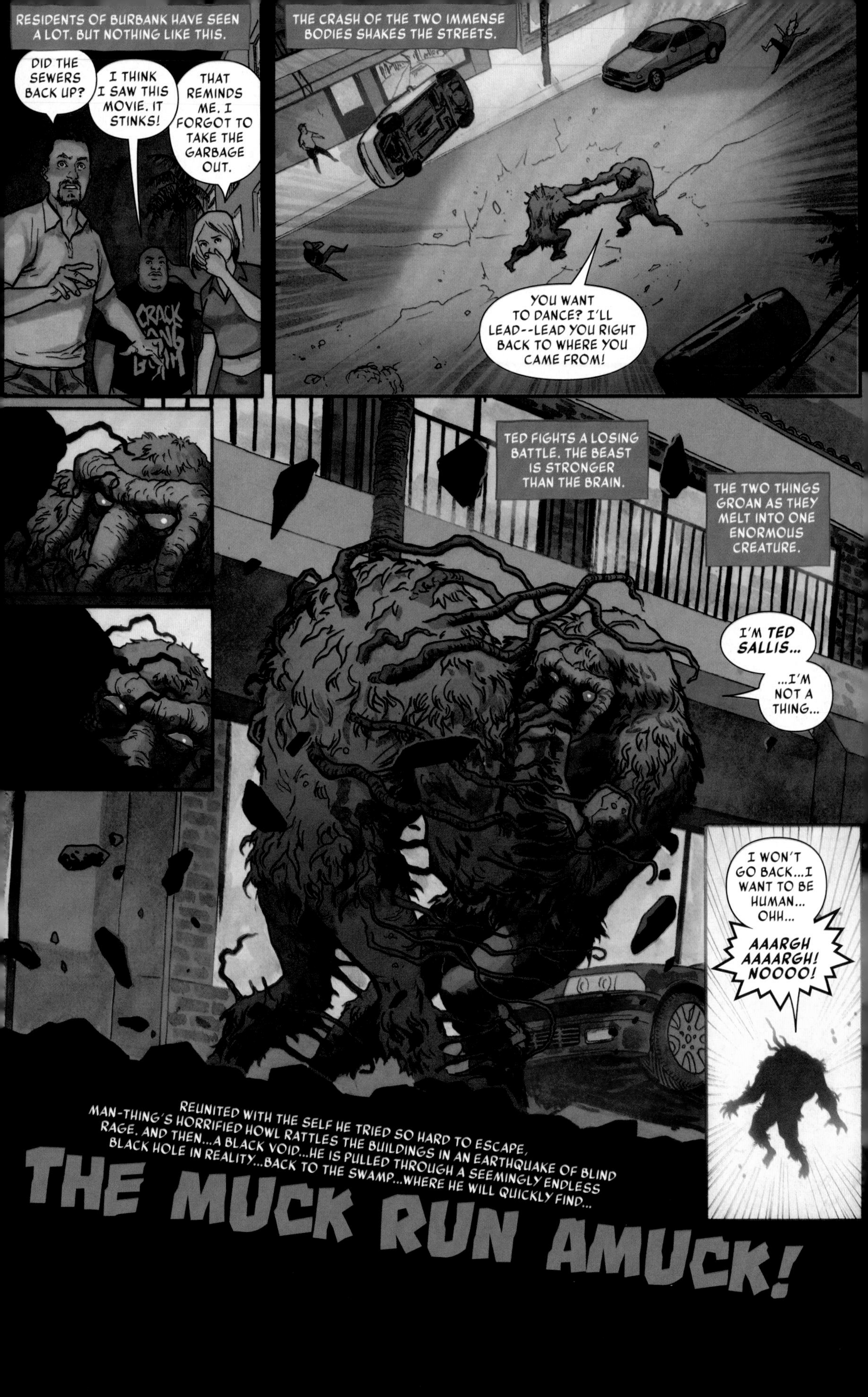
RESIDENTS OF BURBANK HAVE SEEN A LOT. BUT NOTHING LIKE THIS.
DID THE SEWERS BACK UP?
I THINK I SAW THIS MOVIE. IT STINKS!
THAT REMINDS ME. I FORGOT TO TAKE THE GARBAGE OUT.
THE CRASH OF THE TWO IMMENSE BODIES SHAKES THE STREETS.
YOU WANT TO DANCE? I'LL LEAD--LEAD YOU RIGHT BACK TO WHERE YOU CAME FROM!
TED FIGHTS A LOSING BATTLE. THE BEAST IS STRONGER THAN THE BRAIN.
THE TWO THINGS GROAN AS THEY MELT INTO ONE ENORMOUS CREATURE.
I'M TED SALLIS...
...I'M NOT A THING...
I WON'T GO BACK...I WANT TO BE HUMAN... OHH...
AAARGH AAAARGH! NOOOO!
REUNITED WITH THE SELF HE TRIED SO HARD TO ESCAPE, MAN-THING'S HORRIFIED HOWL RATTLES THE BUILDINGS IN AN EARTHQUAKE OF BLIND RAGE. AND THEN...A BLACK VOID...HE IS PULLED THROUGH A SEEMINGLY ENDLESS BLACK HOLE IN REALITY...BACK TO THE SWAMP...WHERE HE WILL QUICKLY FIND...
THE MUCK RUN AMUCK!

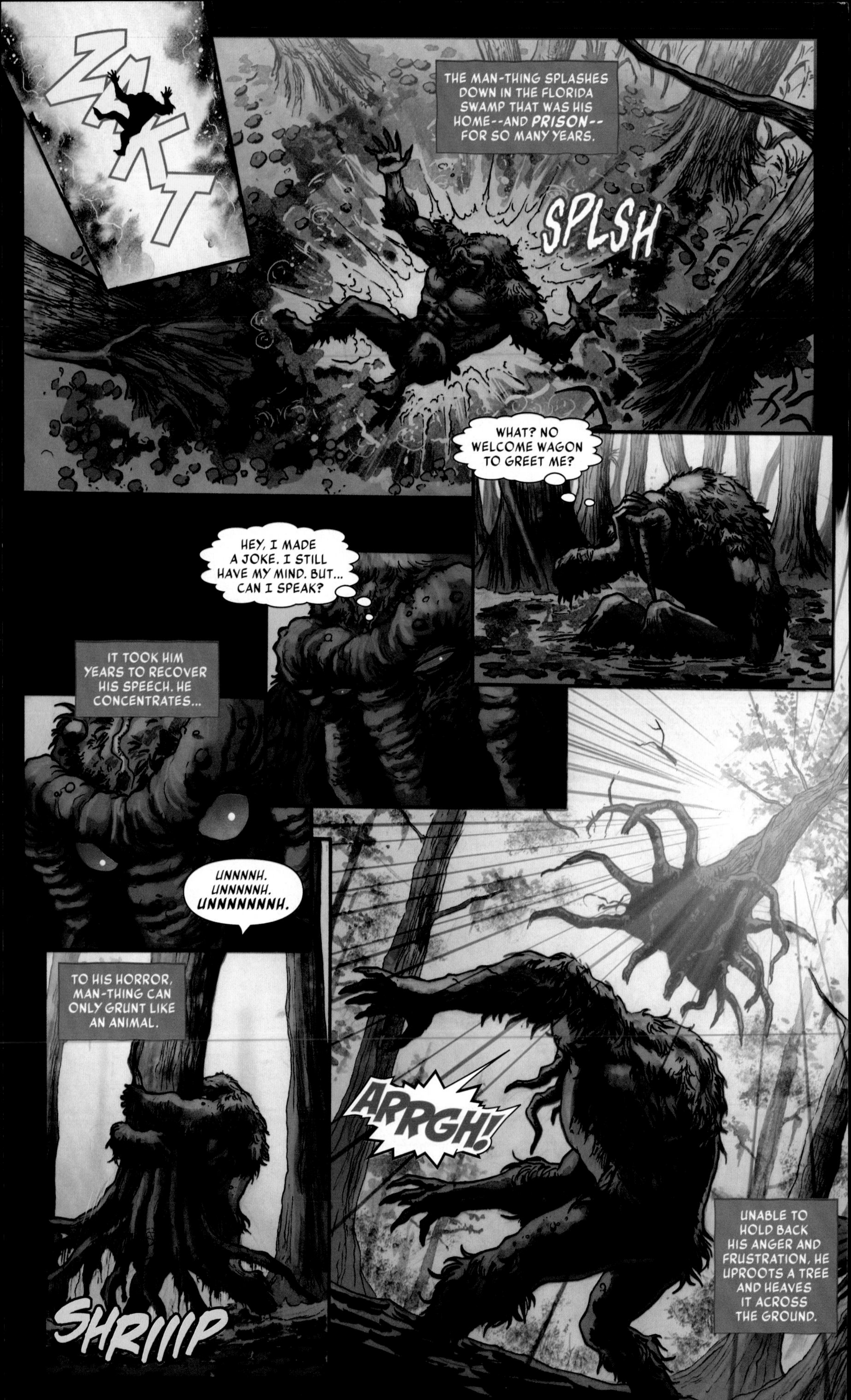
ZAKT
THE MAN-THING SPLASHES DOWN IN THE FLORIDA SWAMP THAT WAS HIS HOME--AND PRISON--FOR SO MANY YEARS.
SPLSH
WHAT? NO WELCOME WAGON TO GREET ME?
HEY, I MADE A JOKE. I STILL HAVE MY MIND. BUT... CAN I SPEAK?
IT TOOK HIM YEARS TO RECOVER HIS SPEECH. HE CONCENTRATES...
UNNNNH. UNNNNNH. UNNNNNNNH.
TO HIS HORROR, MAN-THING CAN ONLY GRUNT LIKE AN ANIMAL.
SHRIIIP
ARRGH!
UNABLE TO HOLD BACK HIS ANGER AND FRUSTRATION, HE UPROOTS A TREE AND HEAVES IT ACROSS THE GROUND.

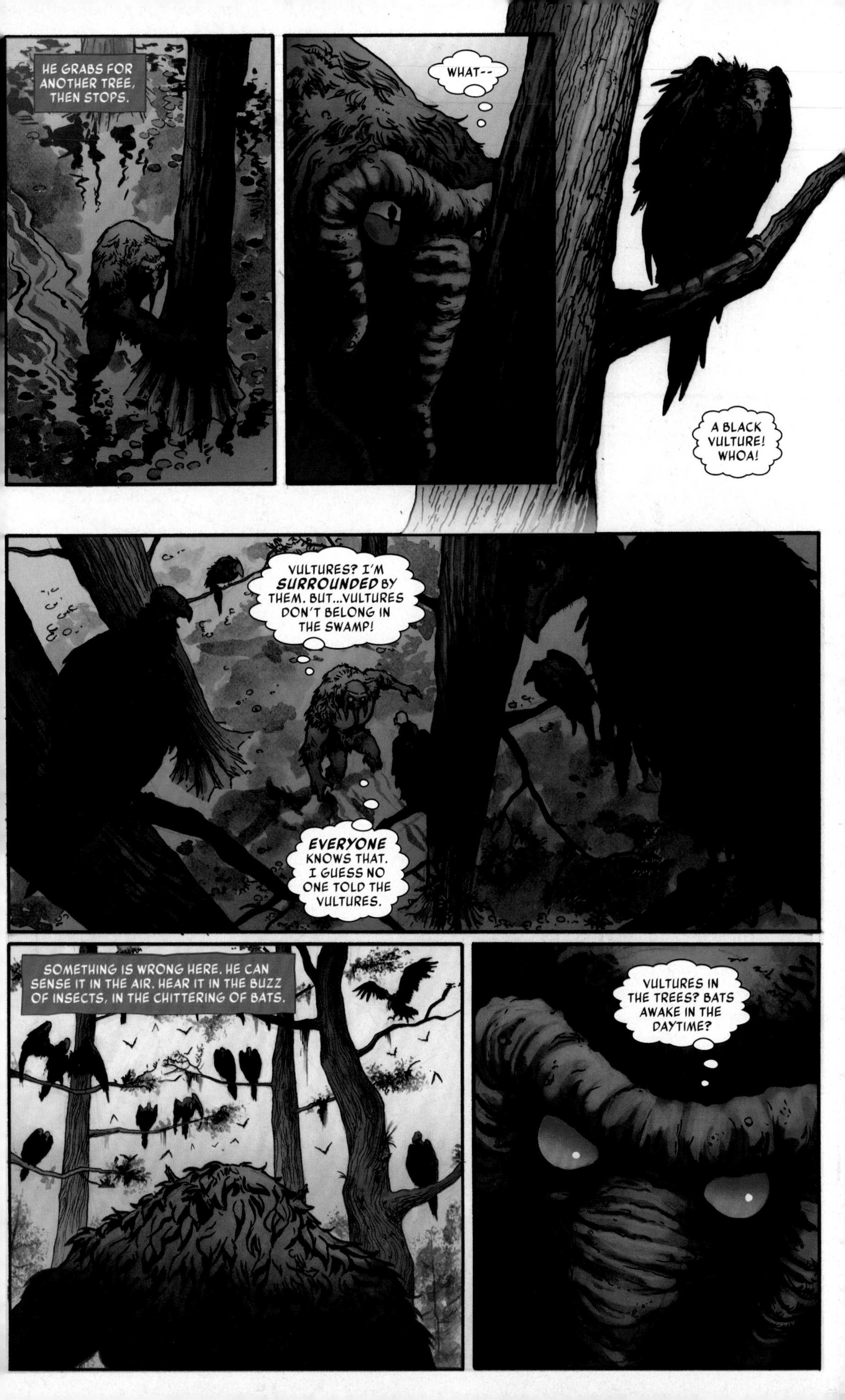
HE GRABS FOR ANOTHER TREE, THEN STOPS.
WHAT--
A BLACK VULTURE! WHOA!
VULTURES? I'M SURROUNDED BY THEM. BUT...VULTURES DON'T BELONG IN THE SWAMP!
EVERYONE KNOWS THAT. I GUESS NO ONE TOLD THE VULTURES.
SOMETHING IS WRONG HERE. HE CAN SENSE IT IN THE AIR, HEAR IT IN THE BUZZ OF INSECTS, IN THE CHITTERING OF BATS.
VULTURES IN THE TREES? BATS AWAKE IN THE DAYTIME?

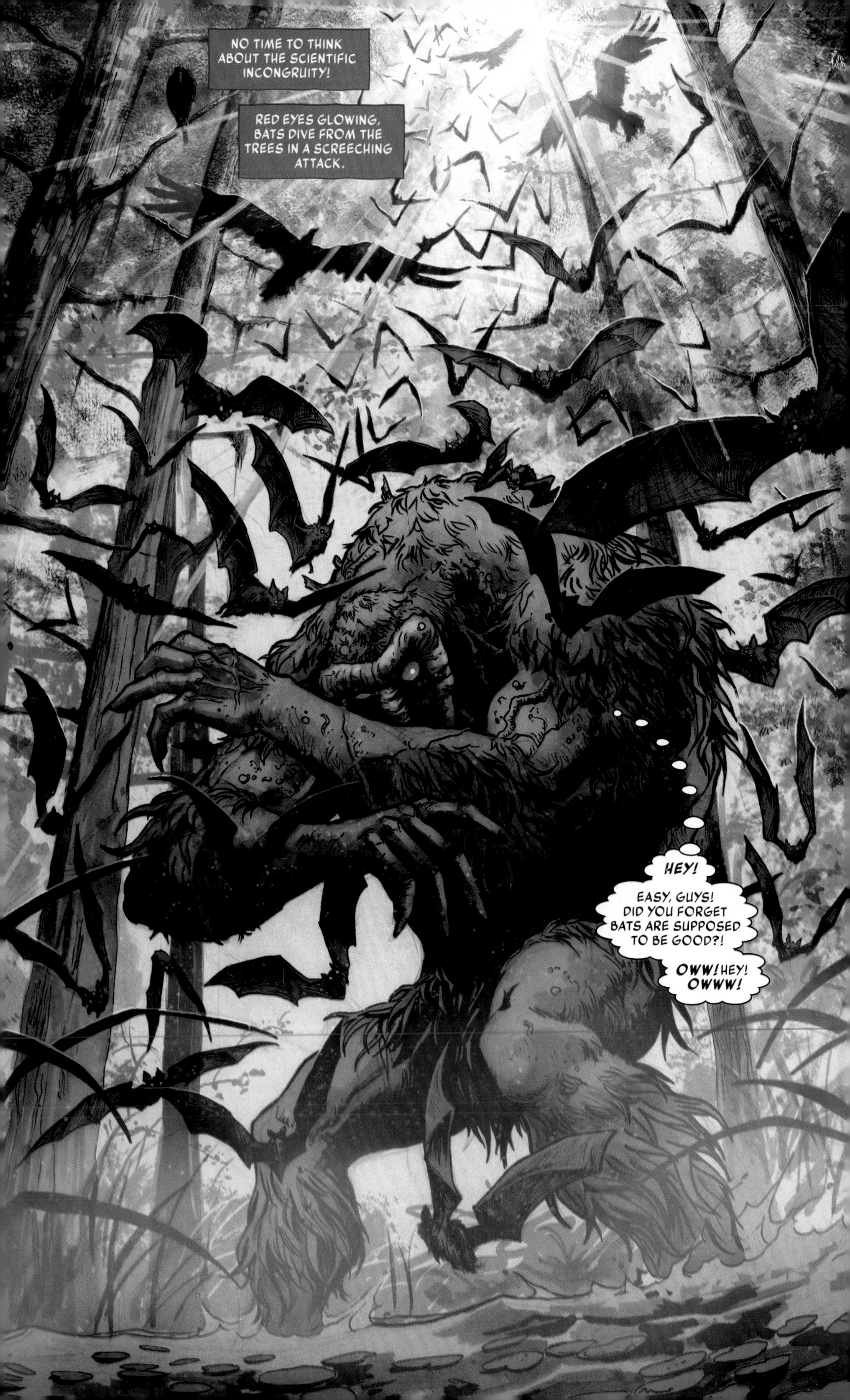
NO TIME TO THINK ABOUT THE SCIENTIFIC INCONGRUITY!
RED EYES GLOWING, BATS DIVE FROM THE TREES IN A SCREECHING ATTACK.
HEY!
EASY, GUYS! DID YOU FORGET BATS ARE SUPPOSED TO BE GOOD?!
OWW! HEY! OWWW!

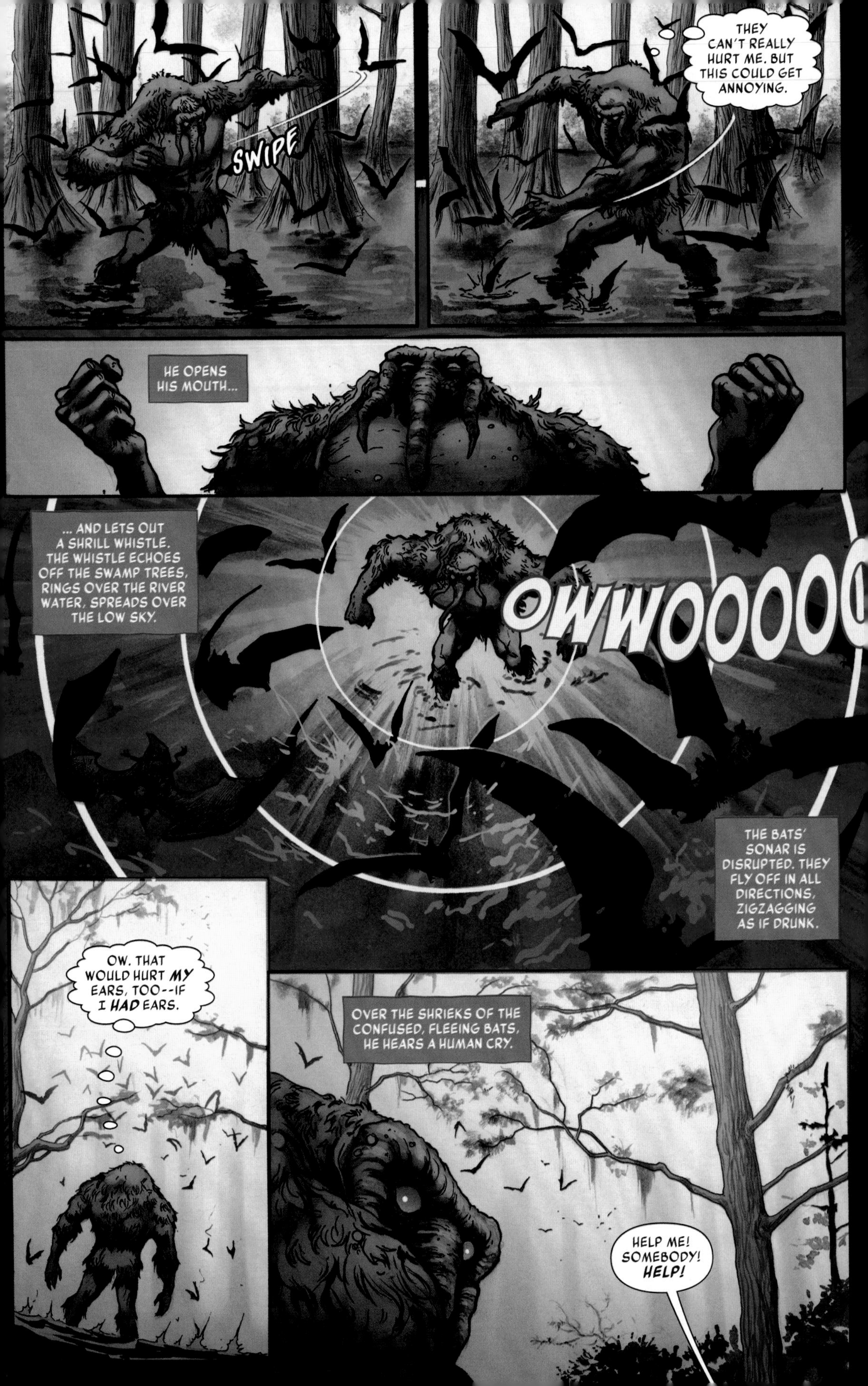
SWIPE
THEY CAN'T REALLY HURT ME. BUT THIS COULD GET ANNOYING.
HE OPENS HIS MOUTH...
... AND LETS OUT A SHRILL WHISTLE. THE WHISTLE ECHOES OFF THE SWAMP TREES, RINGS OVER THE RIVER WATER, SPREADS OVER THE LOW SKY.
OWWOOOOO
THE BATS' SONAR IS DISRUPTED. THEY FLY OFF IN ALL DIRECTIONS, ZIGZAGGING AS IF DRUNK.
OW. THAT WOULD HURT MY EARS, TOO--IF I HAD EARS.
OVER THE SHRIEKS OF THE CONFUSED, FLEEING BATS, HE HEARS A HUMAN CRY.
HELP ME! SOMEBODY! HELP!

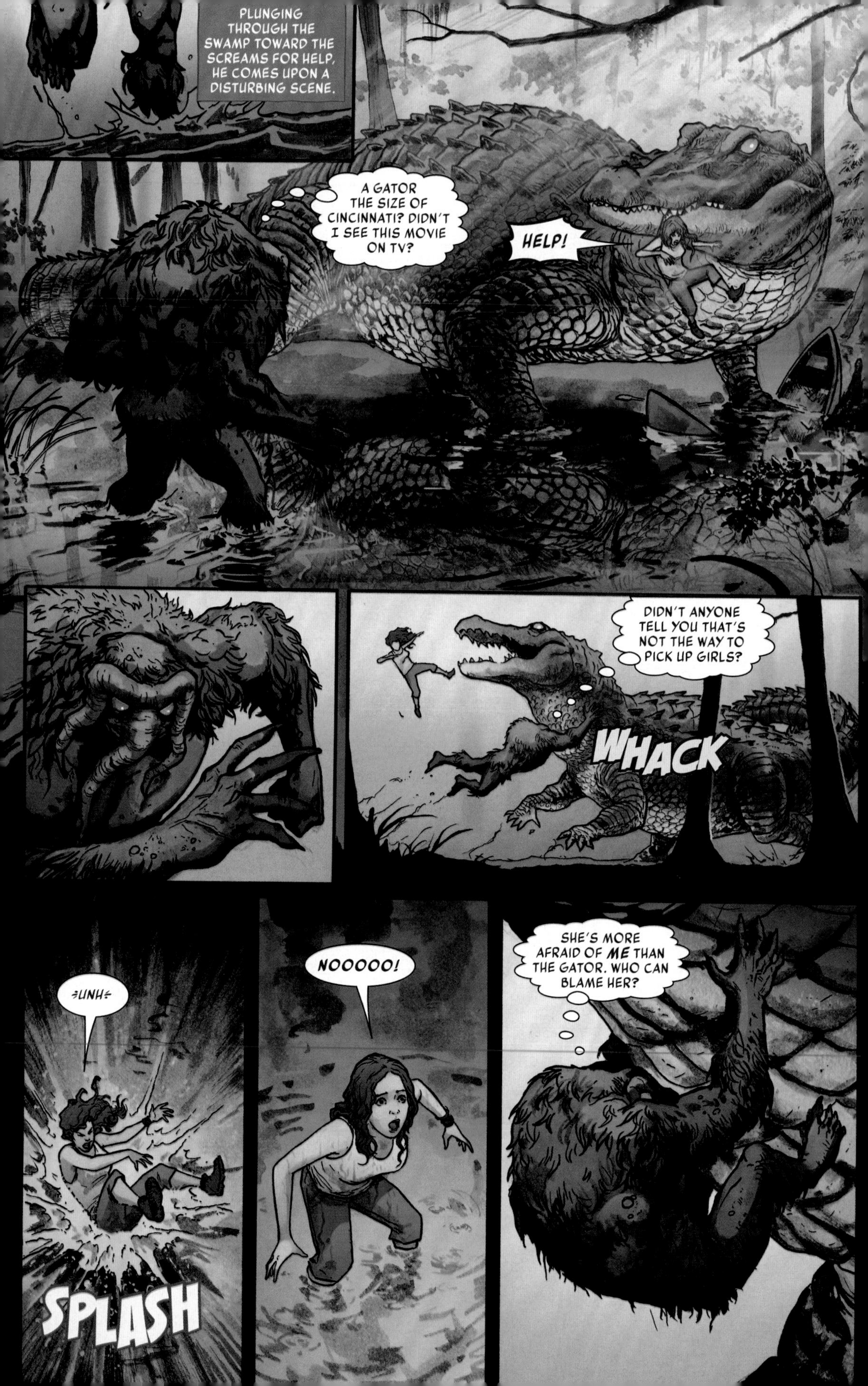
PLUNGING THROUGH THE SWAMP TOWARD THE SCREAMS FOR HELP, HE COMES UPON A DISTURBING SCENE.
A GATOR THE SIZE OF CINCINNATI? DIDN'T I SEE THIS MOVIE ON TV?
HELP!
DIDN'T ANYONE TELL YOU THAT'S NOT THE WAY TO PICK UP GIRLS?
WHACK
UNH
SPLASH
NOOOOO!
SHE'S MORE AFRAID OF ME THAN THE GATOR. WHO CAN BLAME HER?

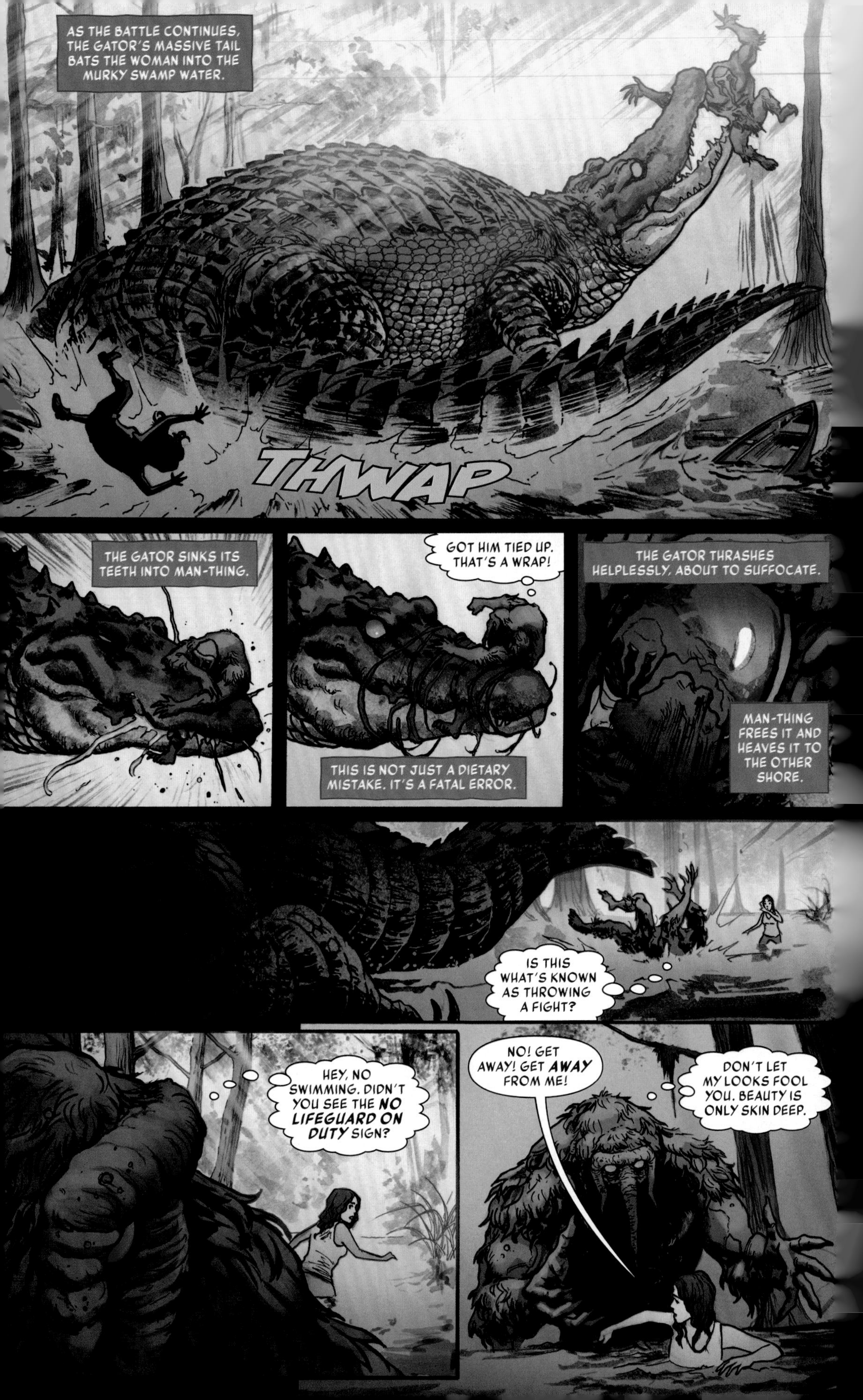
AS THE BATTLE CONTINUES, THE GATOR'S MASSIVE TAIL BATS THE WOMAN INTO THE MURKY SWAMP WATER.
THWAP
THE GATOR SINKS ITS TEETH INTO MAN-THING.
GOT HIM TIED UP. THAT'S A WRAP!
THIS IS NOT JUST A DIETARY MISTAKE. IT'S A FATAL ERROR.
THE GATOR THRASHES HELPLESSLY, ABOUT TO SUFFOCATE.
MAN-THING FREES IT AND HEAVES IT TO THE OTHER SHORE.
IS THIS WHAT'S KNOWN AS THROWING A FIGHT?
HEY, NO SWIMMING. DIDN'T YOU SEE THE NO LIFEGUARD ON DUTY SIGN?
NO! GET AWAY! GET AWAY FROM ME!
DON'T LET MY LOOKS FOOL YOU. BEAUTY IS ONLY SKIN DEEP.

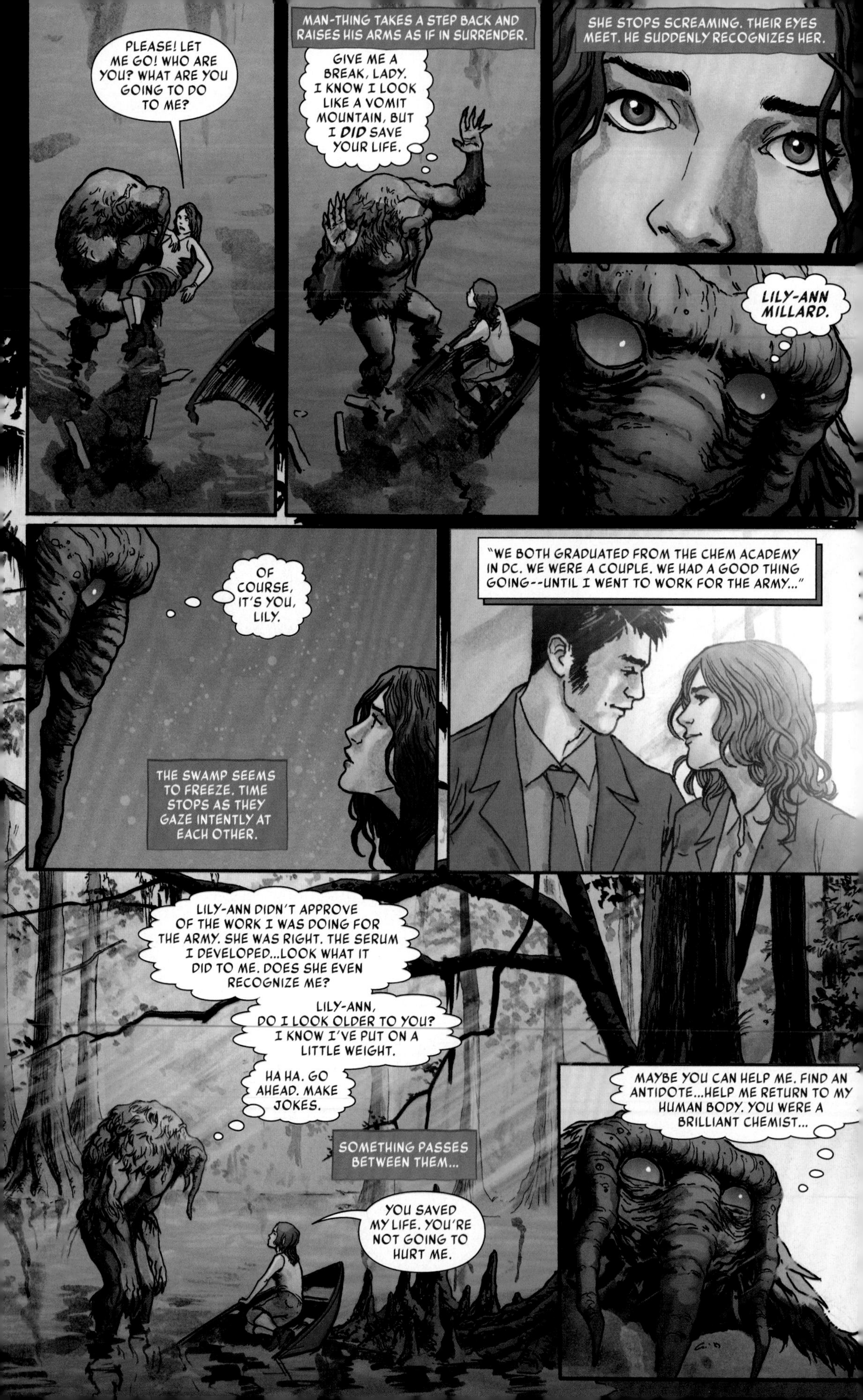
PLEASE! LET ME GO! WHO ARE YOU? WHAT ARE YOU GOING TO DO TO ME?
MAN-THING TAKES A STEP BACK AND RAISES HIS ARMS AS IF IN SURRENDER.
GIVE ME A BREAK, LADY. I KNOW I LOOK LIKE A VOMIT MOUNTAIN, BUT I DID SAVE YOUR LIFE.
SHE STOPS SCREAMING. THEIR EYES MEET. HE SUDDENLY RECOGNIZES HER.
LILY-ANN MILLARD.
OF COURSE, IT'S YOU, LILY.
THE SWAMP SEEMS TO FREEZE. TIME STOPS AS THEY GAZE INTENTLY AT EACH OTHER.
"WE BOTH GRADUATED FROM THE CHEM ACADEMY IN DC. WE WERE A COUPLE. WE HAD A GOOD THING GOING--UNTIL I WENT TO WORK FOR THE ARMY..."
LILY-ANN DIDN'T APPROVE OF THE WORK I WAS DOING FOR THE ARMY. SHE WAS RIGHT. THE SERUM I DEVELOPED...LOOK WHAT IT DID TO ME. DOES SHE EVEN RECOGNIZE ME?
LILY-ANN, DO I LOOK OLDER TO YOU? I KNOW I'VE PUT ON A LITTLE WEIGHT.
HA HA. GO AHEAD. MAKE JOKES.
SOMETHING PASSES BETWEEN THEM...
YOU SAVED MY LIFE. YOU'RE NOT GOING TO HURT ME.
MAYBE YOU CAN HELP ME. FIND AN ANTIDOTE...HELP ME RETURN TO MY HUMAN BODY. YOU WERE A BRILLIANT CHEMIST...

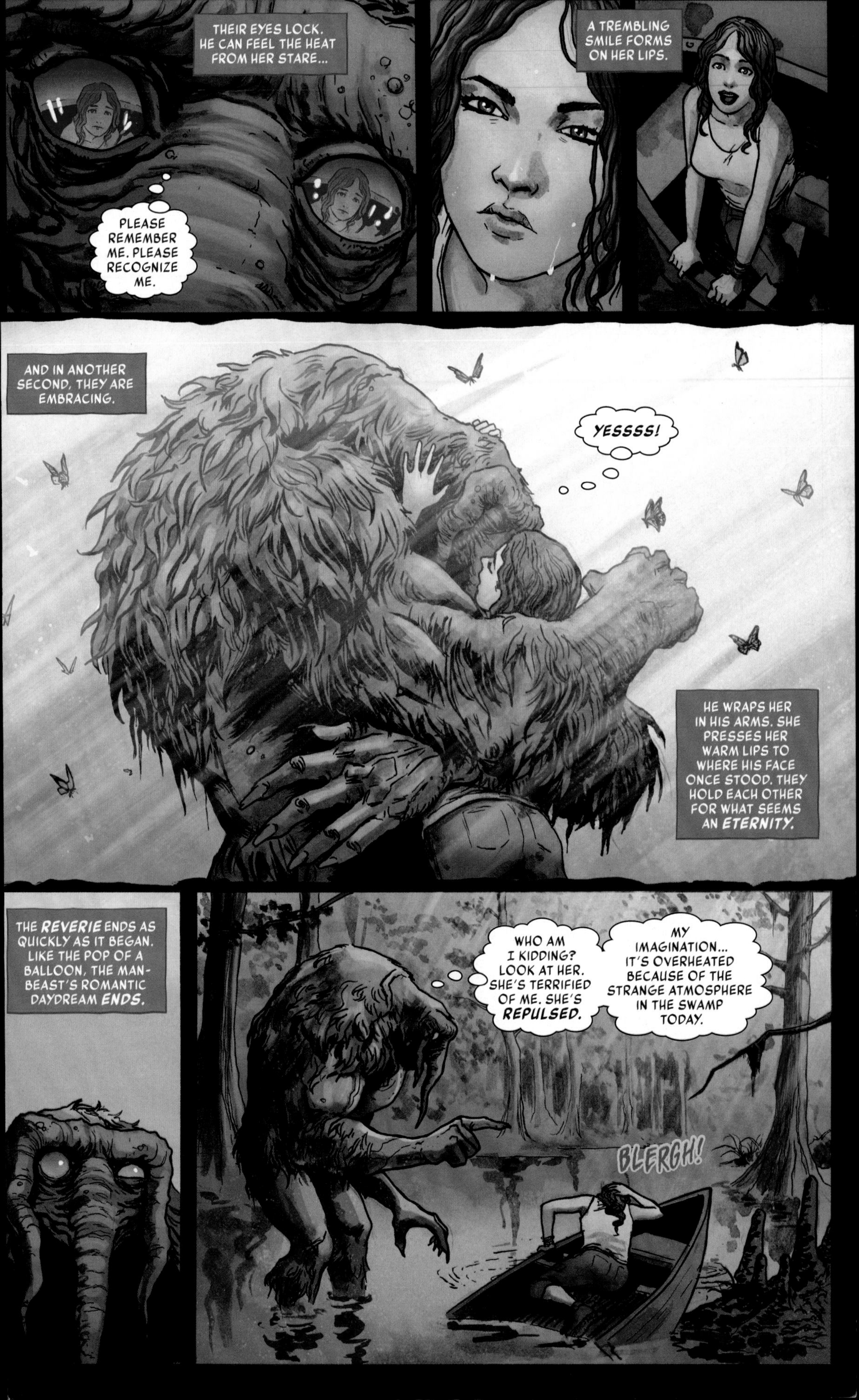
THEIR EYES LOCK. HE CAN FEEL THE HEAT FROM HER STARE...
PLEASE REMEMBER ME. PLEASE RECOGNIZE ME.
A TREMBLING SMILE FORMS ON HER LIPS.
AND IN ANOTHER SECOND, THEY ARE EMBRACING.
YESSSS!
HE WRAPS HER IN HIS ARMS. SHE PRESSES HER WARM LIPS TO WHERE HIS FACE ONCE STOOD. THEY HOLD EACH OTHER FOR WHAT SEEMS AN ETERNITY.
THE REVERIE ENDS AS QUICKLY AS IT BEGAN. LIKE THE POP OF A BALLOON, THE MAN-BEAST'S ROMANTIC DAYDREAM ENDS.
WHO AM I KIDDING? LOOK AT HER. SHE'S TERRIFIED OF ME. SHE'S REPULSED.
MY IMAGINATION... IT'S OVERHEATED BECAUSE OF THE STRANGE ATMOSPHERE IN THE SWAMP TODAY.
BLERGH!

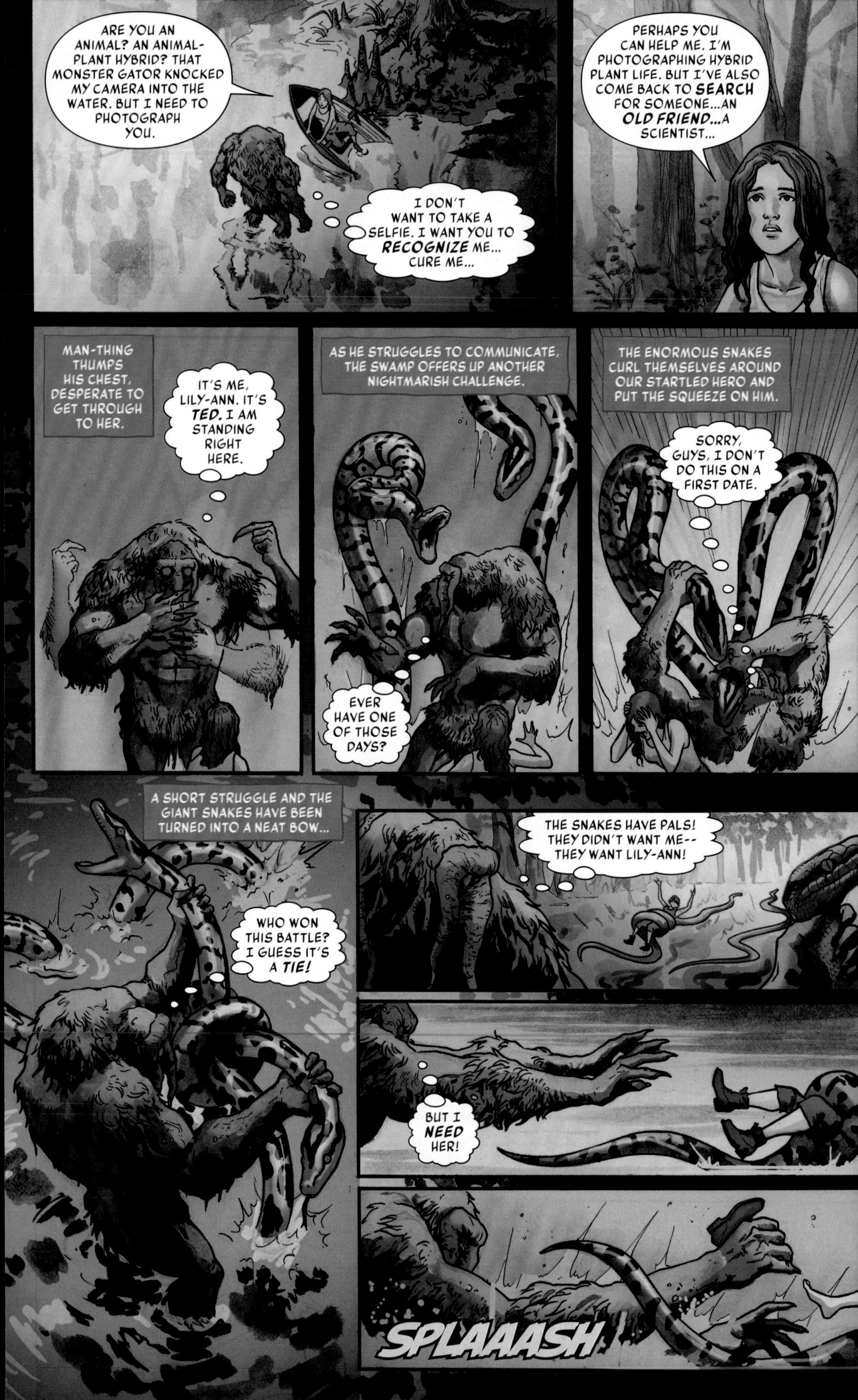
ARE YOU AN ANIMAL? AN ANIMAL-PLANT HYBRID? THAT MONSTER GATOR KNOCKED MY CAMERA INTO THE WATER. BUT I NEED TO PHOTOGRAPH YOU.
I DON'T WANT TO TAKE A SELFIE. I WANT YOU TO RECOGNIZE ME... CURE ME...
PERHAPS YOU CAN HELP ME. I'M PHOTOGRAPHING HYBRID PLANT LIFE. BUT I'VE ALSO COME BACK TO SEARCH FOR SOMEONE...AN OLD FRIEND...A SCIENTIST...
MAN-THING THUMPS HIS CHEST, DESPERATE TO GET THROUGH TO HER.
IT'S ME, LILY-ANN. IT'S TED. I AM STANDING RIGHT HERE.
AS HE STRUGGLES TO COMMUNICATE, THE SWAMP OFFERS UP ANOTHER NIGHTMARISH CHALLENGE.
EVER HAVE ONE OF THOSE DAYS?
THE ENORMOUS SNAKES CURL THEMSELVES AROUND OUR STARTLED HERO AND PUT THE SQUEEZE ON HIM.
SORRY, GUYS, I DON'T DO THIS ON A FIRST DATE.
A SHORT STRUGGLE AND THE GIANT SNAKES HAVE BEEN TURNED INTO A NEAT BOW...
WHO WON THIS BATTLE? I GUESS IT'S A TIE!
THE SNAKES HAVE PALS! THEY DIDN'T WANT ME-- THEY WANT LILY-ANN!
BUT I NEED HER!
SPLAAASH

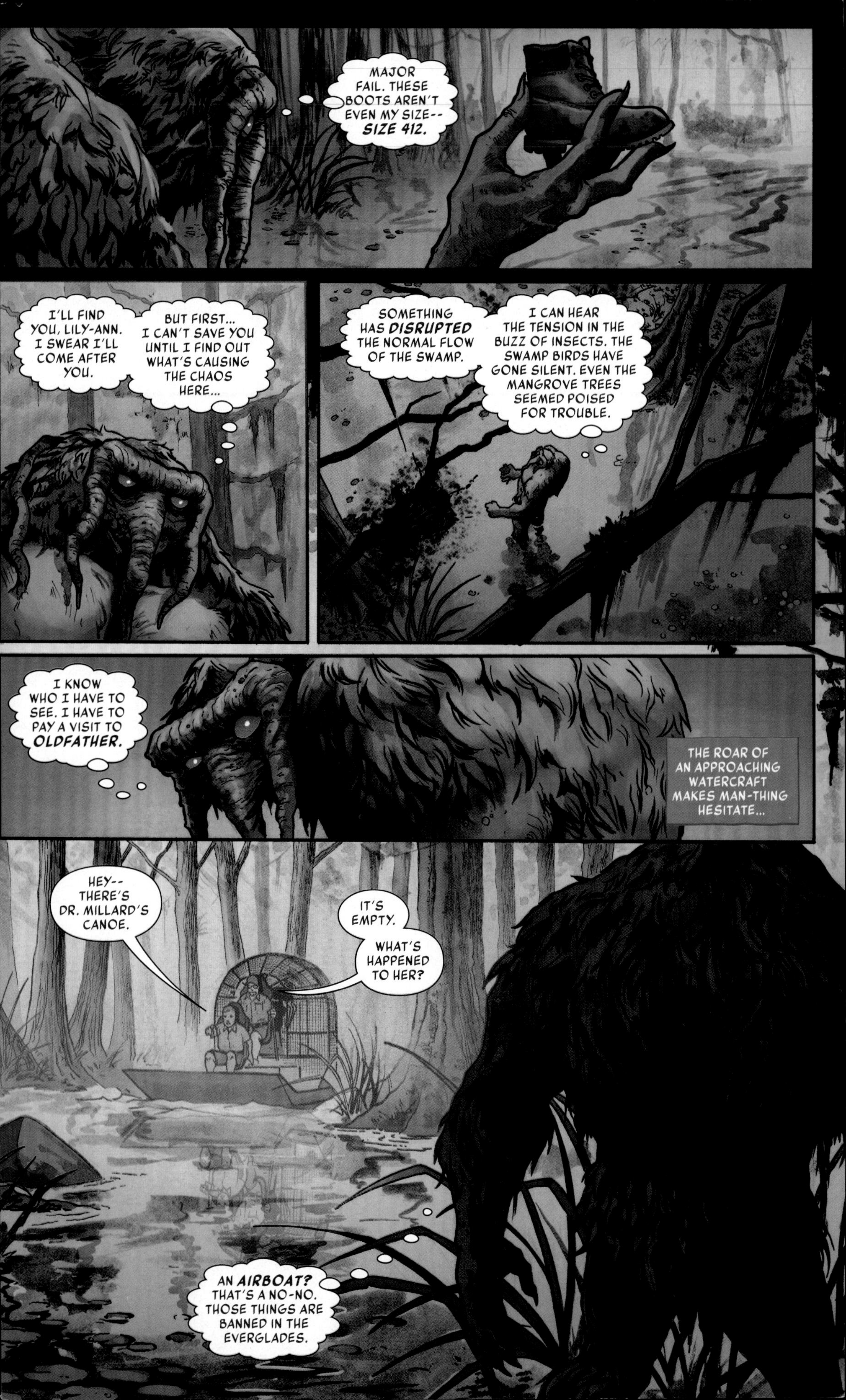
MAJOR FAIL. THESE BOOTS AREN'T EVEN MY SIZE-- SIZE 412.
I'LL FIND YOU, LILY-ANN. I SWEAR I'LL COME AFTER YOU.
BUT FIRST... I CAN'T SAVE YOU UNTIL I FIND OUT WHAT'S CAUSING THE CHAOS HERE...
SOMETHING HAS DISRUPTED THE NORMAL FLOW OF THE SWAMP.
I CAN HEAR THE TENSION IN THE BUZZ OF INSECTS. THE SWAMP BIRDS HAVE GONE SILENT. EVEN THE MANGROVE TREES SEEMED POISED FOR TROUBLE.
I KNOW WHO I HAVE TO SEE. I HAVE TO PAY A VISIT TO OLDFATHER.
THE ROAR OF AN APPROACHING WATERCRAFT MAKES MAN-THING HESITATE...
HEY-- THERE'S DR. MILLARD'S CANOE.
IT'S EMPTY.
WHAT'S HAPPENED TO HER?
AN AIRBOAT? THAT'S A NO-NO. THOSE THINGS ARE BANNED IN THE EVERGLADES.

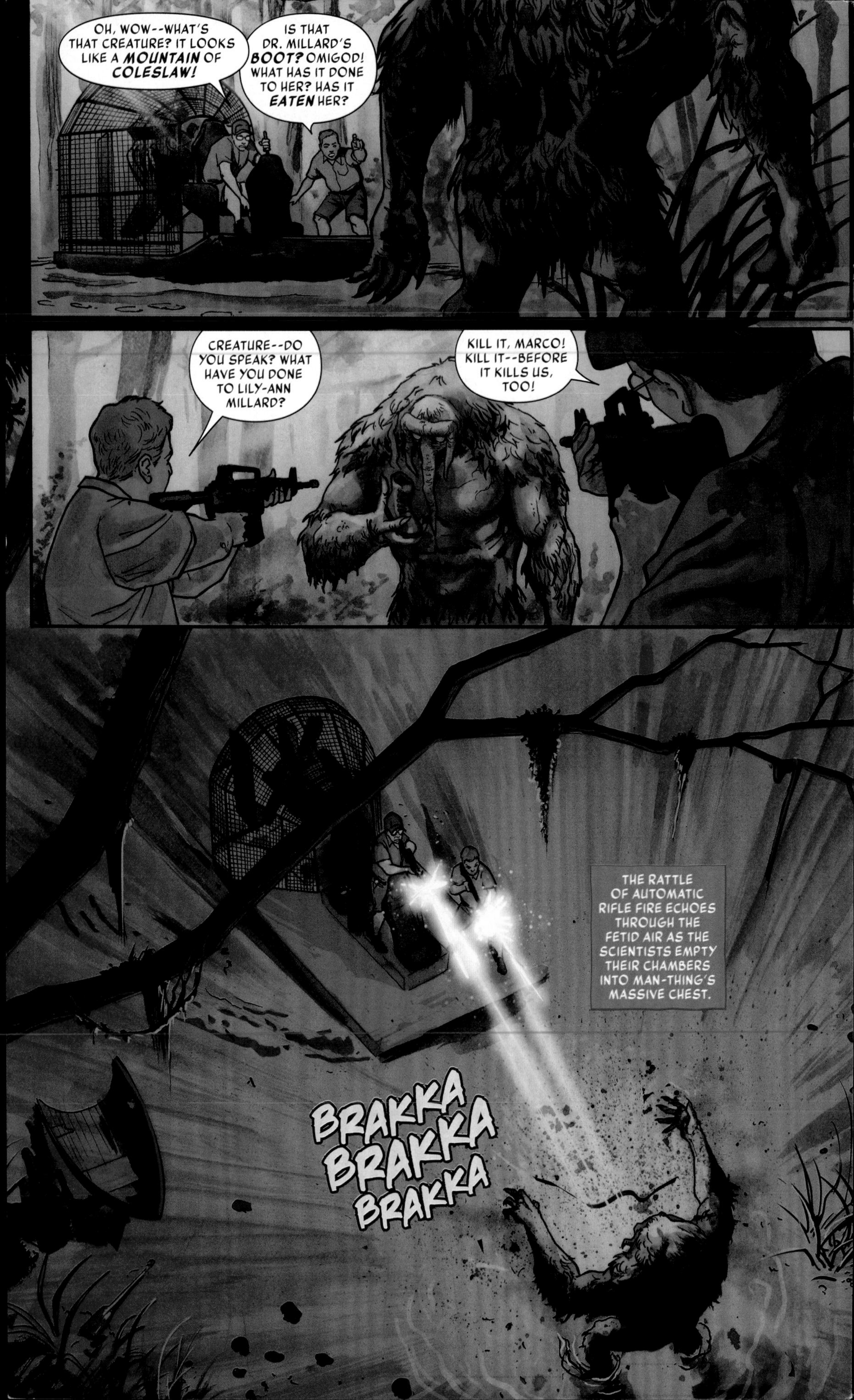
OH, WOW--WHAT'S THAT CREATURE? IT LOOKS LIKE A MOUNTAIN OF COLESLAW!
IS THAT DR. MILLARD'S BOOT? OMIGOD! WHAT HAS IT DONE TO HER? HAS IT EATEN HER?
CREATURE--DO YOU SPEAK? WHAT HAVE YOU DONE TO LILY-ANN MILLARD?
KILL IT, MARCO! KILL IT--BEFORE IT KILLS US, TOO!
THE RATTLE OF AUTOMATIC RIFLE FIRE ECHOES THROUGH THE FETID AIR AS THE SCIENTISTS EMPTY THEIR CHAMBERS INTO MAN-THING'S MASSIVE CHEST.
BRAKKA BRAKKA BRAKKA

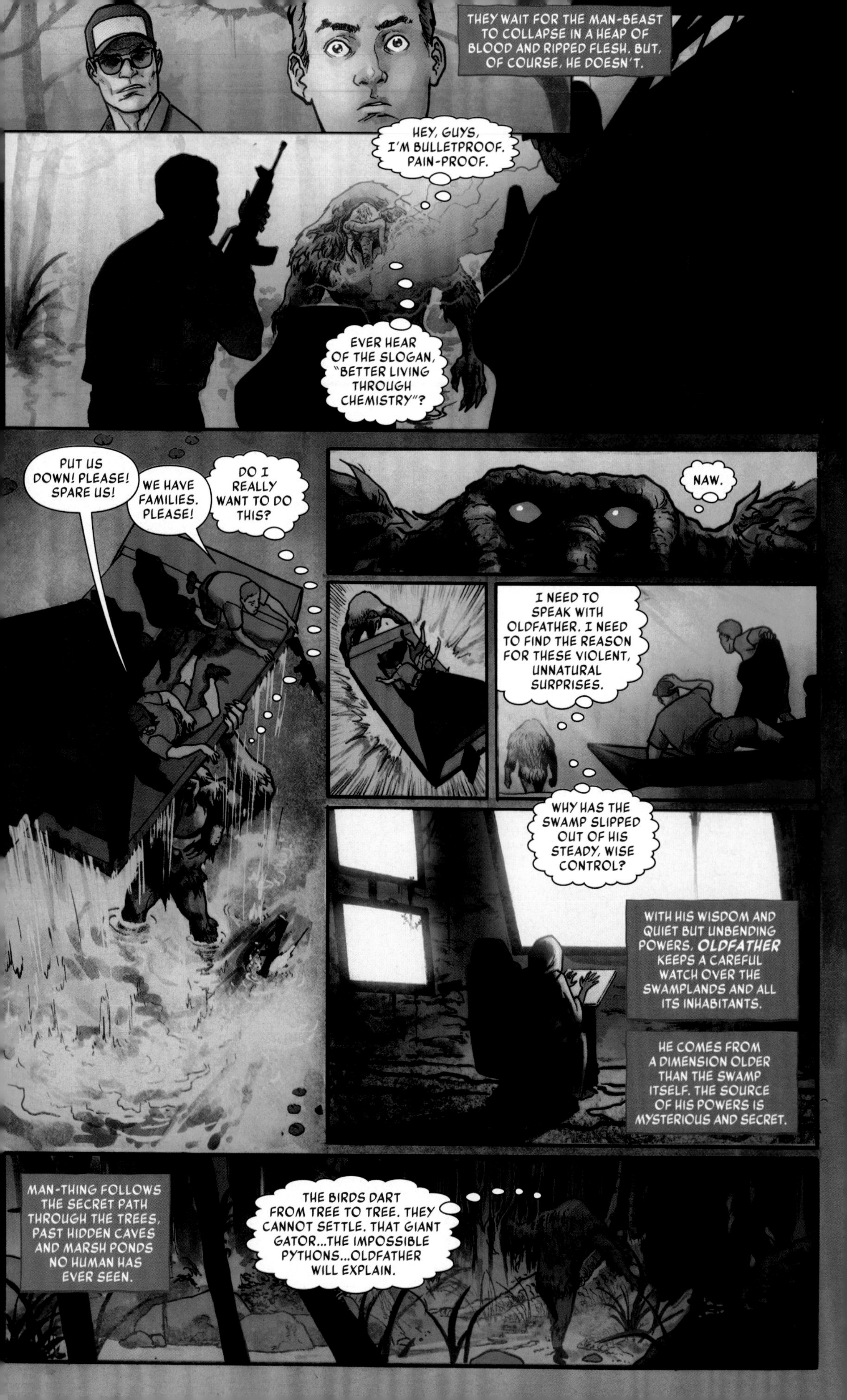
THEY WAIT FOR THE MAN-BEAST TO COLLAPSE IN A HEAP OF BLOOD AND RIPPED FLESH. BUT, OF COURSE, HE DOESN'T.
HEY, GUYS, I'M BULLETPROOF. PAIN-PROOF.
EVER HEAR OF THE SLOGAN, "BETTER LIVING THROUGH CHEMISTRY"?
PUT US DOWN! PLEASE! SPARE US!
WE HAVE FAMILIES. PLEASE!
DO I REALLY WANT TO DO THIS?
NAW.
I NEED TO SPEAK WITH OLDFATHER. I NEED TO FIND THE REASON FOR THESE VIOLENT, UNNATURAL SURPRISES.
WHY HAS THE SWAMP SLIPPED OUT OF HIS STEADY, WISE CONTROL?
WITH HIS WISDOM AND QUIET BUT UNBENDING POWERS, OLDFATHER KEEPS A CAREFUL WATCH OVER THE SWAMPLANDS AND ALL ITS INHABITANTS.
HE COMES FROM A DIMENSION OLDER THAN THE SWAMP ITSELF. THE SOURCE OF HIS POWERS IS MYSTERIOUS AND SECRET.
MAN-THING FOLLOWS THE SECRET PATH THROUGH THE TREES, PAST HIDDEN CAVES AND MARSH PONDS NO HUMAN HAS EVER SEEN.
THE BIRDS DART FROM TREE TO TREE. THEY CANNOT SETTLE. THAT GIANT GATOR...THE IMPOSSIBLE PYTHONS...OLDFATHER WILL EXPLAIN.

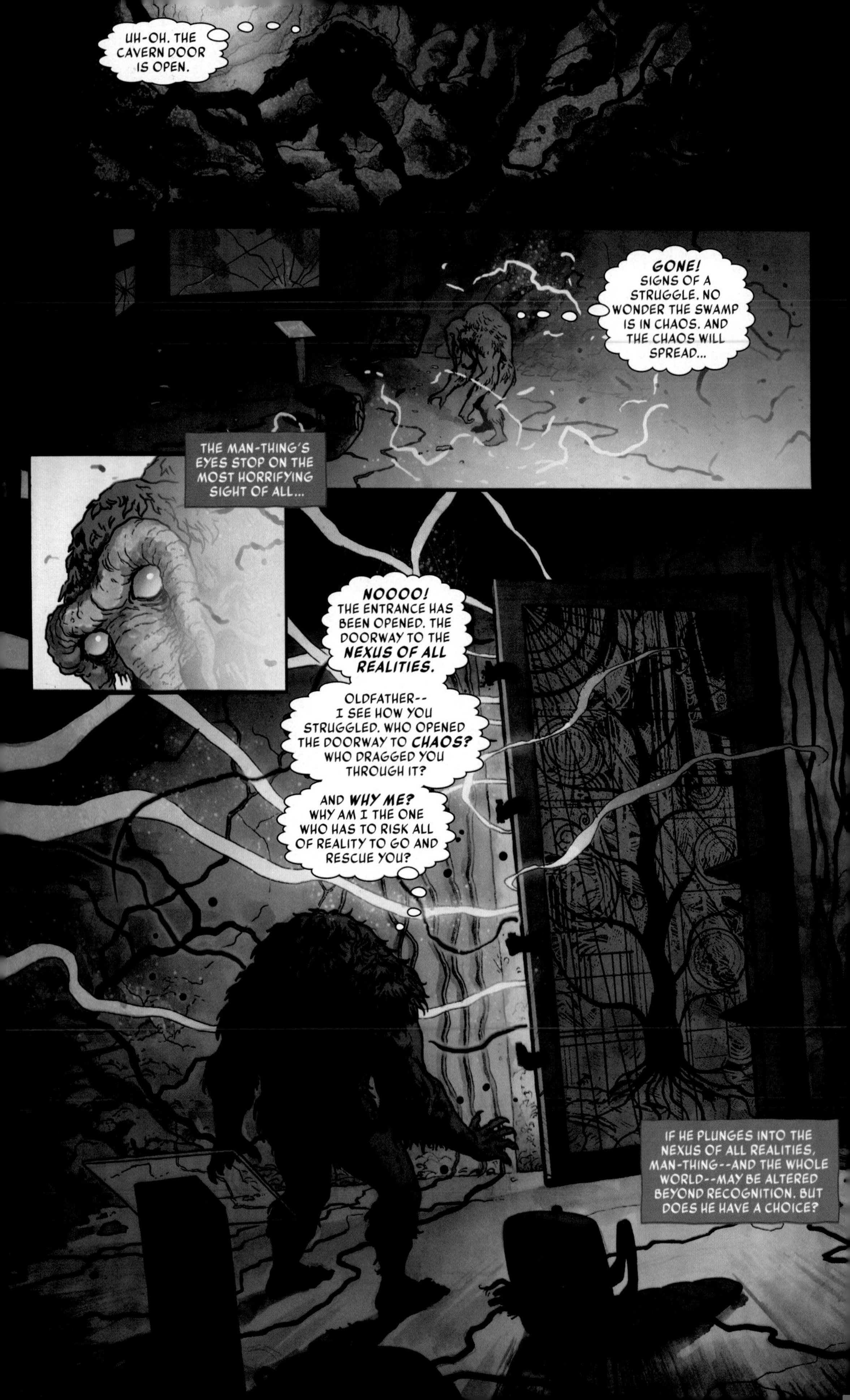

UH-OH. THE CAVERN DOOR IS OPEN.
GONE! SIGNS OF A STRUGGLE. NO WONDER THE SWAMP IS IN CHAOS. AND THE CHAOS WILL SPREAD...
THE MAN-THING'S EYES STOP ON THE MOST HORRIFYING SIGHT OF ALL...
NOOOO! THE ENTRANCE HAS BEEN OPENED. THE DOORWAY TO THE NEXUS OF ALL REALITIES.
OLDFATHER-- I SEE HOW YOU STRUGGLED. WHO OPENED THE DOORWAY TO CHAOS? WHO DRAGGED YOU THROUGH IT?
AND WHY ME? WHY AM I THE ONE WHO HAS TO RISK ALL OF REALITY TO GO AND RESCUE YOU?
IF HE PLUNGES INTO THE NEXUS OF ALL REALITIES, MAN-THING--AND THE WHOLE WORLD--MAY BE ALTERED BEYOND RECOGNITION. BUT DOES HE HAVE A CHOICE?

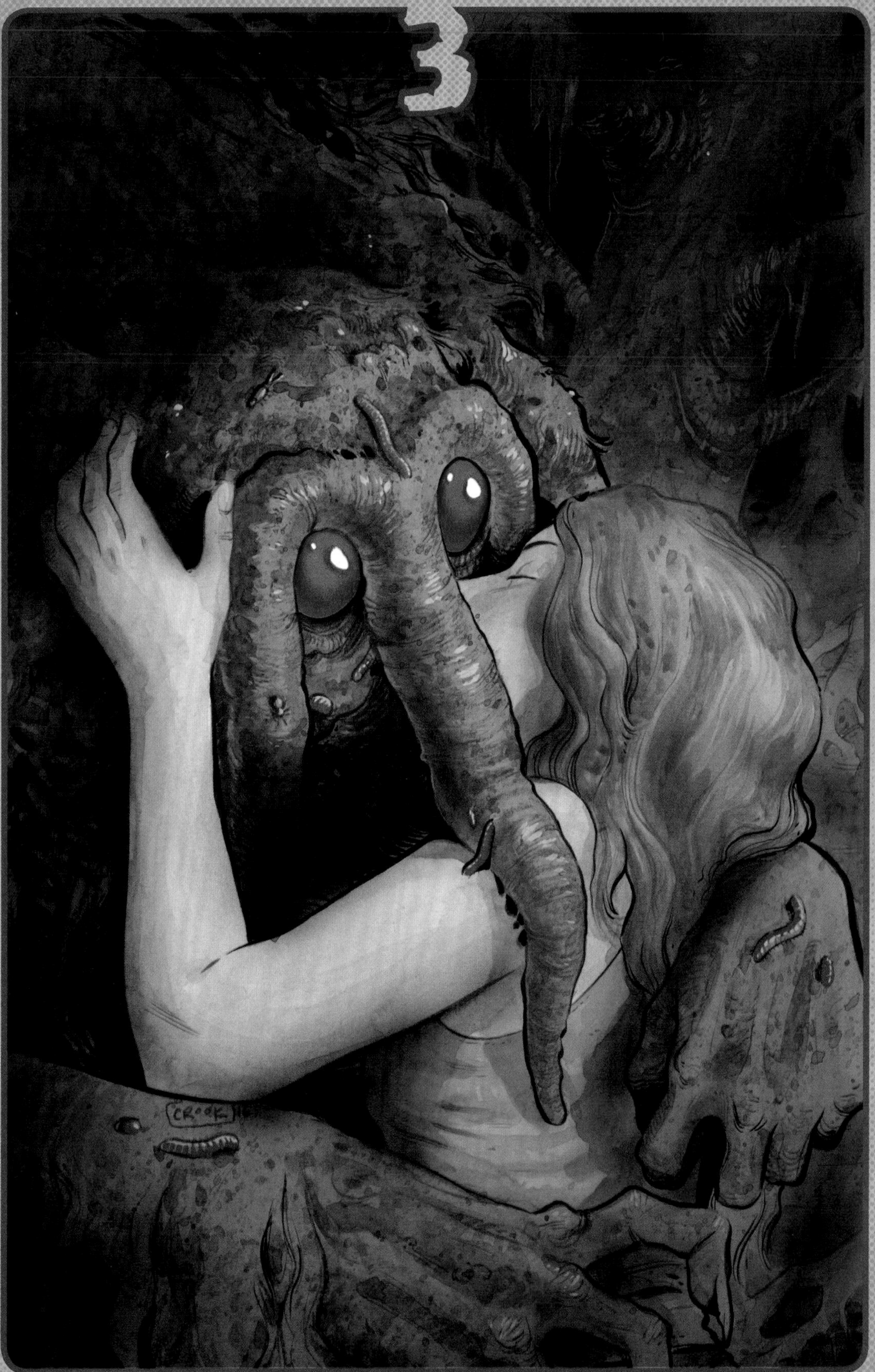
3
CROOK

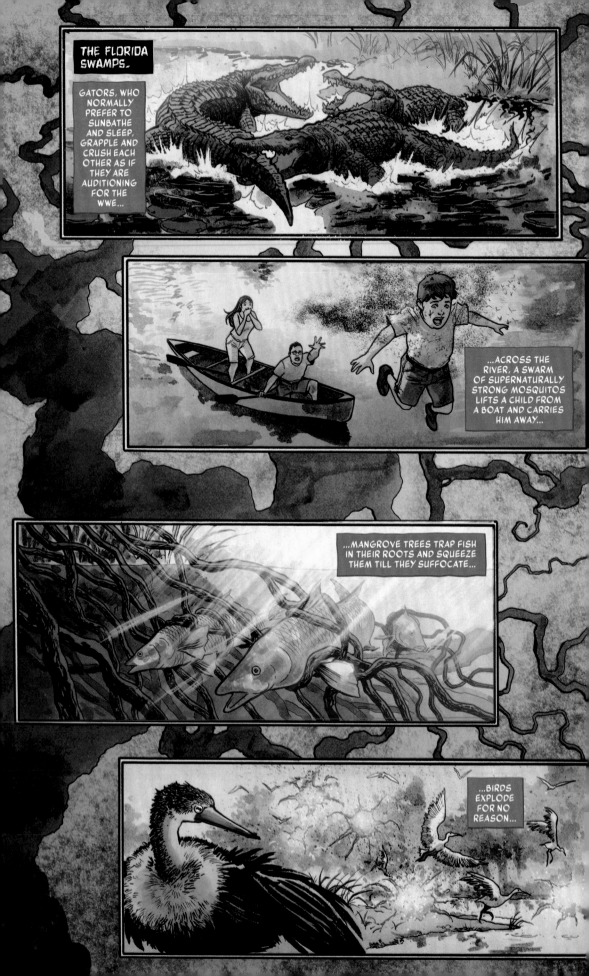

THE FLORIDA SWAMPS.

GATORS, WHO NORMALLY PREFER TO SUNBATHE AND SLEEP, GRAPPLE AND CRUSH EACH OTHER AS IF THEY ARE AUDITIONING FOR THE WWE...

...ACROSS THE RIVER, A SWARM OF SUPERNATURALLY STRONG MOSQUITOS LIFTS A CHILD FROM A BOAT AND CARRIES HIM AWAY...

...MANGROVE TREES TRAP FISH IN THEIR ROOTS AND SQUEEZE THEM TILL THEY SUFFOCATE...

...BIRDS EXPLODE FOR NO REASON...

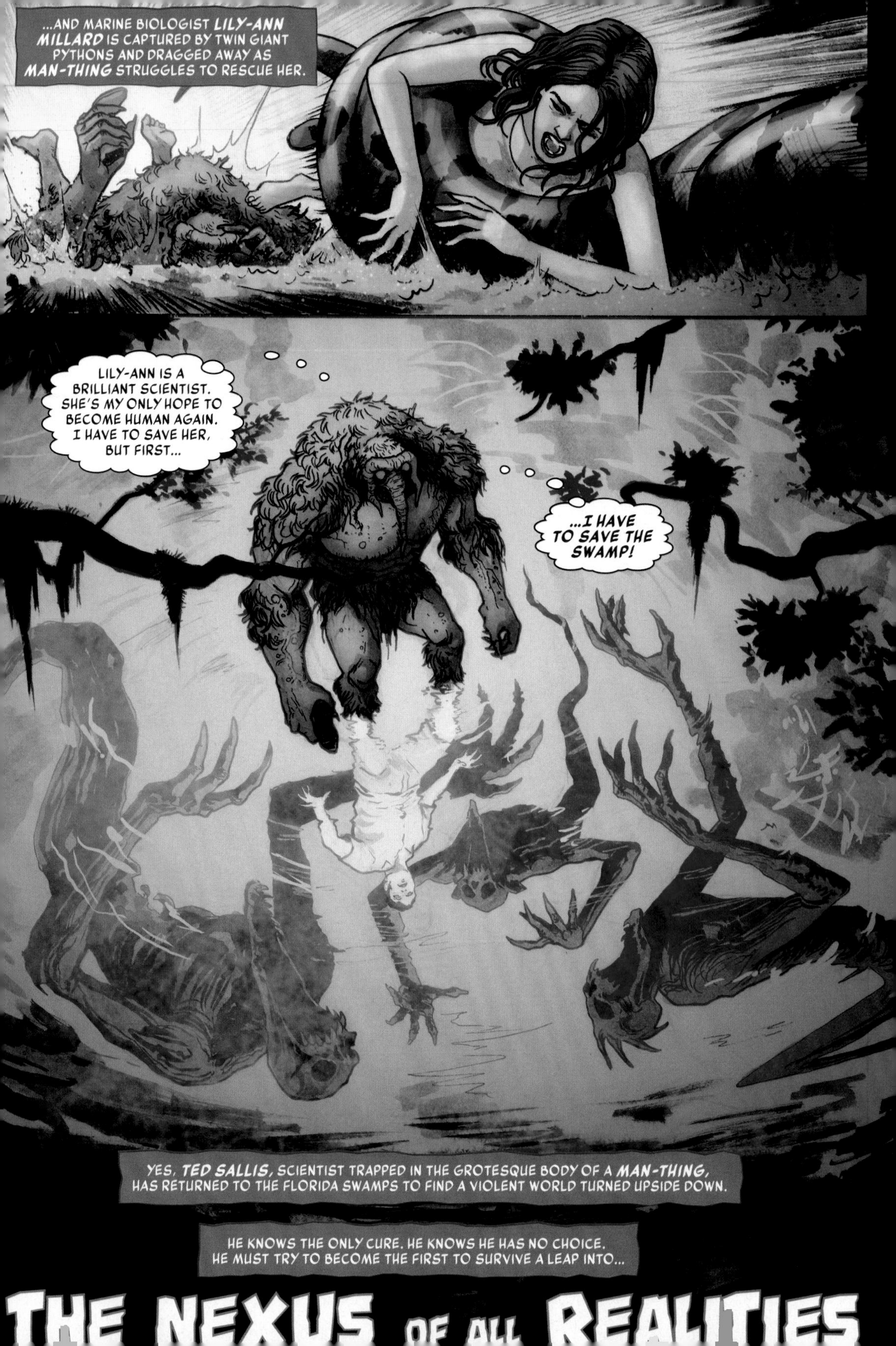
...AND MARINE BIOLOGIST LILY-ANN MILLARD IS CAPTURED BY TWIN GIANT PYTHONS AND DRAGGED AWAY AS MAN-THING STRUGGLES TO RESCUE HER.
LILY-ANN IS A BRILLIANT SCIENTIST. SHE'S MY ONLY HOPE TO BECOME HUMAN AGAIN. I HAVE TO SAVE HER, BUT FIRST...
...I HAVE TO SAVE THE SWAMP!
YES, TED SALLIS, SCIENTIST TRAPPED IN THE GROTESQUE BODY OF A MAN-THING, HAS RETURNED TO THE FLORIDA SWAMPS TO FIND A VIOLENT WORLD TURNED UPSIDE DOWN.
HE KNOWS THE ONLY CURE. HE KNOWS HE HAS NO CHOICE. HE MUST TRY TO BECOME THE FIRST TO SURVIVE A LEAP INTO...
THE NEXUS OF ALL REALITIES

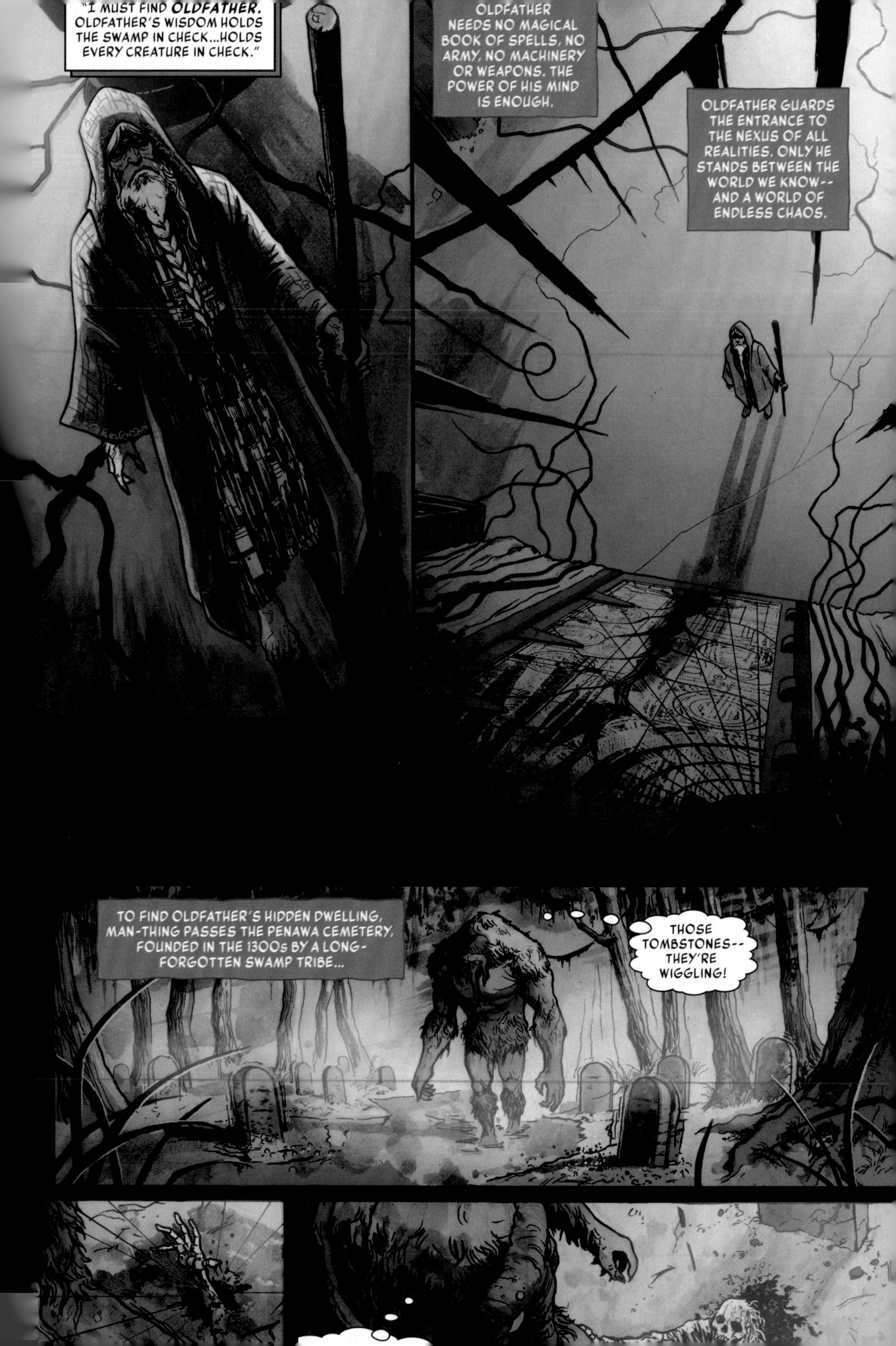
"I MUST FIND OLDFATHER. OLDFATHER'S WISDOM HOLDS THE SWAMP IN CHECK...HOLDS EVERY CREATURE IN CHECK."
OLDFATHER NEEDS NO MAGICAL BOOK OF SPELLS, NO ARMY, NO MACHINERY OR WEAPONS. THE POWER OF HIS MIND IS ENOUGH.
OLDFATHER GUARDS THE ENTRANCE TO THE NEXUS OF ALL REALITIES. ONLY HE STANDS BETWEEN THE WORLD WE KNOW-- AND A WORLD OF ENDLESS CHAOS.
TO FIND OLDFATHER'S HIDDEN DWELLING, MAN-THING PASSES THE PENAWA CEMETERY, FOUNDED IN THE 1300s BY A LONG-FORGOTTEN SWAMP TRIBE...
THOSE TOMBSTONES-- THEY'RE WIGGLING!

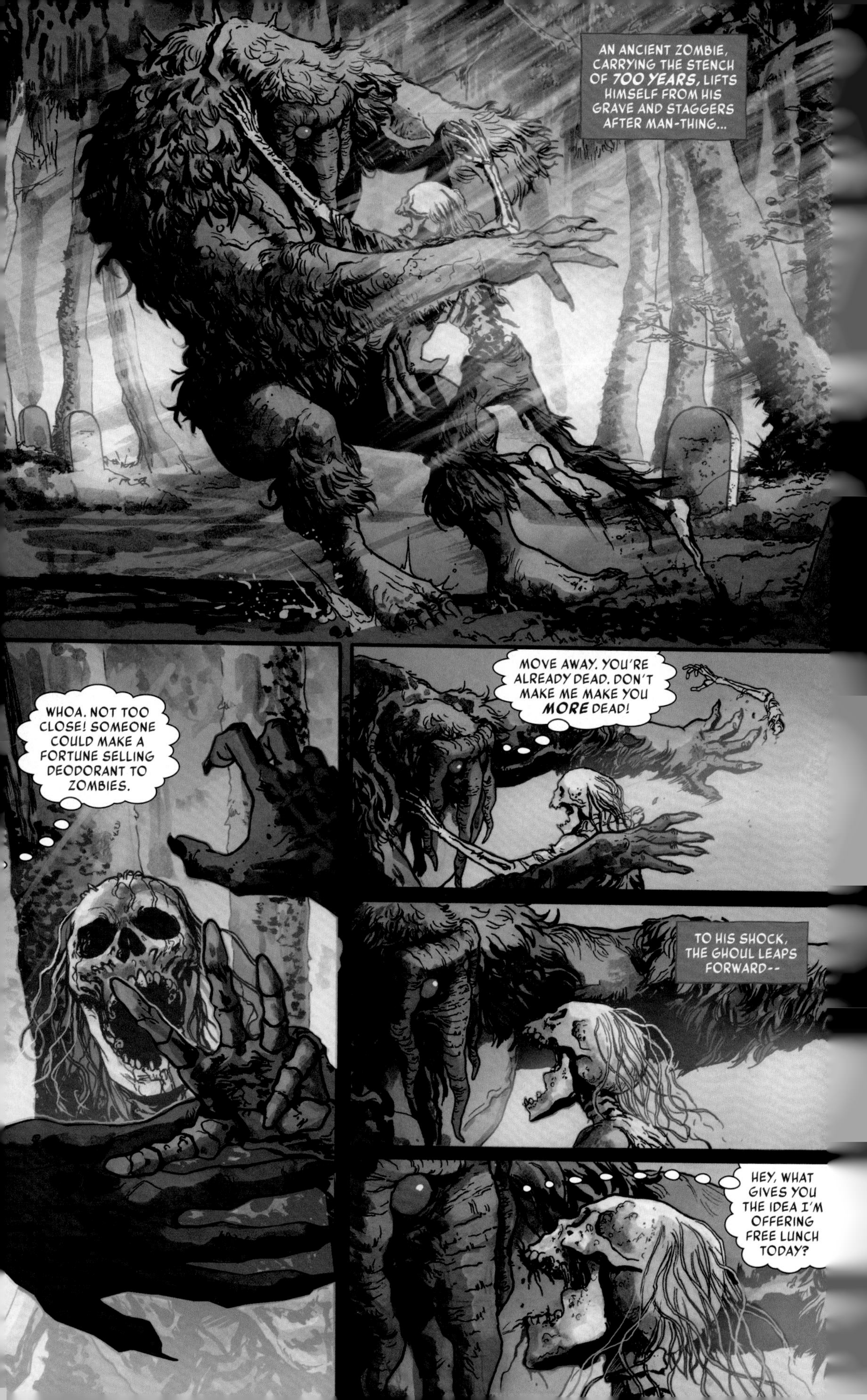
AN ANCIENT ZOMBIE, CARRYING THE STENCH OF 700 YEARS, LIFTS HIMSELF FROM HIS GRAVE AND STAGGERS AFTER MAN-THING...
WHOA. NOT TOO CLOSE! SOMEONE COULD MAKE A FORTUNE SELLING DEODORANT TO ZOMBIES.
MOVE AWAY. YOU'RE ALREADY DEAD. DON'T MAKE ME MAKE YOU MORE DEAD!
TO HIS SHOCK, THE GHOUL LEAPS FORWARD--
HEY, WHAT GIVES YOU THE IDEA I'M OFFERING FREE LUNCH TODAY?

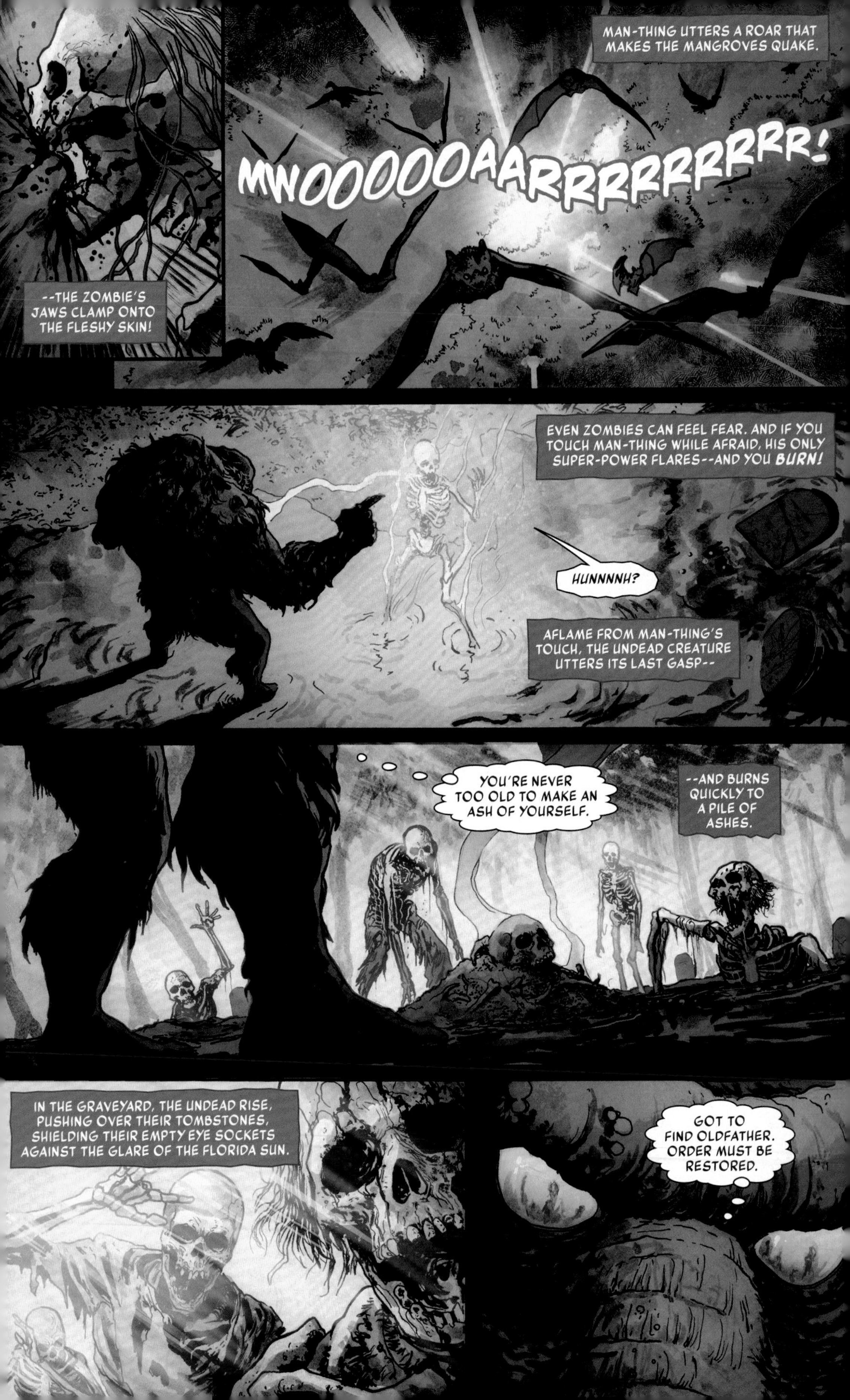
--THE ZOMBIE'S JAWS CLAMP ONTO THE FLESHY SKIN!
MAN-THING UTTERS A ROAR THAT MAKES THE MANGROVES QUAKE.
MWOOOOOOAARRRRRRRR!
EVEN ZOMBIES CAN FEEL FEAR. AND IF YOU TOUCH MAN-THING WHILE AFRAID, HIS ONLY SUPER-POWER FLARES--AND YOU BURN!
HUNNNNH?
AFLAME FROM MAN-THING'S TOUCH, THE UNDEAD CREATURE UTTERS ITS LAST GASP--
YOU'RE NEVER TOO OLD TO MAKE AN ASH OF YOURSELF.
--AND BURNS QUICKLY TO A PILE OF ASHES.
IN THE GRAVEYARD, THE UNDEAD RISE, PUSHING OVER THEIR TOMBSTONES, SHIELDING THEIR EMPTY EYE SOCKETS AGAINST THE GLARE OF THE FLORIDA SUN.
GOT TO FIND OLDFATHER. ORDER MUST BE RESTORED.

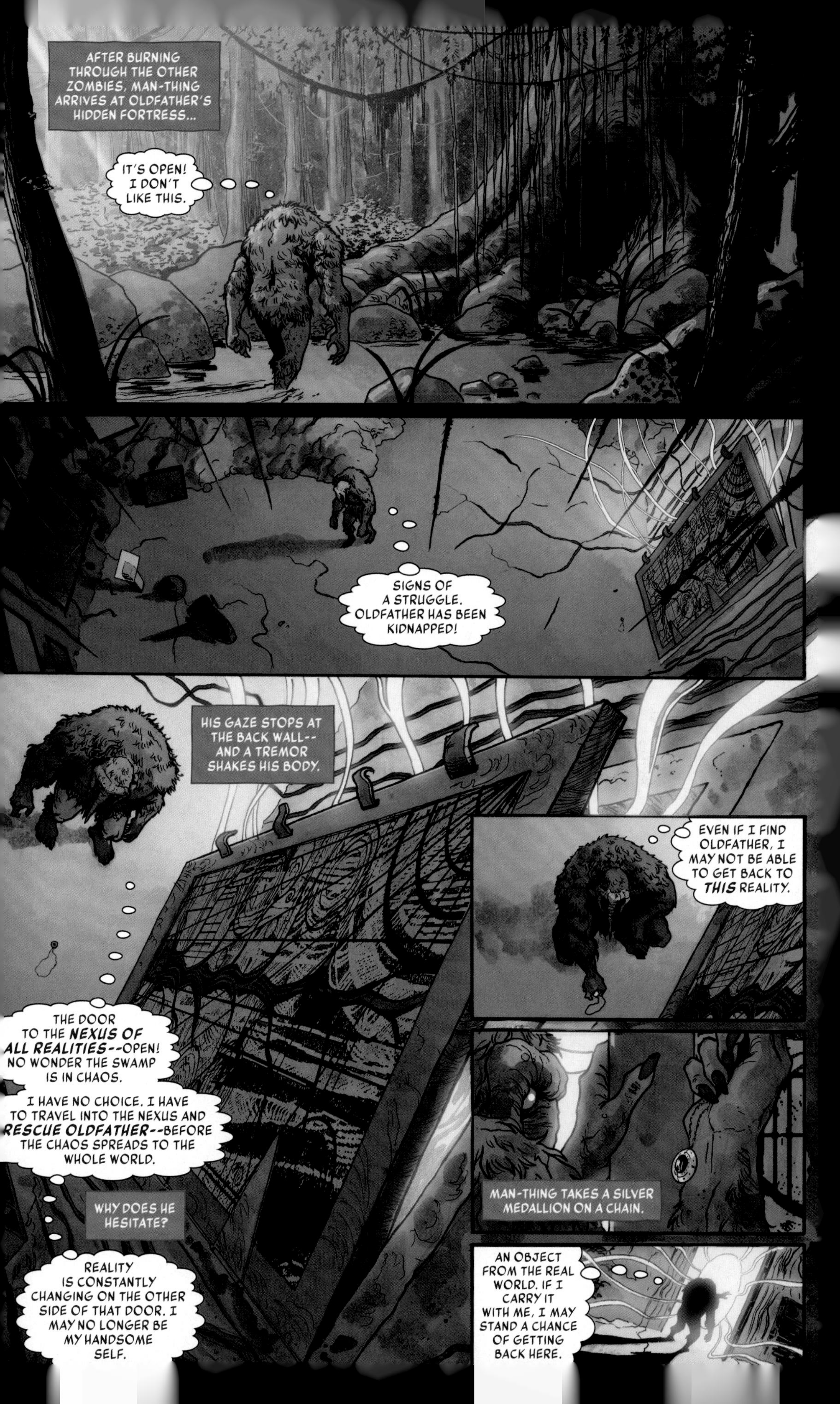
AFTER BURNING THROUGH THE OTHER ZOMBIES, MAN-THING ARRIVES AT OLDFATHER'S HIDDEN FORTRESS...
IT'S OPEN! I DON'T LIKE THIS.
SIGNS OF A STRUGGLE. OLDFATHER HAS BEEN KIDNAPPED!
HIS GAZE STOPS AT THE BACK WALL-- AND A TREMOR SHAKES HIS BODY.
THE DOOR TO THE NEXUS OF ALL REALITIES--OPEN! NO WONDER THE SWAMP IS IN CHAOS.
I HAVE NO CHOICE. I HAVE TO TRAVEL INTO THE NEXUS AND RESCUE OLDFATHER--BEFORE THE CHAOS SPREADS TO THE WHOLE WORLD.
WHY DOES HE HESITATE?
REALITY IS CONSTANTLY CHANGING ON THE OTHER SIDE OF THAT DOOR. I MAY NO LONGER BE MY HANDSOME SELF.
EVEN IF I FIND OLDFATHER, I MAY NOT BE ABLE TO GET BACK TO THIS REALITY.
MAN-THING TAKES A SILVER MEDALLION ON A CHAIN.
AN OBJECT FROM THE REAL WORLD. IF I CARRY IT WITH ME, I MAY STAND A CHANCE OF GETTING BACK HERE.

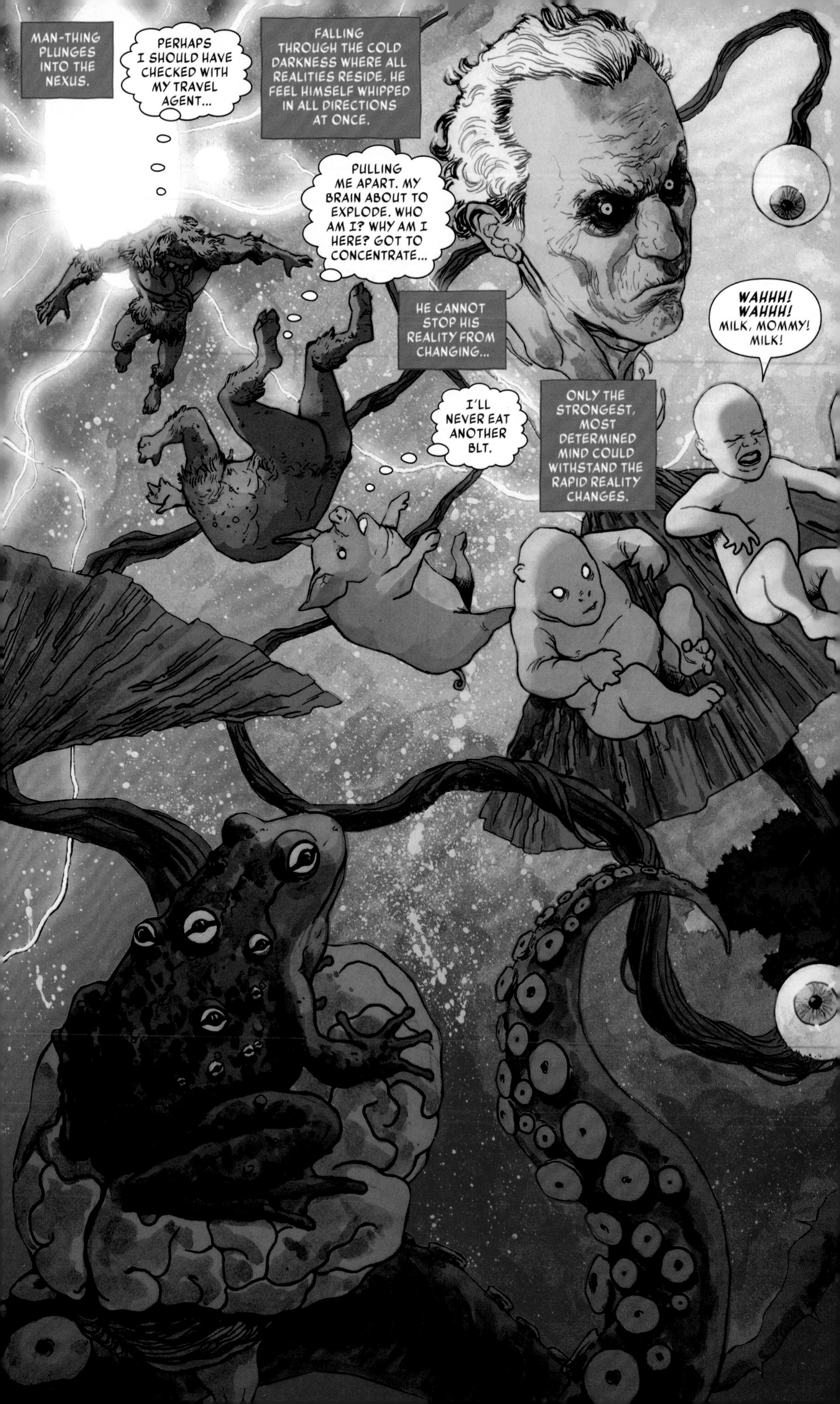

MAN-THING PLUNGES INTO THE NEXUS.
PERHAPS I SHOULD HAVE CHECKED WITH MY TRAVEL AGENT...
FALLING THROUGH THE COLD DARKNESS WHERE ALL REALITIES RESIDE, HE FEEL HIMSELF WHIPPED IN ALL DIRECTIONS AT ONCE.
PULLING ME APART. MY BRAIN ABOUT TO EXPLODE. WHO AM I? WHY AM I HERE? GOT TO CONCENTRATE...
HE CANNOT STOP HIS REALITY FROM CHANGING...
I'LL NEVER EAT ANOTHER BLT.
ONLY THE STRONGEST, MOST DETERMINED MIND COULD WITHSTAND THE RAPID REALITY CHANGES.
WAHHH! WAHHH! MILK, MOMMY! MILK!

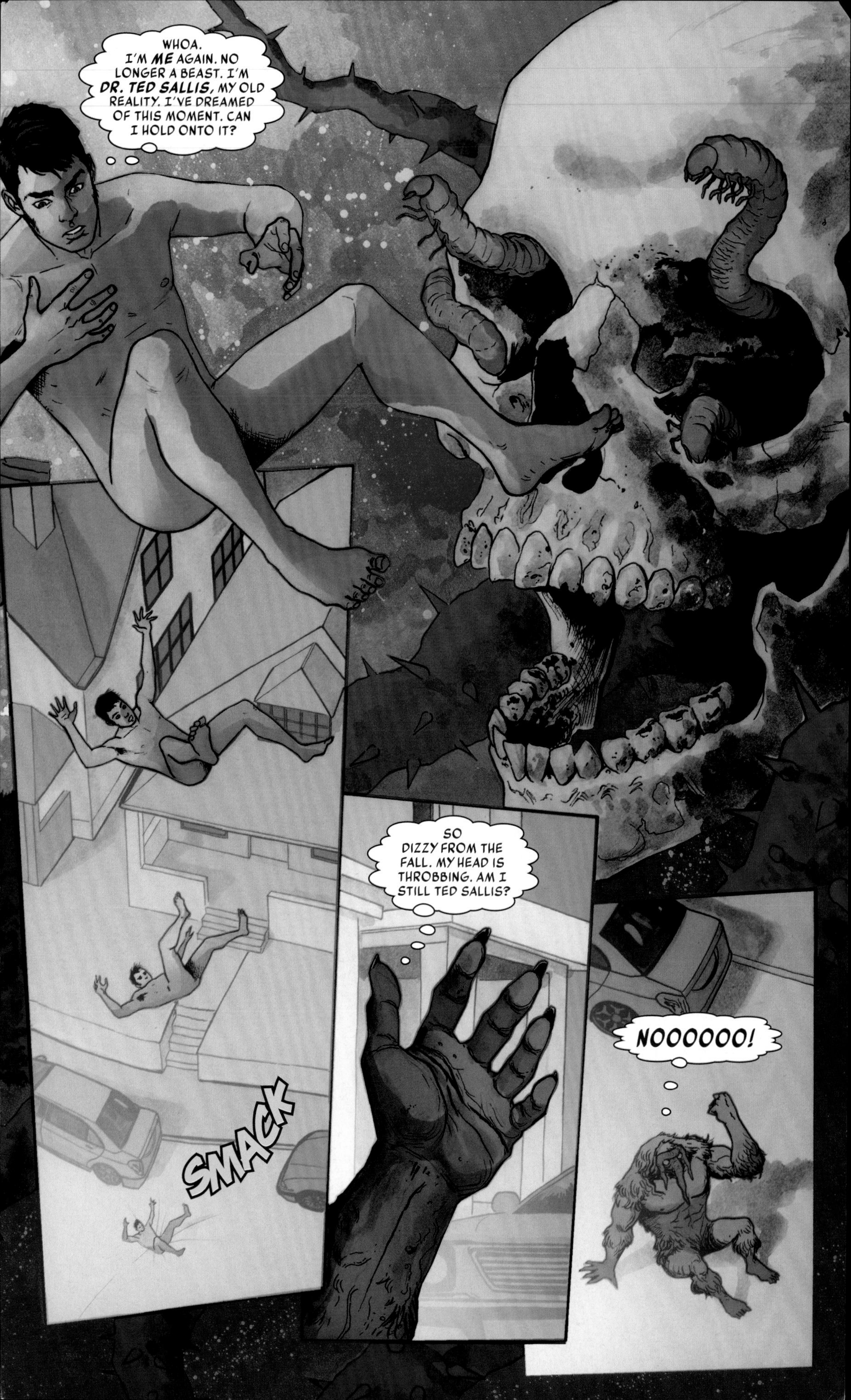
WHOA. I'M **ME** AGAIN. NO LONGER A BEAST. I'M **DR. TED SALLIS**, MY OLD REALITY. I'VE DREAMED OF THIS MOMENT. CAN I HOLD ONTO IT?
SMACK
SO DIZZY FROM THE FALL. MY HEAD IS THROBBING. AM I STILL TED SALLIS?
NOOOOOO!

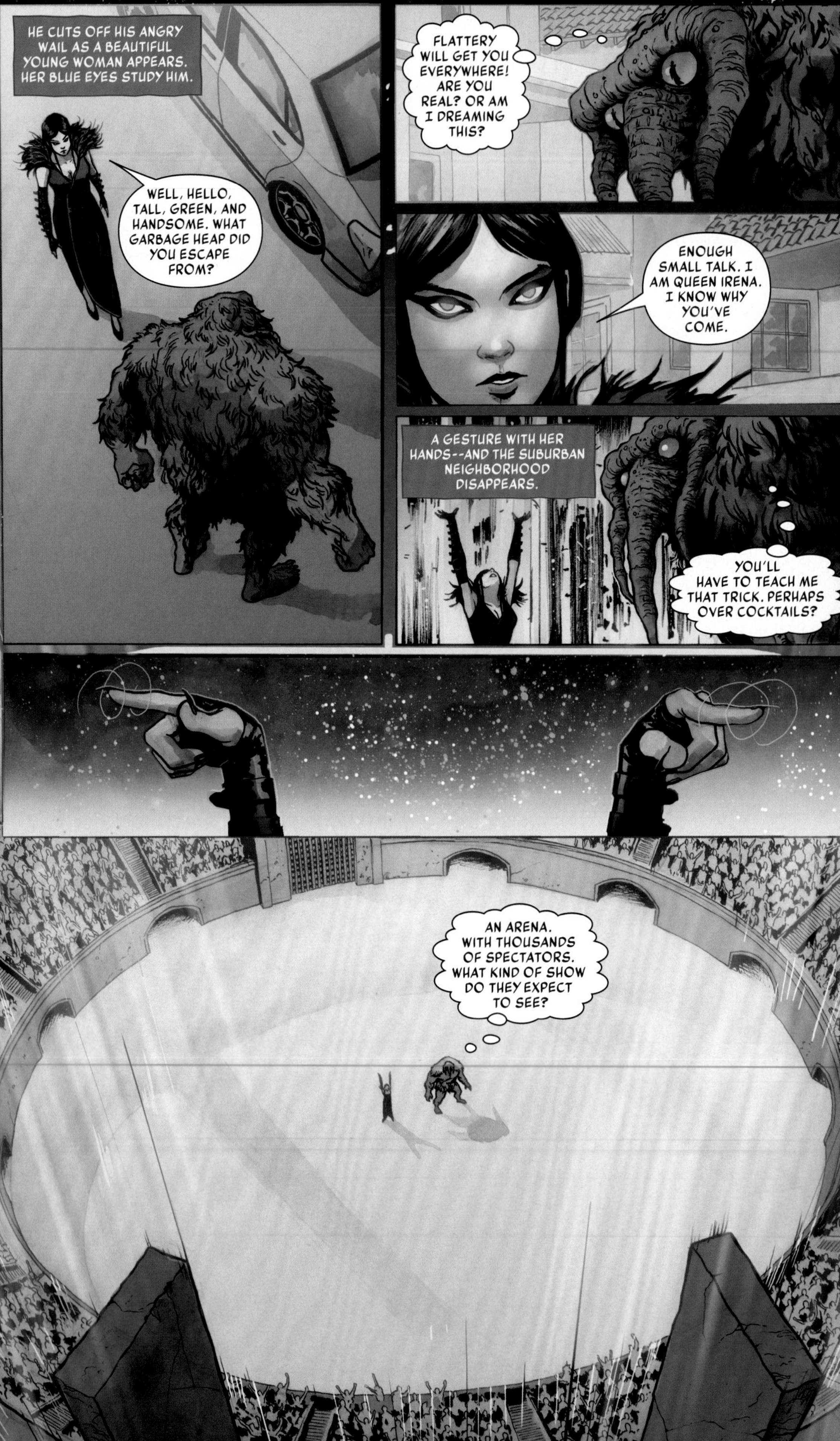
HE CUTS OFF HIS ANGRY WAIL AS A BEAUTIFUL YOUNG WOMAN APPEARS. HER BLUE EYES STUDY HIM.
WELL, HELLO, TALL, GREEN, AND HANDSOME. WHAT GARBAGE HEAP DID YOU ESCAPE FROM?
FLATTERY WILL GET YOU EVERYWHERE! ARE YOU REAL? OR AM I DREAMING THIS?
ENOUGH SMALL TALK. I AM QUEEN IRENA. I KNOW WHY YOU'VE COME.
A GESTURE WITH HER HANDS--AND THE SUBURBAN NEIGHBORHOOD DISAPPEARS.
YOU'LL HAVE TO TEACH ME THAT TRICK. PERHAPS OVER COCKTAILS?
AN ARENA. WITH THOUSANDS OF SPECTATORS. WHAT KIND OF SHOW DO THEY EXPECT TO SEE?

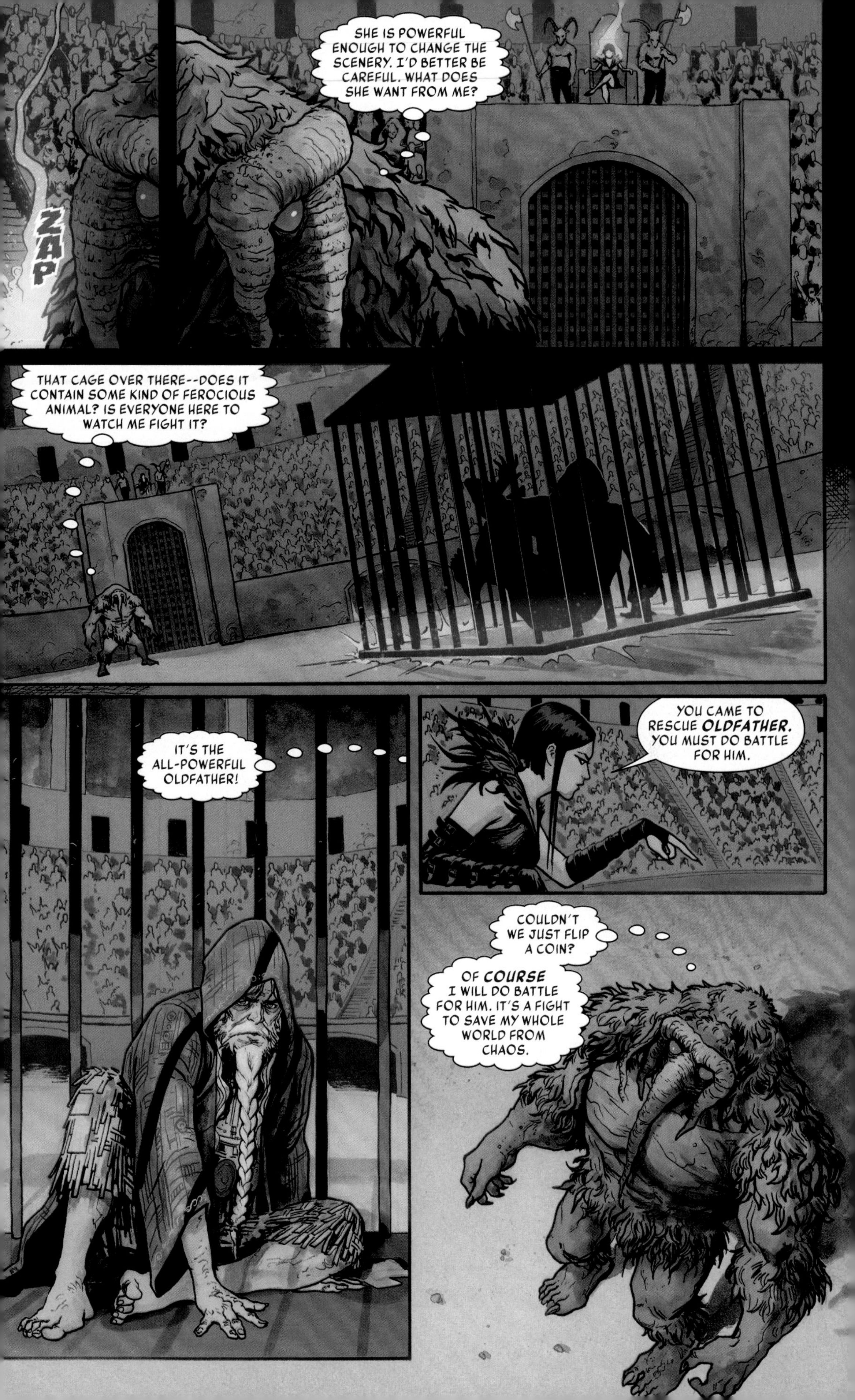
ZAP
SHE IS POWERFUL ENOUGH TO CHANGE THE SCENERY. I'D BETTER BE CAREFUL. WHAT DOES SHE WANT FROM ME?
THAT CAGE OVER THERE--DOES IT CONTAIN SOME KIND OF FEROCIOUS ANIMAL? IS EVERYONE HERE TO WATCH ME FIGHT IT?
IT'S THE ALL-POWERFUL OLDFATHER!
YOU CAME TO RESCUE OLDFATHER. YOU MUST DO BATTLE FOR HIM.
COULDN'T WE JUST FLIP A COIN?
OF COURSE I WILL DO BATTLE FOR HIM. IT'S A FIGHT TO SAVE MY WHOLE WORLD FROM CHAOS.

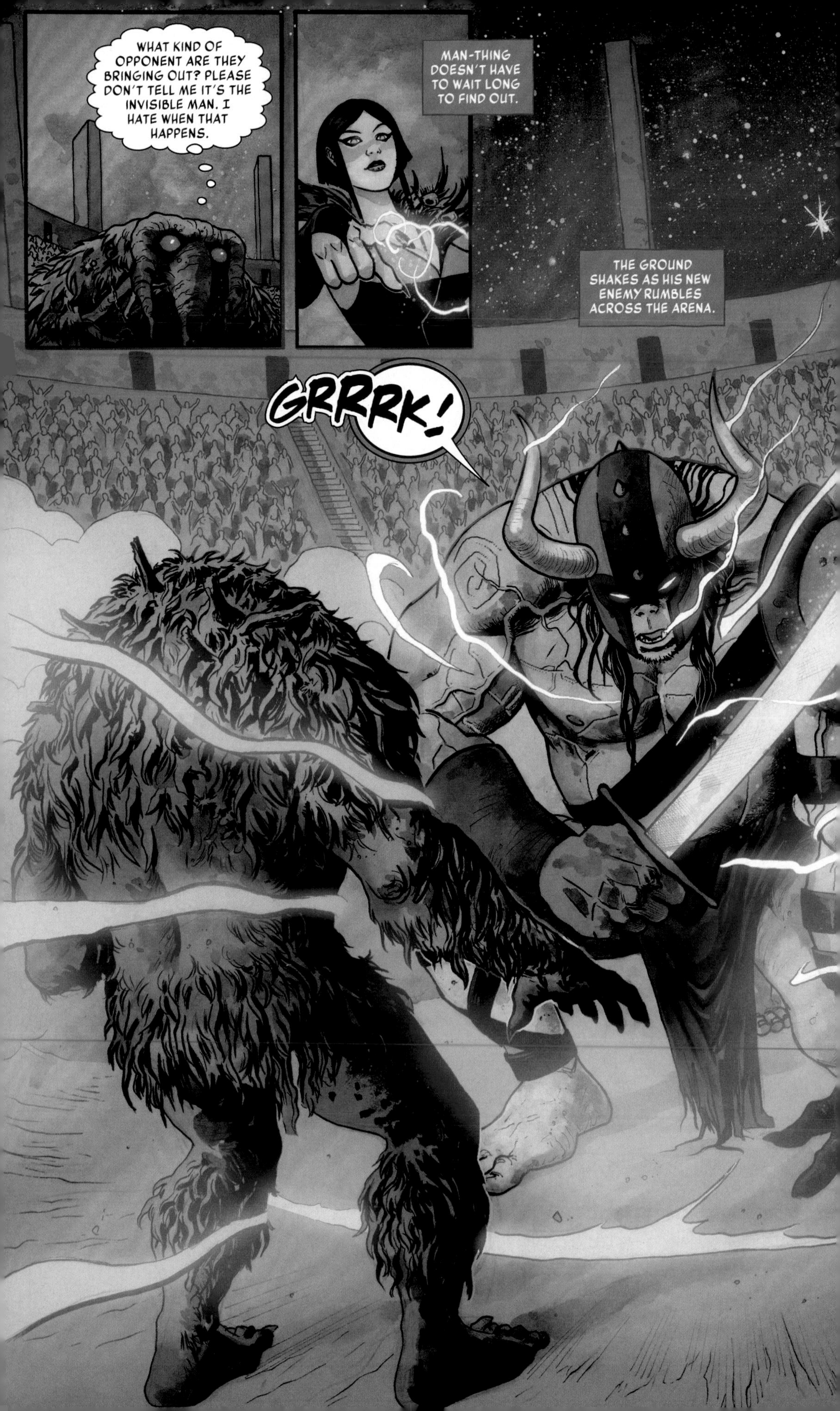

WHAT KIND OF OPPONENT ARE THEY BRINGING OUT? PLEASE DON'T TELL ME IT'S THE INVISIBLE MAN. I HATE WHEN THAT HAPPENS.
MAN-THING DOESN'T HAVE TO WAIT LONG TO FIND OUT.
THE GROUND SHAKES AS HIS NEW ENEMY RUMBLES ACROSS THE ARENA.
GRRRK!

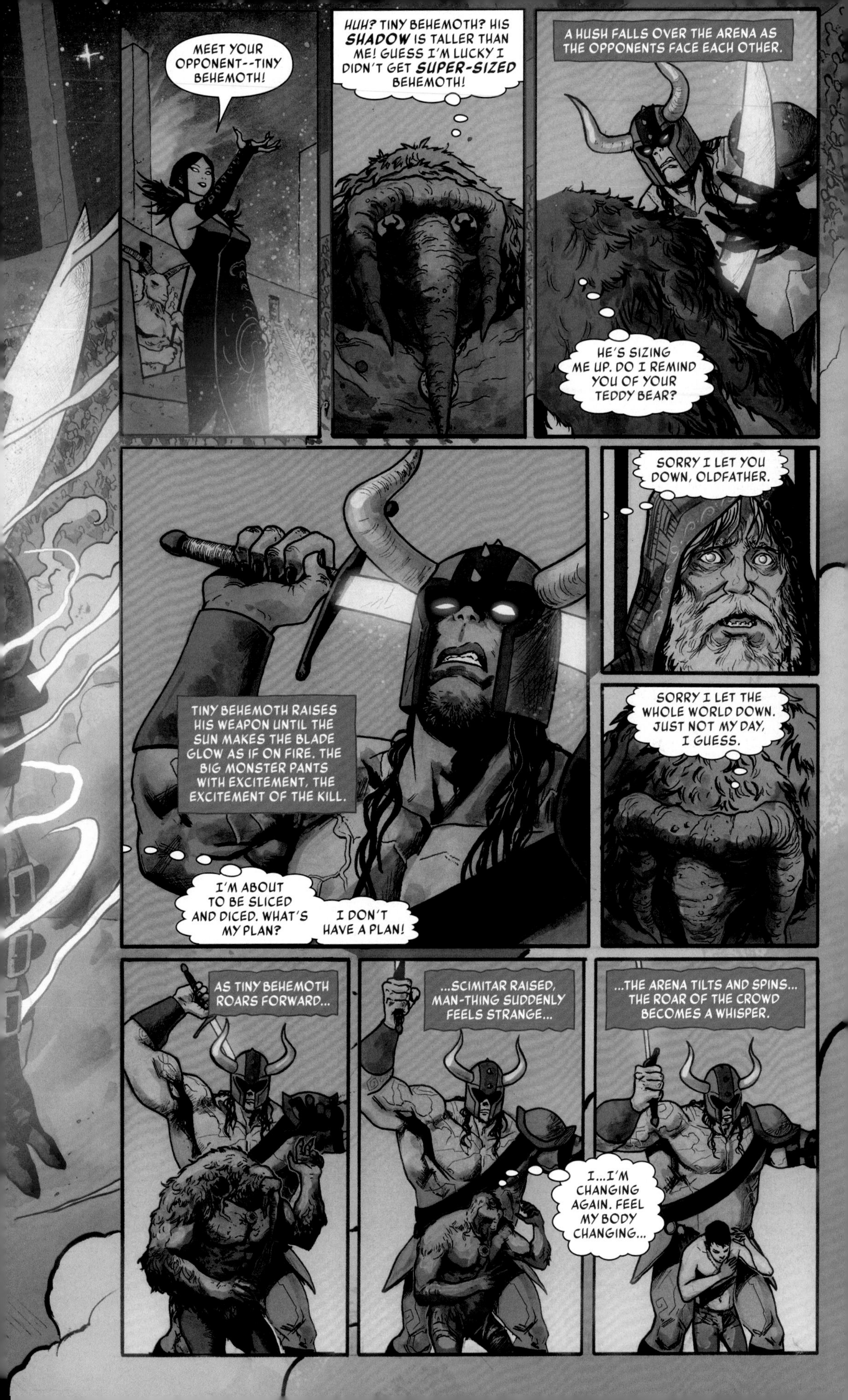
MEET YOUR OPPONENT--TINY BEHEMOTH!
HUH? TINY BEHEMOTH? HIS SHADOW IS TALLER THAN ME! GUESS I'M LUCKY I DIDN'T GET SUPER-SIZED BEHEMOTH!
A HUSH FALLS OVER THE ARENA AS THE OPPONENTS FACE EACH OTHER.
HE'S SIZING ME UP. DO I REMIND YOU OF YOUR TEDDY BEAR?
TINY BEHEMOTH RAISES HIS WEAPON UNTIL THE SUN MAKES THE BLADE GLOW AS IF ON FIRE. THE BIG MONSTER PANTS WITH EXCITEMENT, THE EXCITEMENT OF THE KILL.
I'M ABOUT TO BE SLICED AND DICED. WHAT'S MY PLAN?
I DON'T HAVE A PLAN!
SORRY I LET YOU DOWN, OLDFATHER.
SORRY I LET THE WHOLE WORLD DOWN. JUST NOT MY DAY, I GUESS.
AS TINY BEHEMOTH ROARS FORWARD...
...SCIMITAR RAISED, MAN-THING SUDDENLY FEELS STRANGE...
...THE ARENA TILTS AND SPINS... THE ROAR OF THE CROWD BECOMES A WHISPER.
I...I'M CHANGING AGAIN. FEEL MY BODY CHANGING...

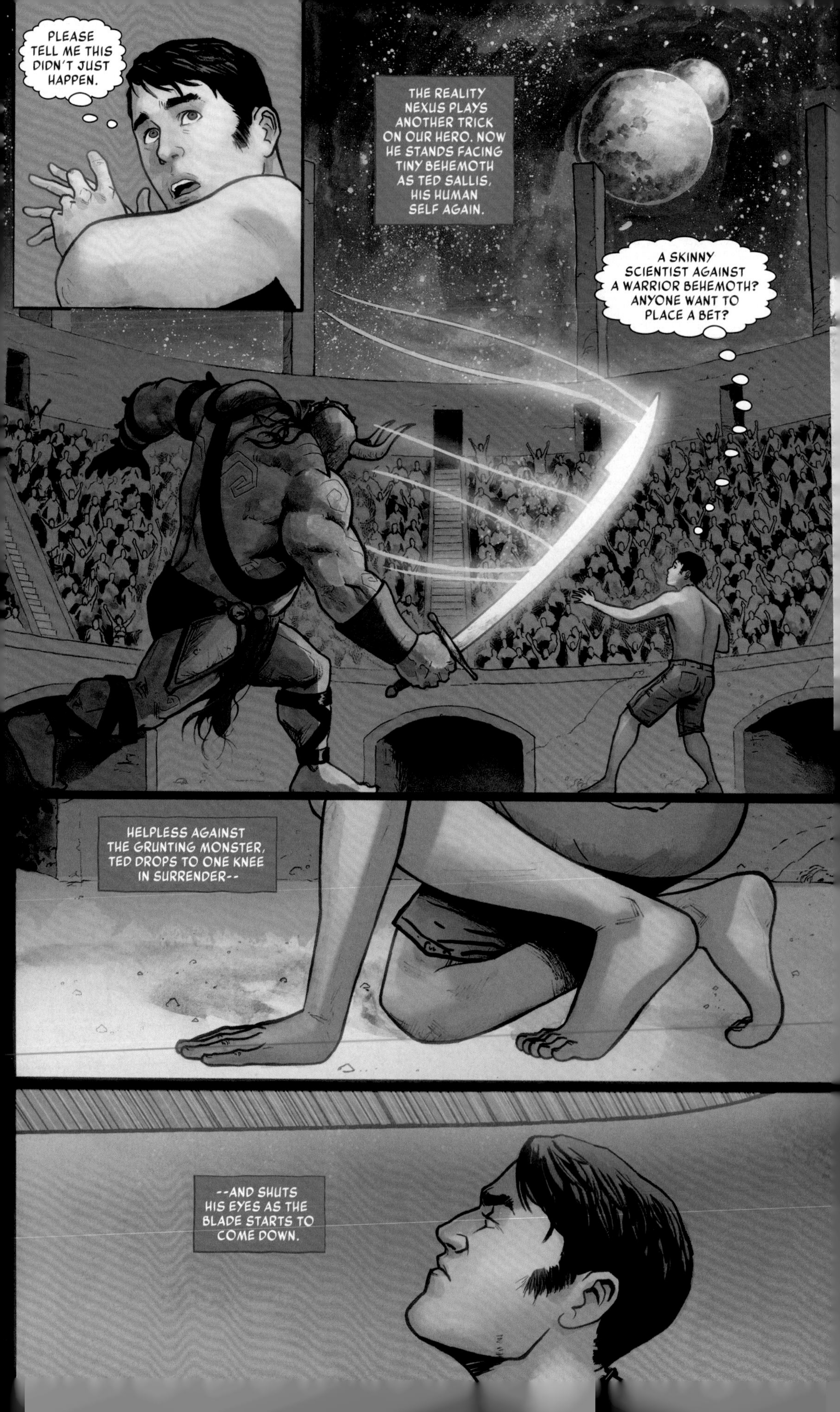
PLEASE TELL ME THIS DIDN'T JUST HAPPEN.
THE REALITY NEXUS PLAYS ANOTHER TRICK ON OUR HERO. NOW HE STANDS FACING TINY BEHEMOTH AS TED SALLIS, HIS HUMAN SELF AGAIN.
A SKINNY SCIENTIST AGAINST A WARRIOR BEHEMOTH? ANYONE WANT TO PLACE A BET?
HELPLESS AGAINST THE GRUNTING MONSTER, TED DROPS TO ONE KNEE IN SURRENDER--
--AND SHUTS HIS EYES AS THE BLADE STARTS TO COME DOWN.

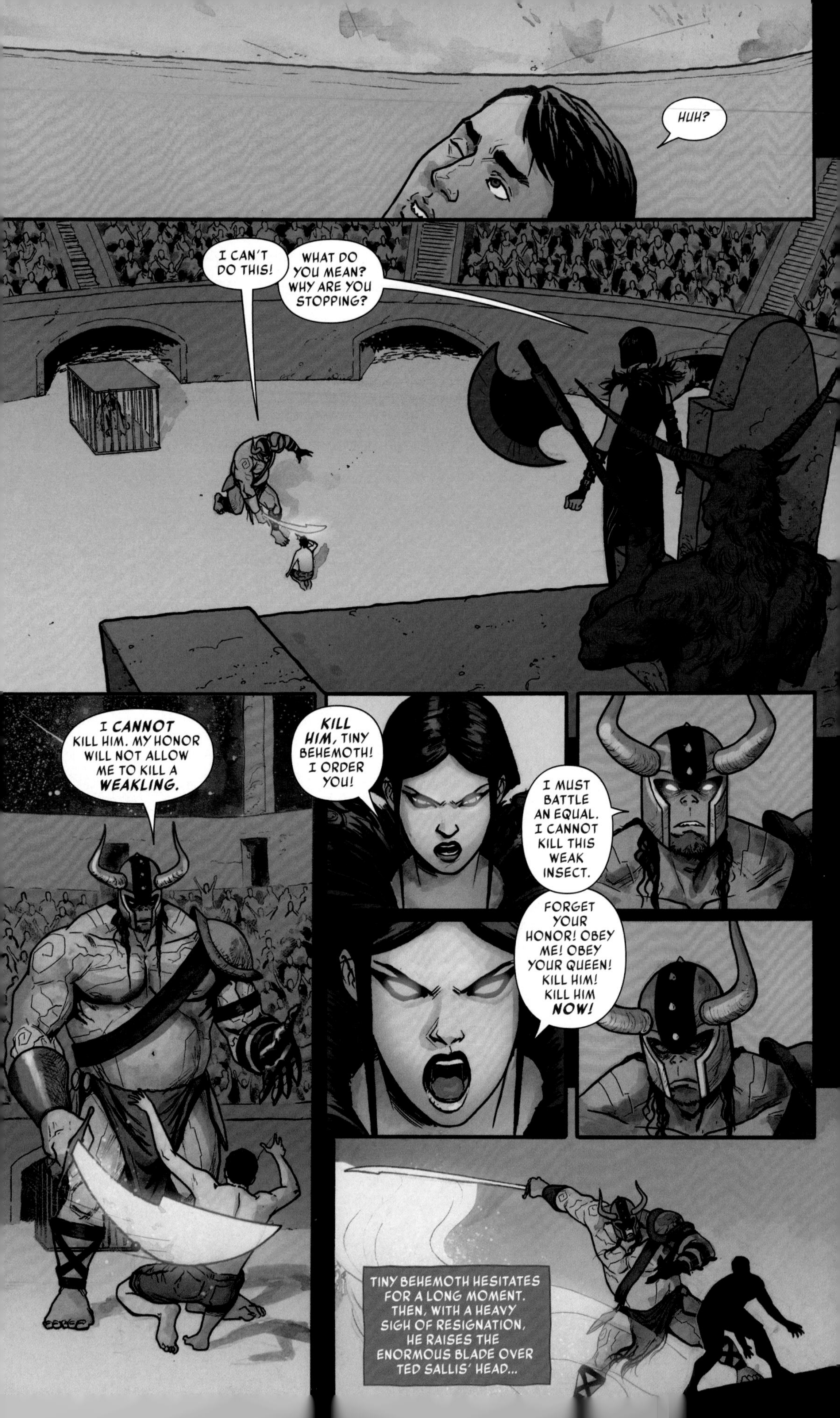
HUH?
I CAN'T DO THIS!
WHAT DO YOU MEAN? WHY ARE YOU STOPPING?
I CANNOT KILL HIM. MY HONOR WILL NOT ALLOW ME TO KILL A WEAKLING.
KILL HIM, TINY BEHEMOTH! I ORDER YOU!
I MUST BATTLE AN EQUAL. I CANNOT KILL THIS WEAK INSECT.
FORGET YOUR HONOR! OBEY ME! OBEY YOUR QUEEN! KILL HIM! KILL HIM NOW!
TINY BEHEMOTH HESITATES FOR A LONG MOMENT. THEN, WITH A HEAVY SIGH OF RESIGNATION, HE RAISES THE ENORMOUS BLADE OVER TED SALLIS' HEAD...

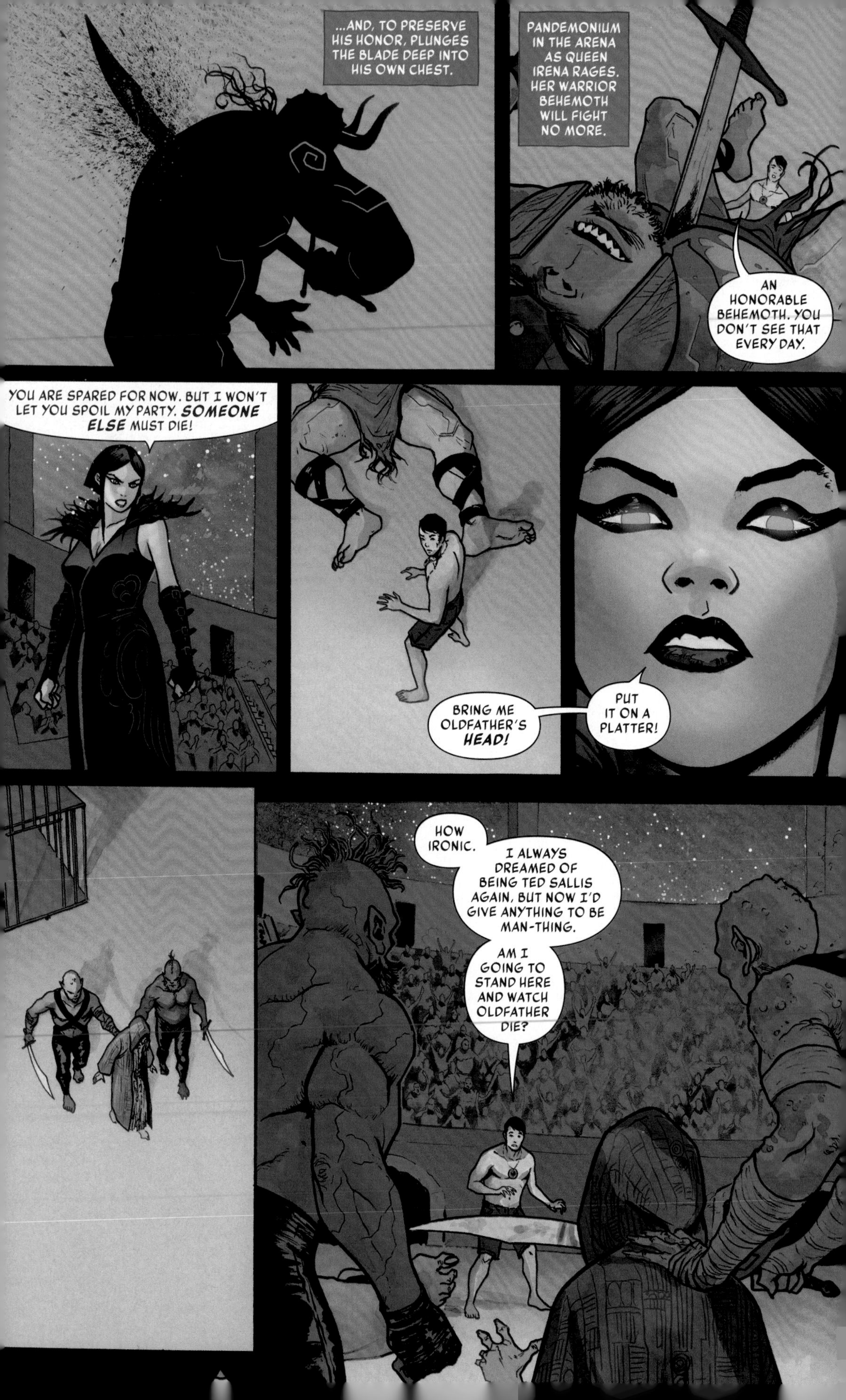
...AND, TO PRESERVE HIS HONOR, PLUNGES THE BLADE DEEP INTO HIS OWN CHEST.
PANDEMONIUM IN THE ARENA AS QUEEN IRENA RAGES. HER WARRIOR BEHEMOTH WILL FIGHT NO MORE.
AN HONORABLE BEHEMOTH. YOU DON'T SEE THAT EVERY DAY.
YOU ARE SPARED FOR NOW. BUT I WON'T LET YOU SPOIL MY PARTY. SOMEONE ELSE MUST DIE!
BRING ME OLDFATHER'S HEAD!
PUT IT ON A PLATTER!
HOW IRONIC.
I ALWAYS DREAMED OF BEING TED SALLIS AGAIN, BUT NOW I'D GIVE ANYTHING TO BE MAN-THING.
AM I GOING TO STAND HERE AND WATCH OLDFATHER DIE?

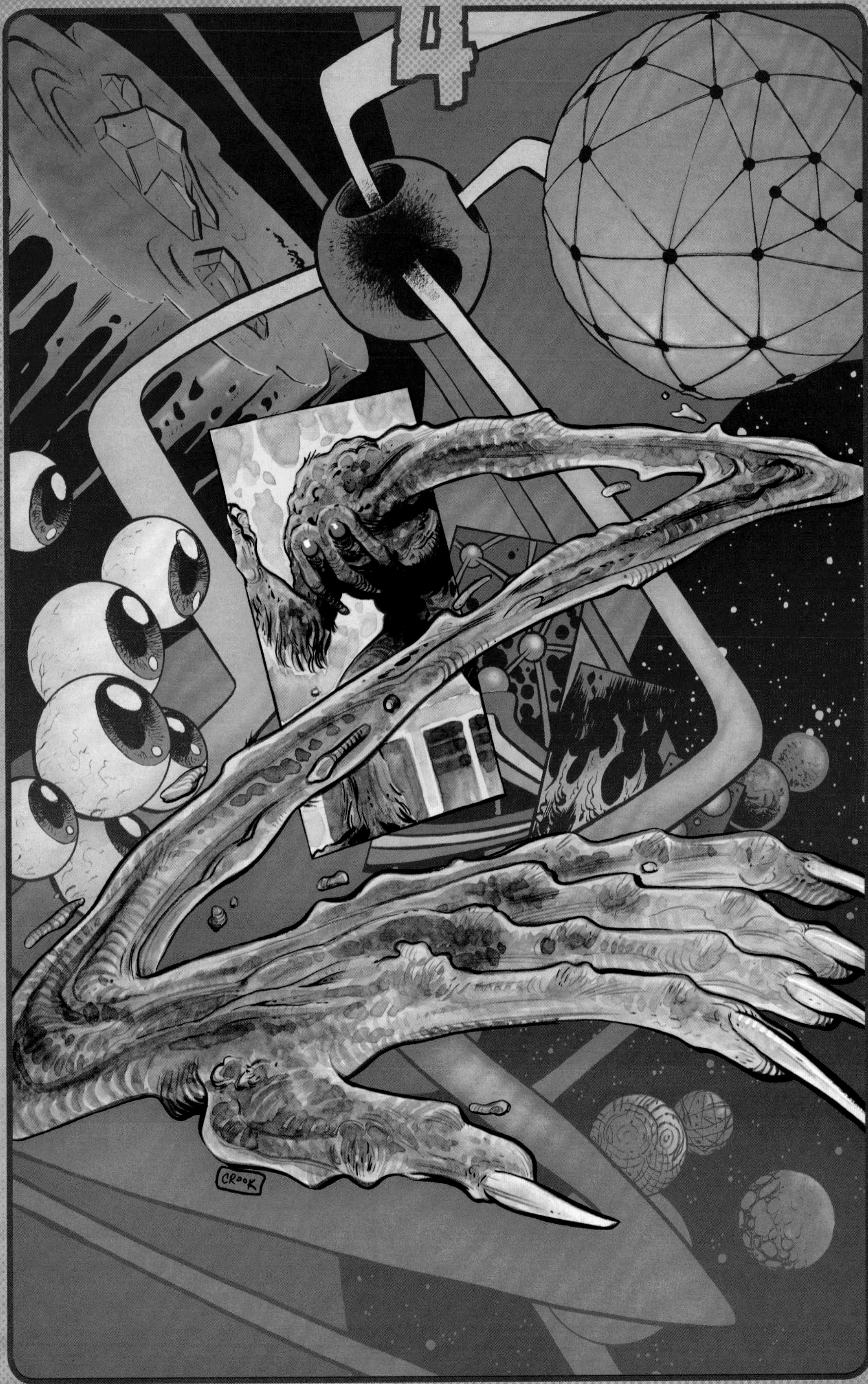
4
CROOK

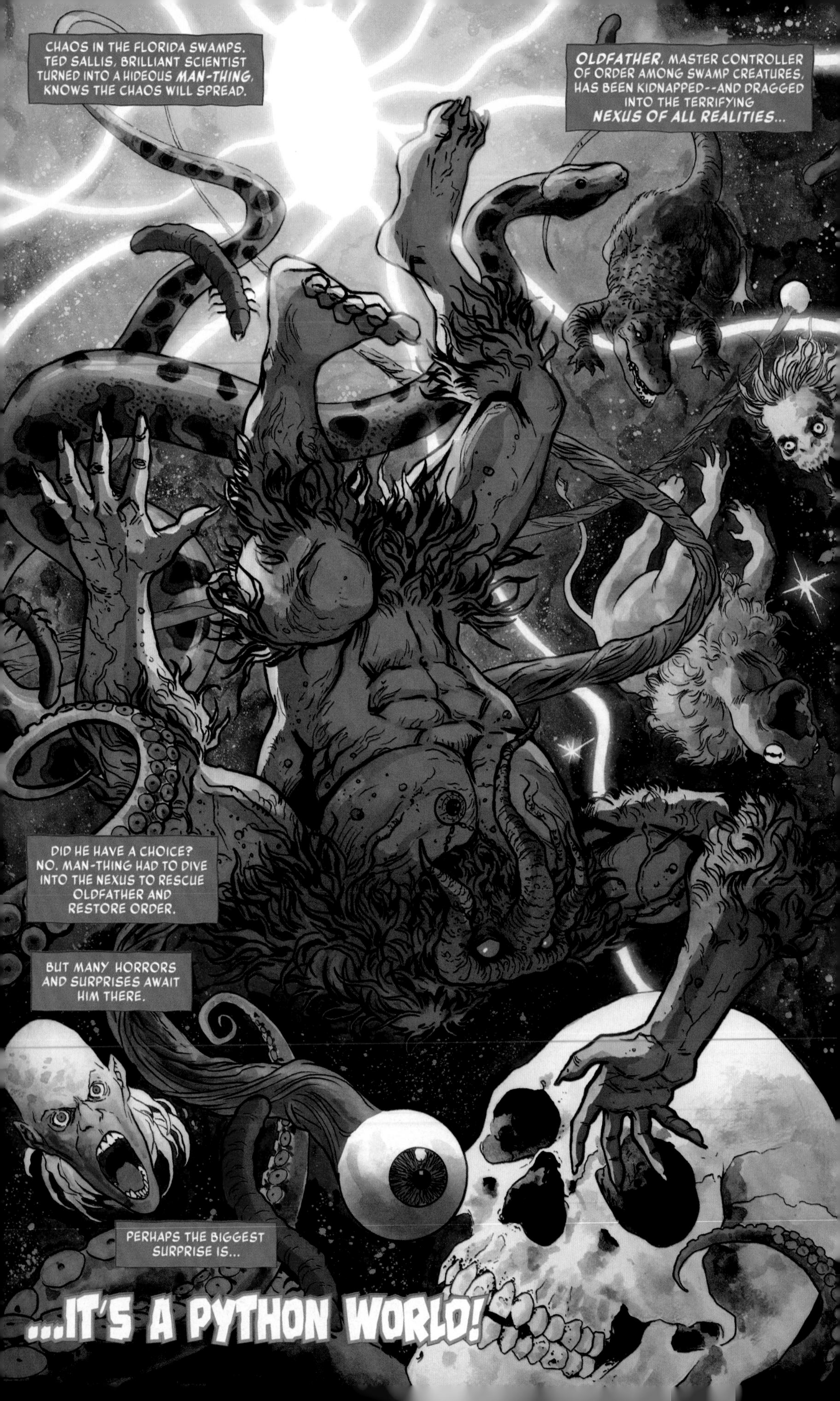
CHAOS IN THE FLORIDA SWAMPS. TED SALLIS, BRILLIANT SCIENTIST TURNED INTO A HIDEOUS MAN-THING, KNOWS THE CHAOS WILL SPREAD.
OLDFATHER, MASTER CONTROLLER OF ORDER AMONG SWAMP CREATURES, HAS BEEN KIDNAPPED--AND DRAGGED INTO THE TERRIFYING NEXUS OF ALL REALITIES...
DID HE HAVE A CHOICE? NO. MAN-THING HAD TO DIVE INTO THE NEXUS TO RESCUE OLDFATHER AND RESTORE ORDER.
BUT MANY HORRORS AND SURPRISES AWAIT HIM THERE.
PERHAPS THE BIGGEST SURPRISE IS...
...IT'S A PYTHON WORLD!

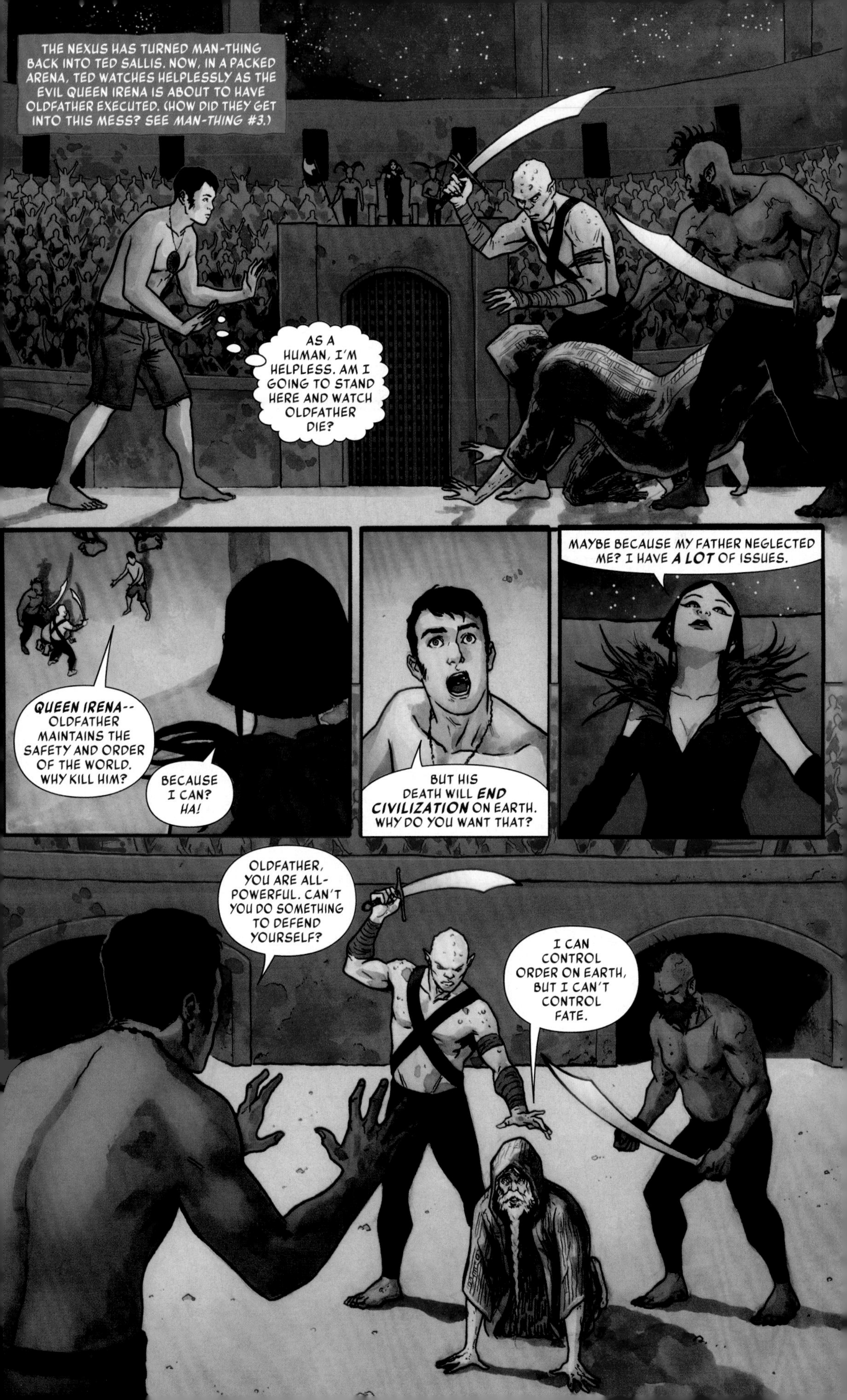
THE NEXUS HAS TURNED MAN-THING BACK INTO TED SALLIS. NOW, IN A PACKED ARENA, TED WATCHES HELPLESSLY AS THE EVIL QUEEN IRENA IS ABOUT TO HAVE OLDFATHER EXECUTED. (HOW DID THEY GET INTO THIS MESS? SEE *MAN-THING #3.*)
AS A HUMAN, I'M HELPLESS. AM I GOING TO STAND HERE AND WATCH OLDFATHER DIE?
QUEEN IRENA-- OLDFATHER MAINTAINS THE SAFETY AND ORDER OF THE WORLD. WHY KILL HIM?
BECAUSE I CAN? HA!
BUT HIS DEATH WILL ***END CIVILIZATION*** ON EARTH. WHY DO YOU WANT THAT?
MAYBE BECAUSE MY FATHER NEGLECTED ME? I HAVE ***A LOT*** OF ISSUES.
OLDFATHER, YOU ARE ALL-POWERFUL. CAN'T YOU DO SOMETHING TO DEFEND YOURSELF?
I CAN CONTROL ORDER ON EARTH, BUT I CAN'T CONTROL FATE.

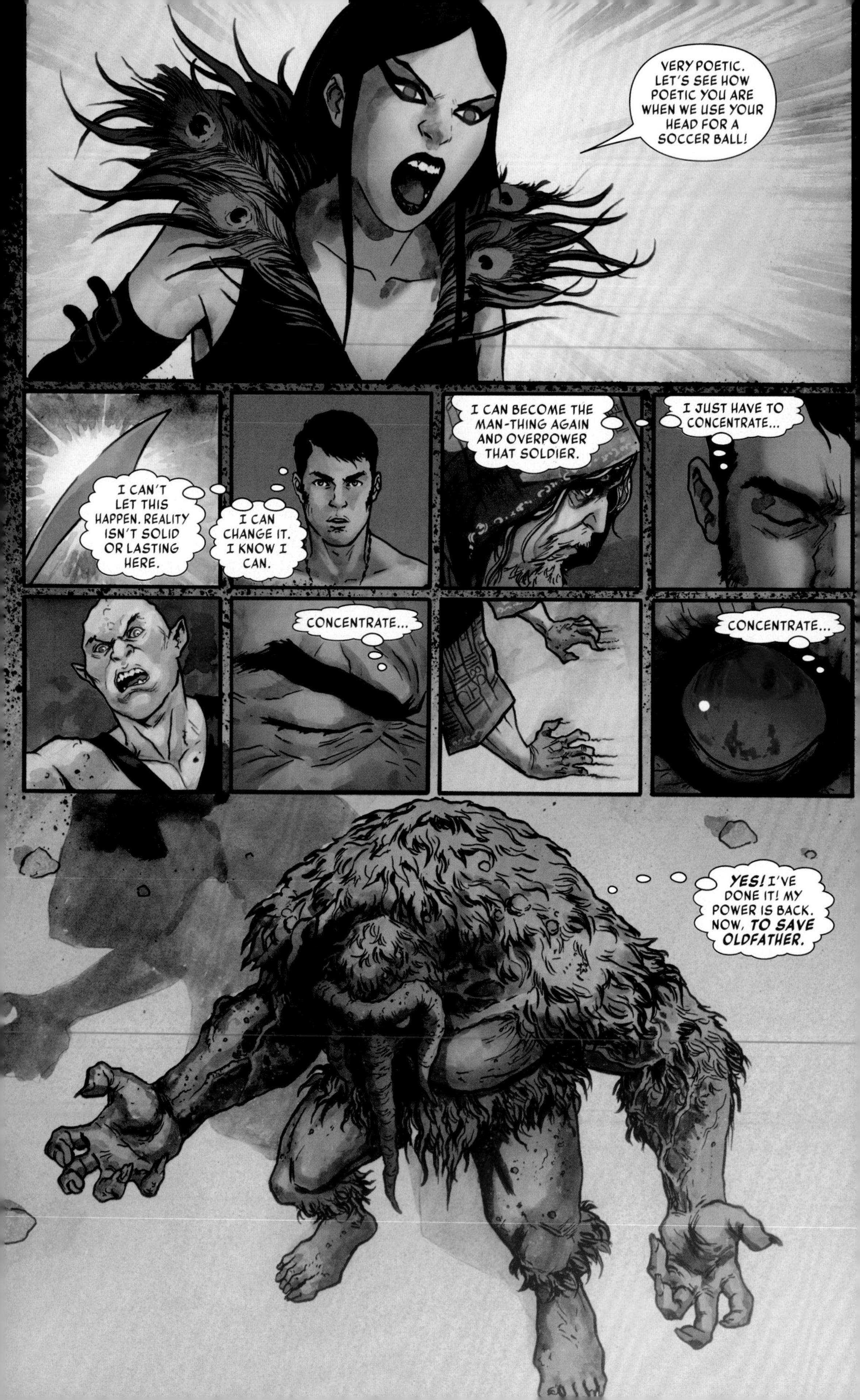
VERY POETIC. LET'S SEE HOW POETIC YOU ARE WHEN WE USE YOUR HEAD FOR A SOCCER BALL!
I CAN'T LET THIS HAPPEN. REALITY ISN'T SOLID OR LASTING HERE.
I CAN CHANGE IT. I KNOW I CAN.
I CAN BECOME THE MAN-THING AGAIN AND OVERPOWER THAT SOLDIER.
I JUST HAVE TO CONCENTRATE...
CONCENTRATE...
CONCENTRATE...
YES! I'VE DONE IT! MY POWER IS BACK. NOW, *TO SAVE OLDFATHER.*

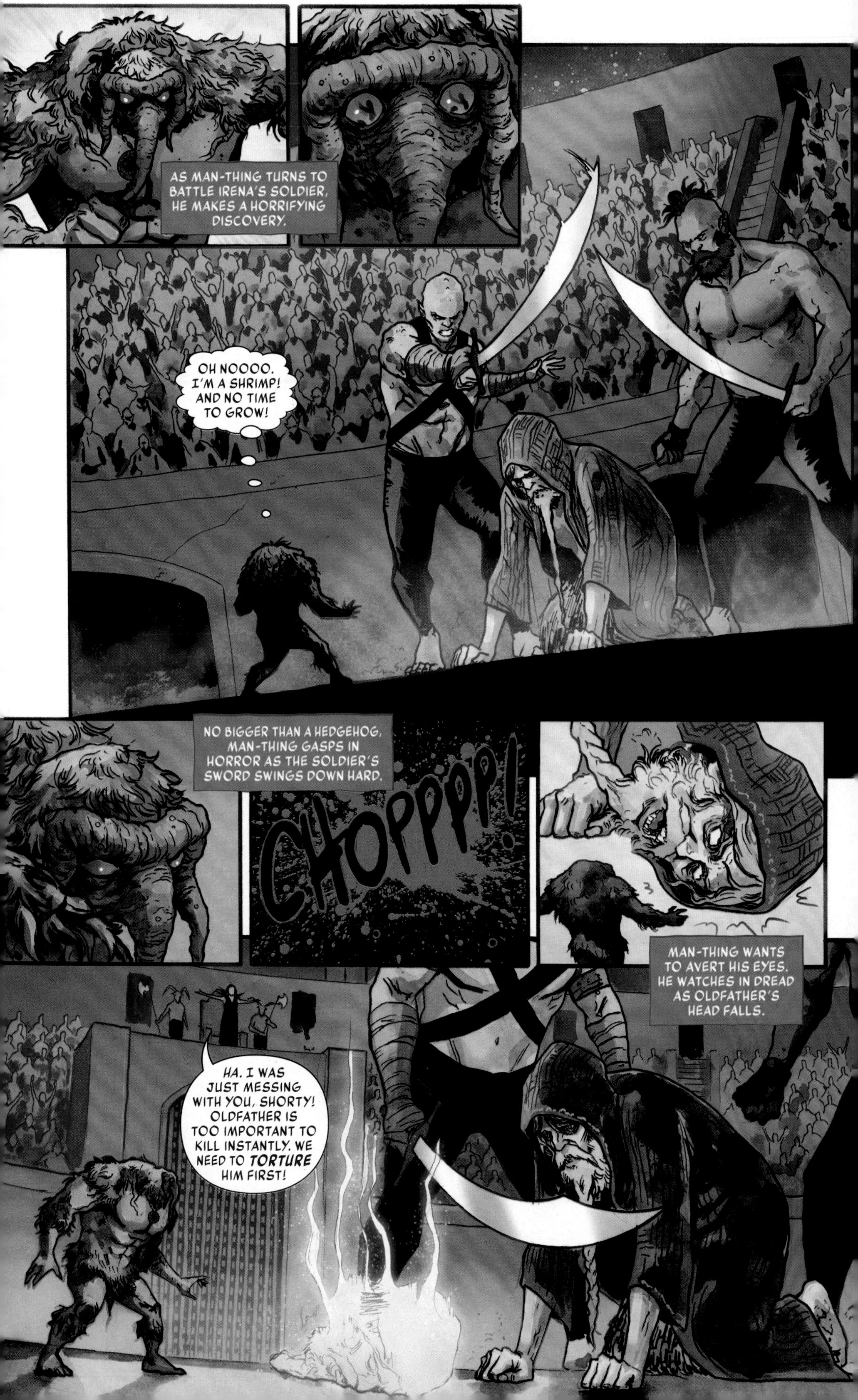

AS MAN-THING TURNS TO BATTLE IRENA'S SOLDIER, HE MAKES A HORRIFYING DISCOVERY.
OH NOOOO. I'M A SHRIMP! AND NO TIME TO GROW!
NO BIGGER THAN A HEDGEHOG, MAN-THING GASPS IN HORROR AS THE SOLDIER'S SWORD SWINGS DOWN HARD.
CHOPPPP!
MAN-THING WANTS TO AVERT HIS EYES. HE WATCHES IN DREAD AS OLDFATHER'S HEAD FALLS.
HA. I WAS JUST MESSING WITH YOU, SHORTY! OLDFATHER IS TOO IMPORTANT TO KILL INSTANTLY. WE NEED TO TORTURE HIM FIRST!

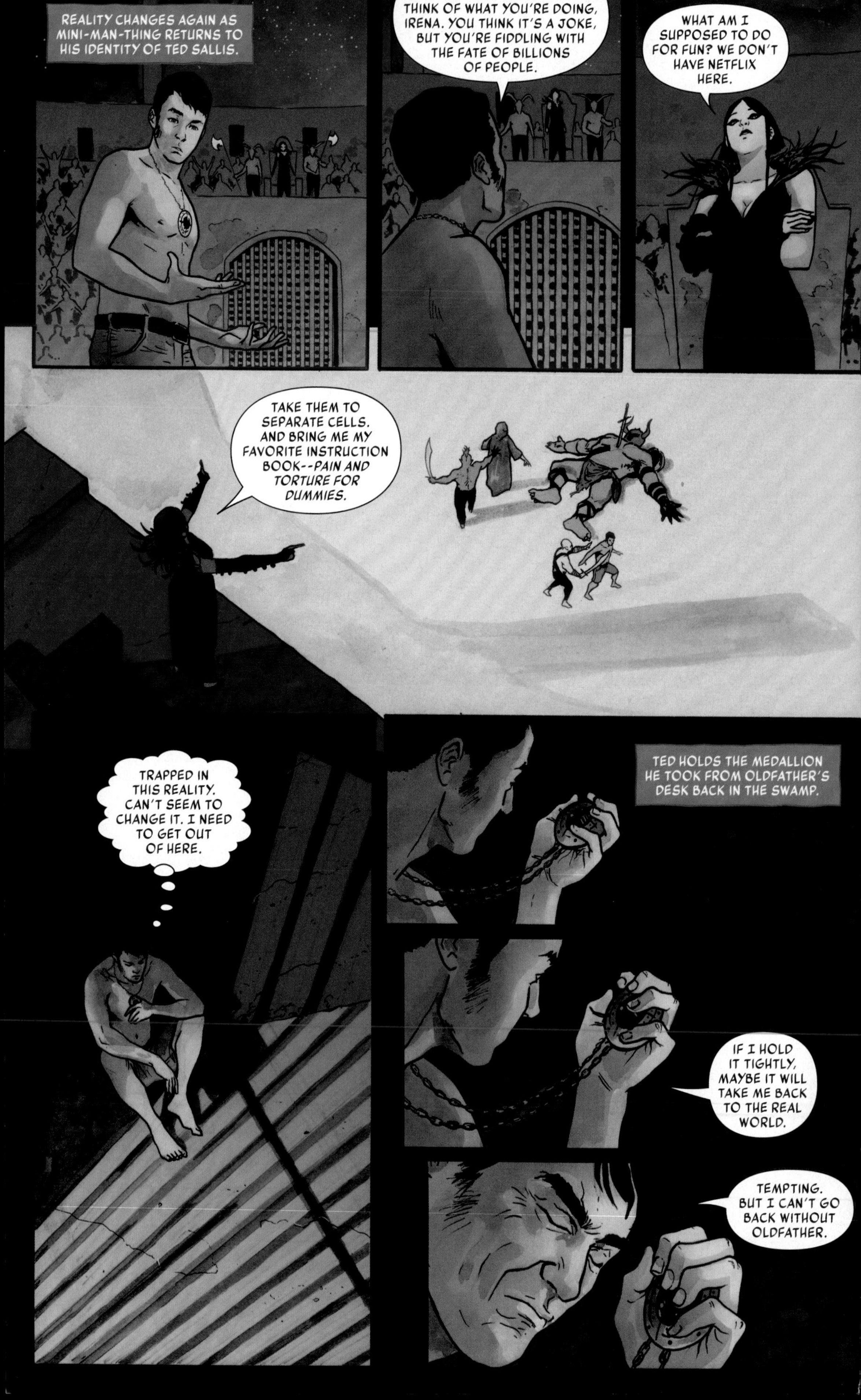
REALITY CHANGES AGAIN AS MINI-MAN-THING RETURNS TO HIS IDENTITY OF TED SALLIS.
THINK OF WHAT YOU'RE DOING, IRENA. YOU THINK IT'S A JOKE, BUT YOU'RE FIDDLING WITH THE FATE OF BILLIONS OF PEOPLE.
WHAT AM I SUPPOSED TO DO FOR FUN? WE DON'T HAVE NETFLIX HERE.
TAKE THEM TO SEPARATE CELLS. AND BRING ME MY FAVORITE INSTRUCTION BOOK--PAIN AND TORTURE FOR DUMMIES.
TRAPPED IN THIS REALITY. CAN'T SEEM TO CHANGE IT. I NEED TO GET OUT OF HERE.
TED HOLDS THE MEDALLION HE TOOK FROM OLDFATHER'S DESK BACK IN THE SWAMP.
IF I HOLD IT TIGHTLY, MAYBE IT WILL TAKE ME BACK TO THE REAL WORLD.
TEMPTING. BUT I CAN'T GO BACK WITHOUT OLDFATHER.

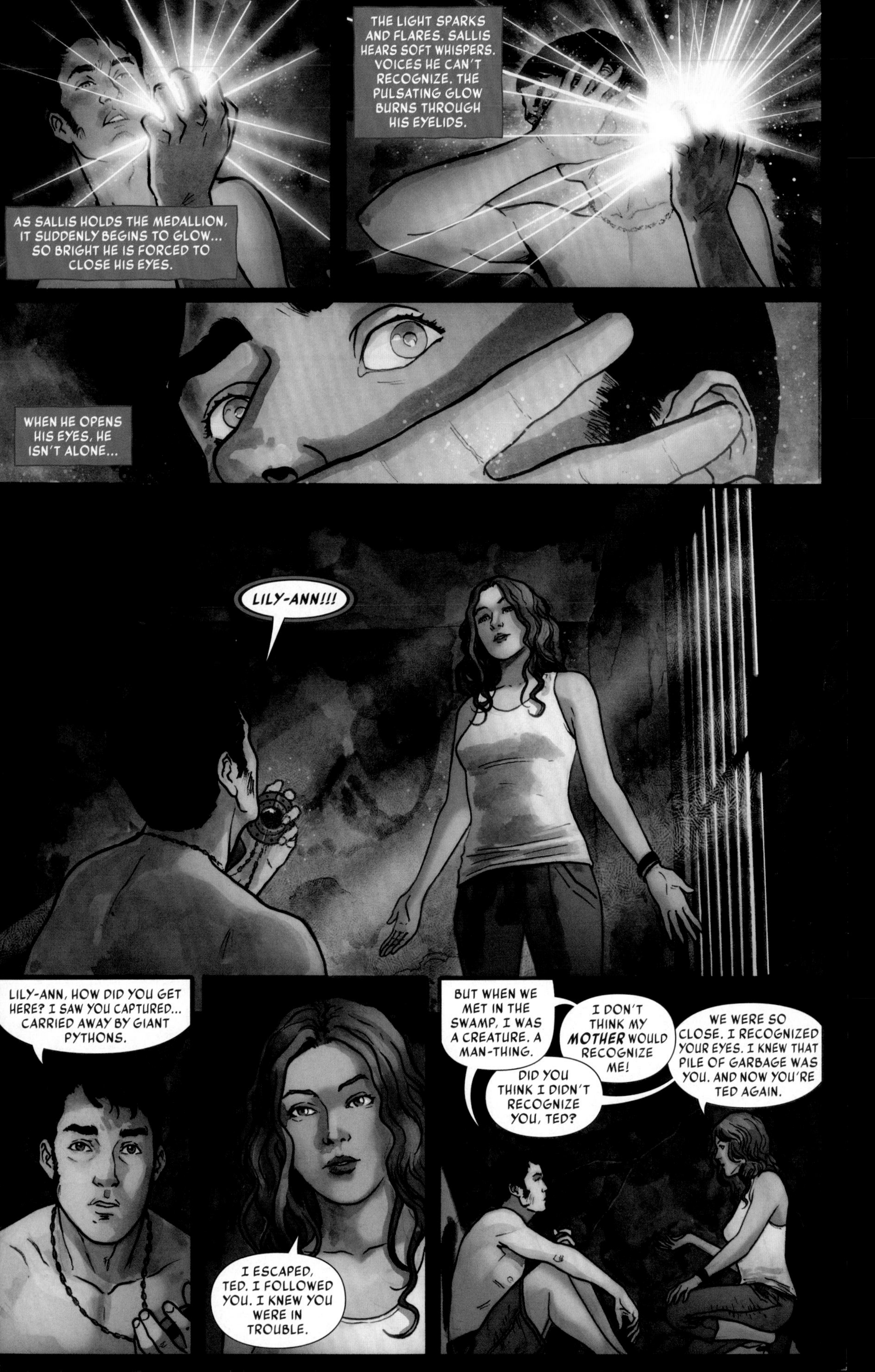
AS SALLIS HOLDS THE MEDALLION, IT SUDDENLY BEGINS TO GLOW... SO BRIGHT HE IS FORCED TO CLOSE HIS EYES.
THE LIGHT SPARKS AND FLARES. SALLIS HEARS SOFT WHISPERS. VOICES HE CAN'T RECOGNIZE. THE PULSATING GLOW BURNS THROUGH HIS EYELIDS.
WHEN HE OPENS HIS EYES, HE ISN'T ALONE...
LILY-ANN!!!
LILY-ANN, HOW DID YOU GET HERE? I SAW YOU CAPTURED... CARRIED AWAY BY GIANT PYTHONS.
I ESCAPED, TED. I FOLLOWED YOU. I KNEW YOU WERE IN TROUBLE.
BUT WHEN WE MET IN THE SWAMP, I WAS A CREATURE. A MAN-THING.
I DON'T THINK MY MOTHER WOULD RECOGNIZE ME!
DID YOU THINK I DIDN'T RECOGNIZE YOU, TED?
WE WERE SO CLOSE. I RECOGNIZED YOUR EYES. I KNEW THAT PILE OF GARBAGE WAS YOU. AND NOW YOU'RE TED AGAIN.

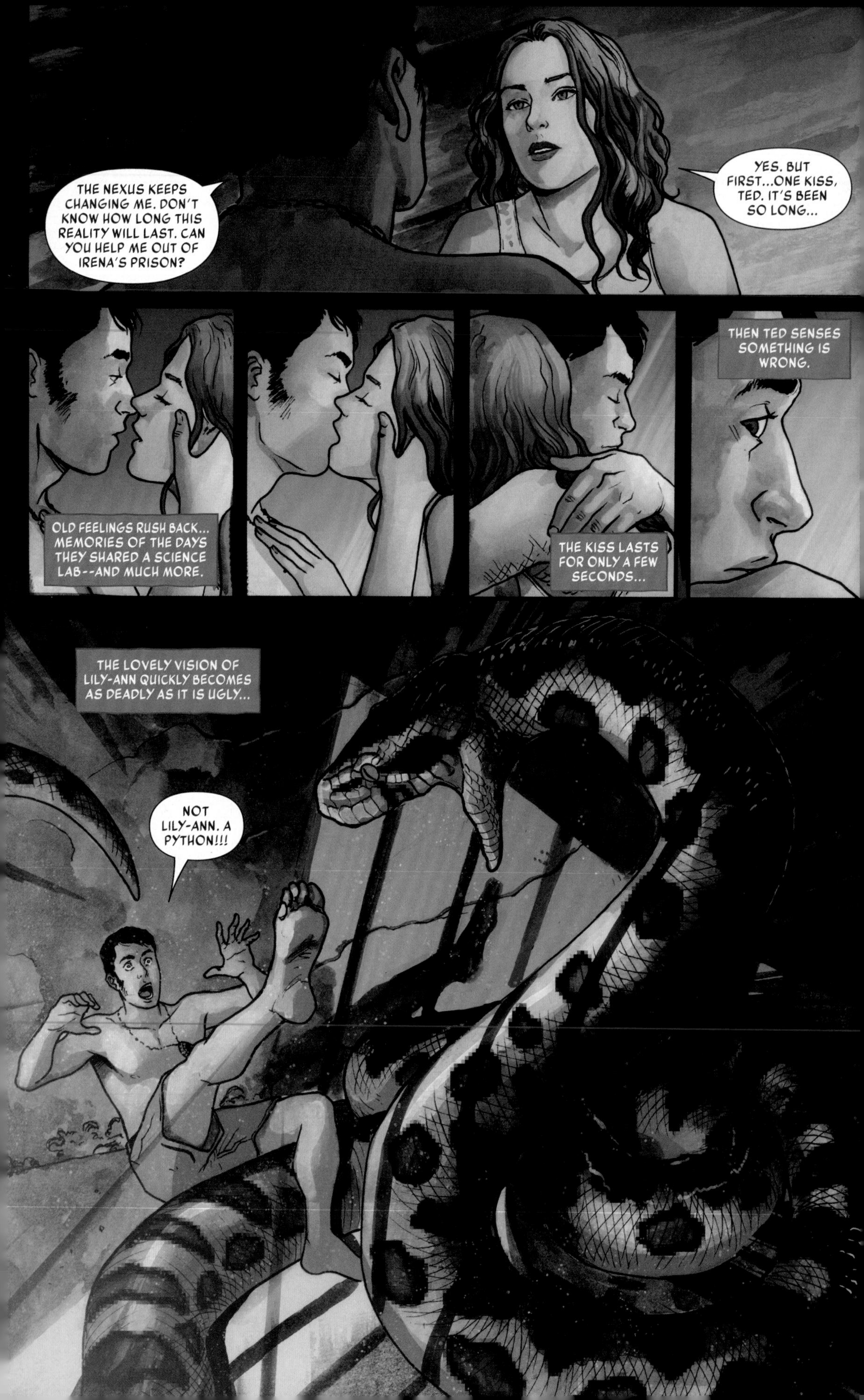
THE NEXUS KEEPS CHANGING ME. DON'T KNOW HOW LONG THIS REALITY WILL LAST. CAN YOU HELP ME OUT OF IRENA'S PRISON?
YES. BUT FIRST...ONE KISS, TED. IT'S BEEN SO LONG...
OLD FEELINGS RUSH BACK... MEMORIES OF THE DAYS THEY SHARED A SCIENCE LAB--AND MUCH MORE.
THE KISS LASTS FOR ONLY A FEW SECONDS...
THEN TED SENSES SOMETHING IS WRONG.
THE LOVELY VISION OF LILY-ANN QUICKLY BECOMES AS DEADLY AS IT IS UGLY...
NOT LILY-ANN. A PYTHON!!!

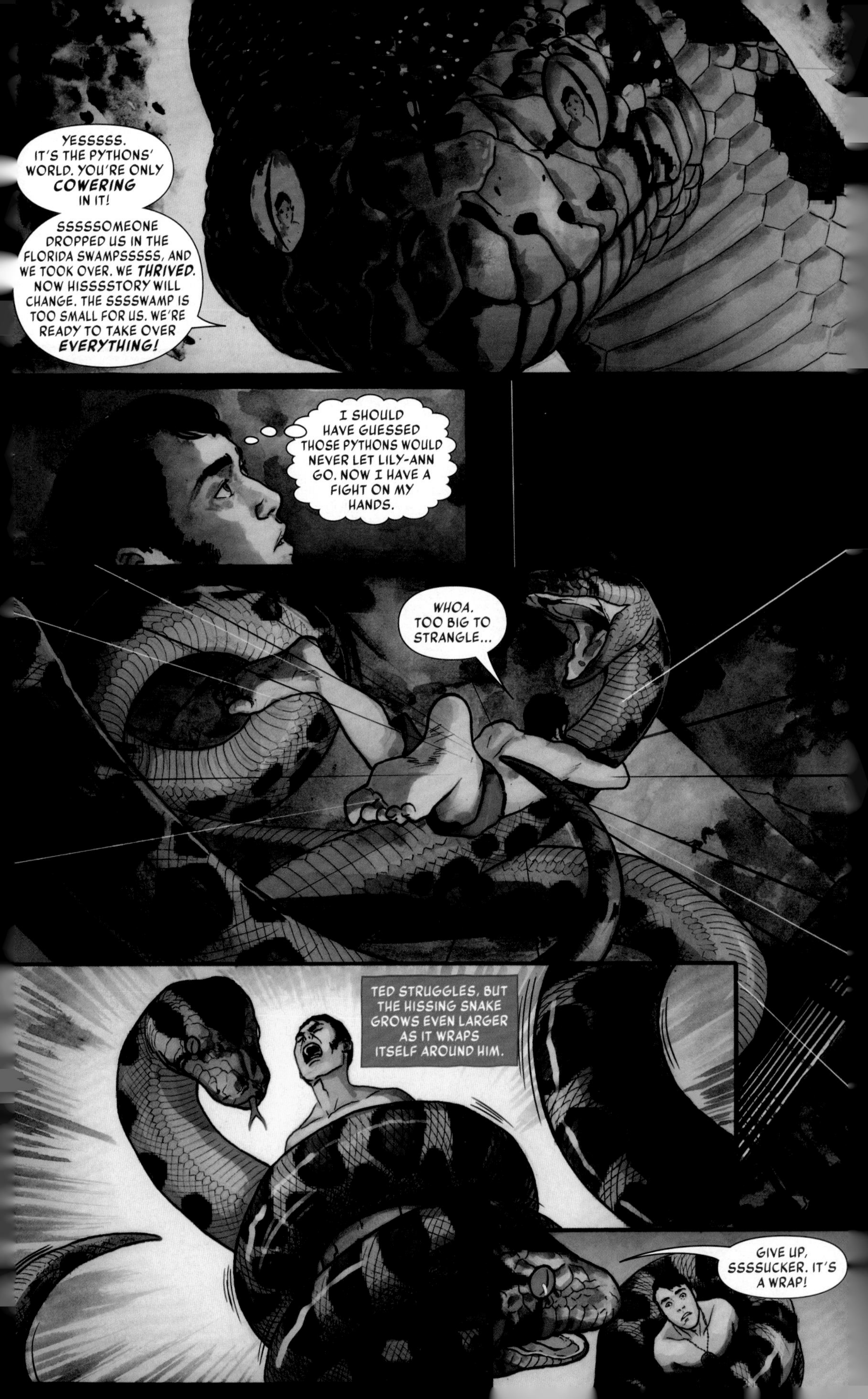
YESSSSS. IT'S THE PYTHONS' WORLD. YOU'RE ONLY ***COWERING*** IN IT!
SSSSSOMEONE DROPPED US IN THE FLORIDA SWAMPSSSSS, AND WE TOOK OVER. WE ***THRIVED***. NOW HISSSSTORY WILL CHANGE. THE SSSSWAMP IS TOO SMALL FOR US. WE'RE READY TO TAKE OVER ***EVERYTHING!***
I SHOULD HAVE GUESSED THOSE PYTHONS WOULD NEVER LET LILY-ANN GO. NOW I HAVE A FIGHT ON MY HANDS.
WHOA. TOO BIG TO STRANGLE...
TED STRUGGLES, BUT THE HISSING SNAKE GROWS EVEN LARGER AS IT WRAPS ITSELF AROUND HIM.
GIVE UP, SSSSUCKER. IT'S A WRAP!

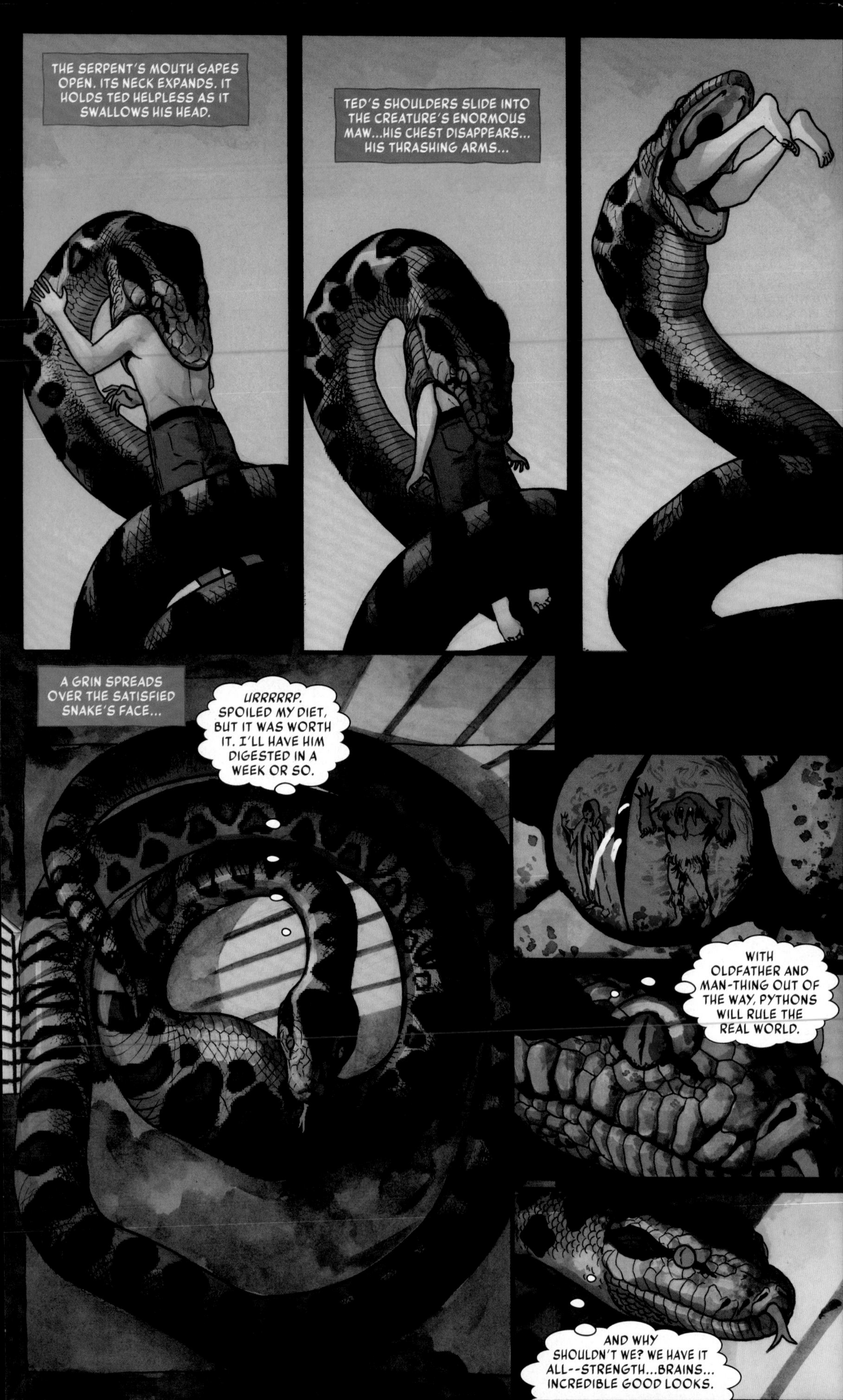
THE SERPENT'S MOUTH GAPES OPEN. ITS NECK EXPANDS. IT HOLDS TED HELPLESS AS IT SWALLOWS HIS HEAD.
TED'S SHOULDERS SLIDE INTO THE CREATURE'S ENORMOUS MAW...HIS CHEST DISAPPEARS... HIS THRASHING ARMS...
A GRIN SPREADS OVER THE SATISFIED SNAKE'S FACE...
URRRRRP. SPOILED MY DIET, BUT IT WAS WORTH IT. I'LL HAVE HIM DIGESTED IN A WEEK OR SO.
WITH OLDFATHER AND MAN-THING OUT OF THE WAY, PYTHONS WILL RULE THE REAL WORLD.
AND WHY SHOULDN'T WE? WE HAVE IT ALL--STRENGTH...BRAINS... INCREDIBLE GOOD LOOKS.

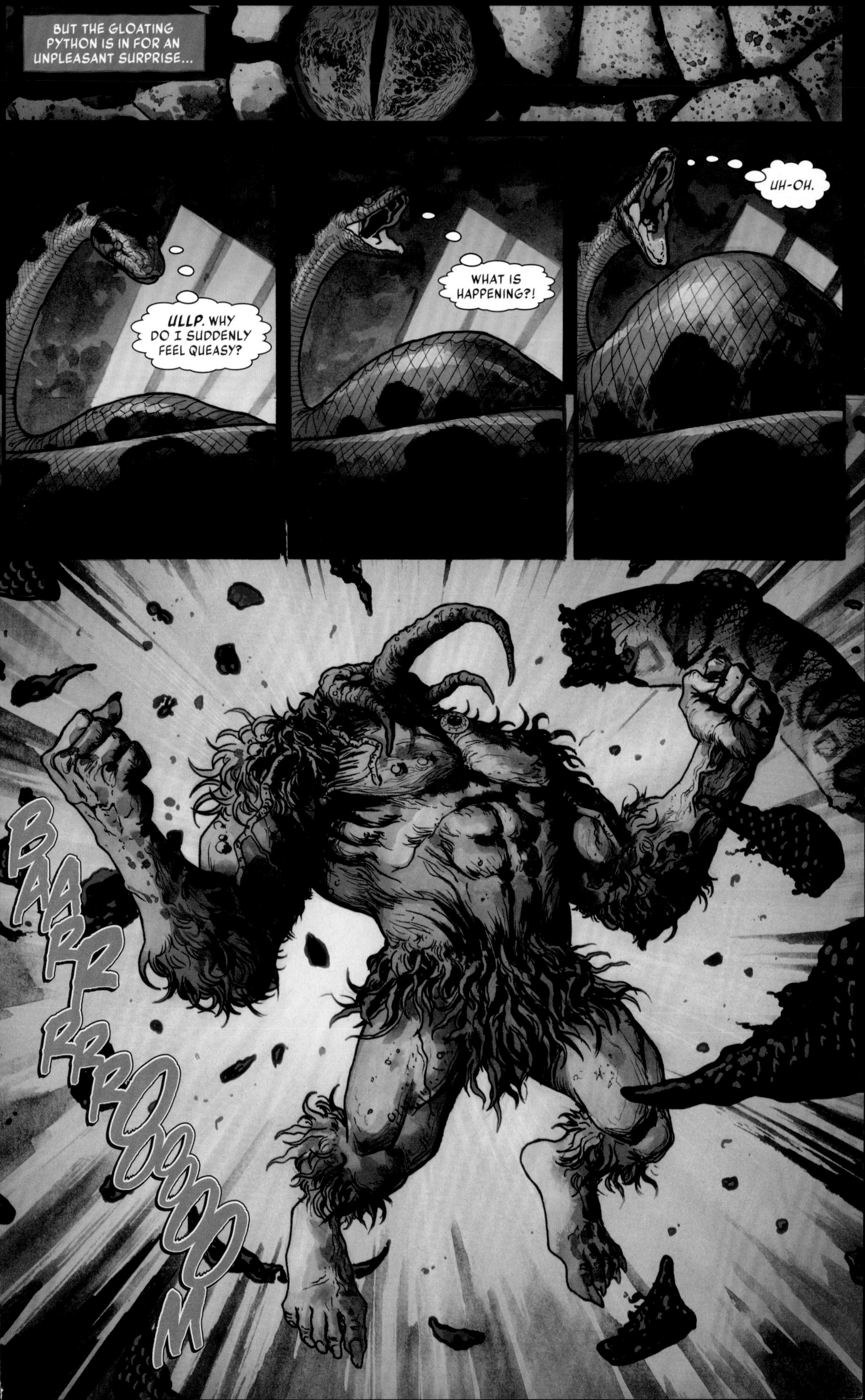
BUT THE GLOATING PYTHON IS IN FOR AN UNPLEASANT SURPRISE...
ULLP. WHY DO I SUDDENLY FEEL QUEASY?
WHAT IS HAPPENING?!
UH-OH.
BAARRRROOOOOM

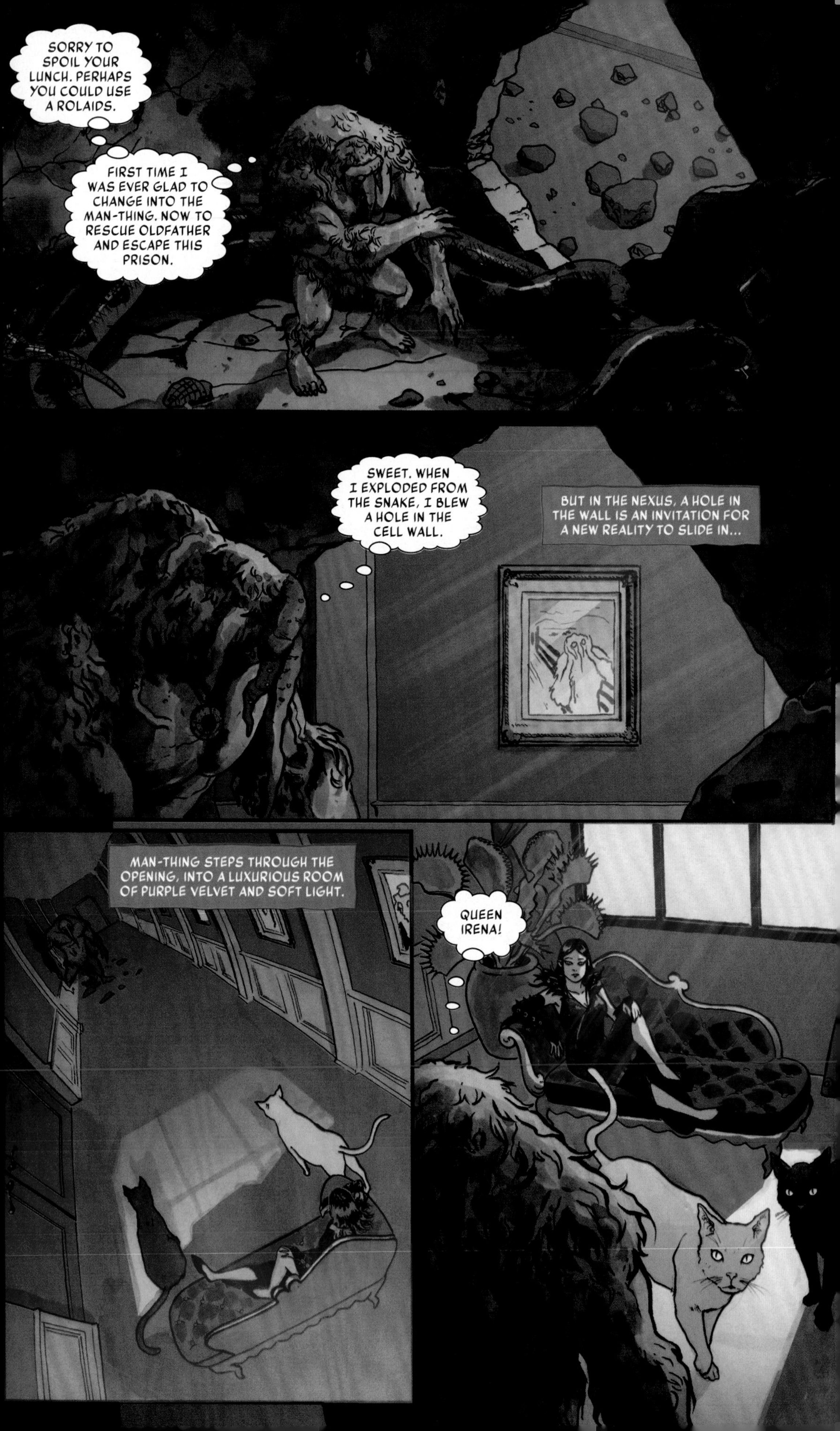
SORRY TO SPOIL YOUR LUNCH. PERHAPS YOU COULD USE A ROLAIDS.
FIRST TIME I WAS EVER GLAD TO CHANGE INTO THE MAN-THING. NOW TO RESCUE OLDFATHER AND ESCAPE THIS PRISON.
SWEET. WHEN I EXPLODED FROM THE SNAKE, I BLEW A HOLE IN THE CELL WALL.
BUT IN THE NEXUS, A HOLE IN THE WALL IS AN INVITATION FOR A NEW REALITY TO SLIDE IN...
MAN-THING STEPS THROUGH THE OPENING, INTO A LUXURIOUS ROOM OF PURPLE VELVET AND SOFT LIGHT.
QUEEN IRENA!

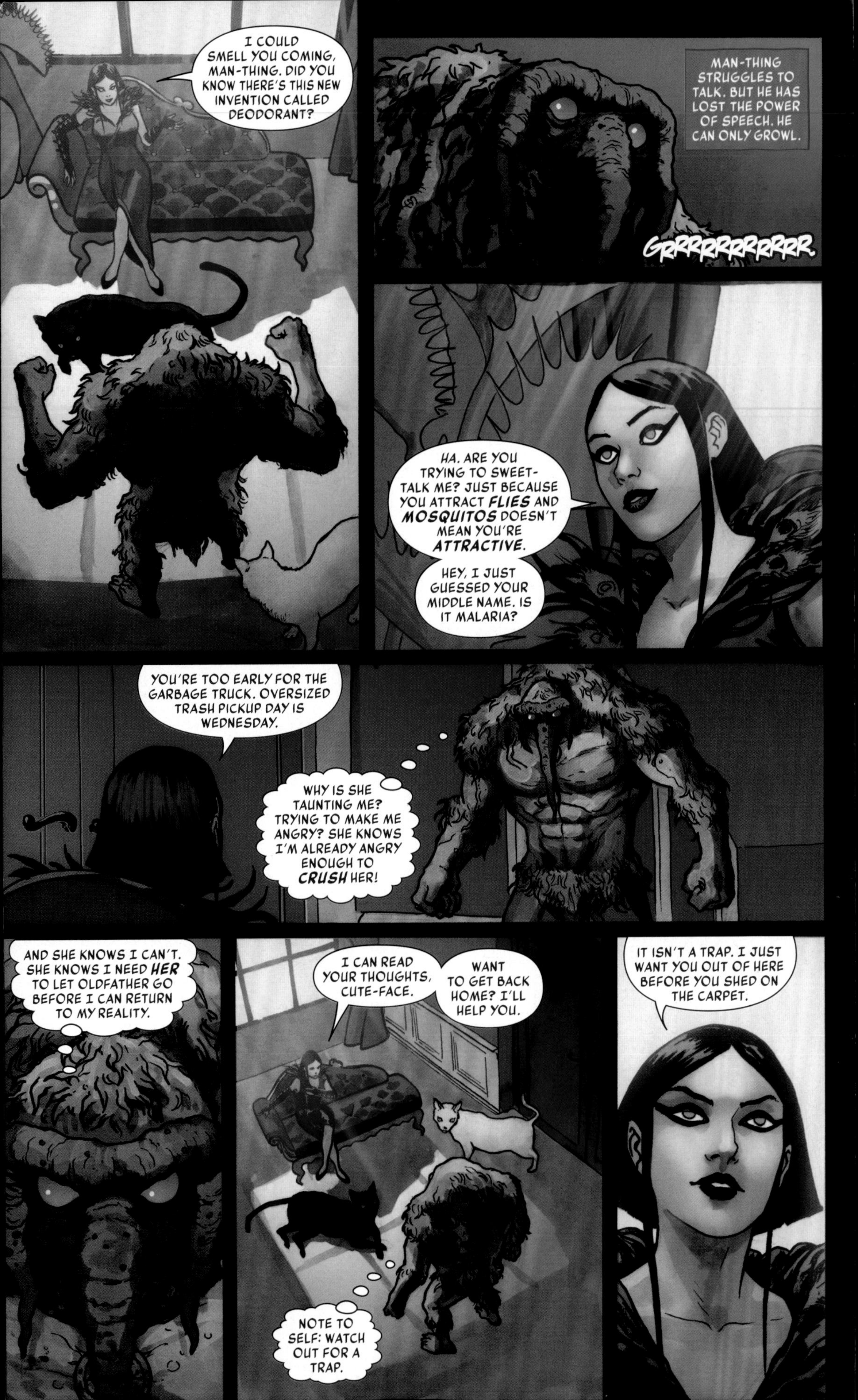
I COULD SMELL YOU COMING, MAN-THING. DID YOU KNOW THERE'S THIS NEW INVENTION CALLED DEODORANT?
MAN-THING STRUGGLES TO TALK. BUT HE HAS LOST THE POWER OF SPEECH. HE CAN ONLY GROWL.
GRRRRRRRRRRR.
HA. ARE YOU TRYING TO SWEET-TALK ME? JUST BECAUSE YOU ATTRACT FLIES AND MOSQUITOS DOESN'T MEAN YOU'RE ATTRACTIVE.
HEY, I JUST GUESSED YOUR MIDDLE NAME. IS IT MALARIA?
YOU'RE TOO EARLY FOR THE GARBAGE TRUCK. OVERSIZED TRASH PICKUP DAY IS WEDNESDAY.
WHY IS SHE TAUNTING ME? TRYING TO MAKE ME ANGRY? SHE KNOWS I'M ALREADY ANGRY ENOUGH TO CRUSH HER!
AND SHE KNOWS I CAN'T. SHE KNOWS I NEED HER TO LET OLDFATHER GO BEFORE I CAN RETURN TO MY REALITY.
I CAN READ YOUR THOUGHTS, CUTE-FACE.
WANT TO GET BACK HOME? I'LL HELP YOU.
NOTE TO SELF: WATCH OUT FOR A TRAP.
IT ISN'T A TRAP. I JUST WANT YOU OUT OF HERE BEFORE YOU SHED ON THE CARPET.

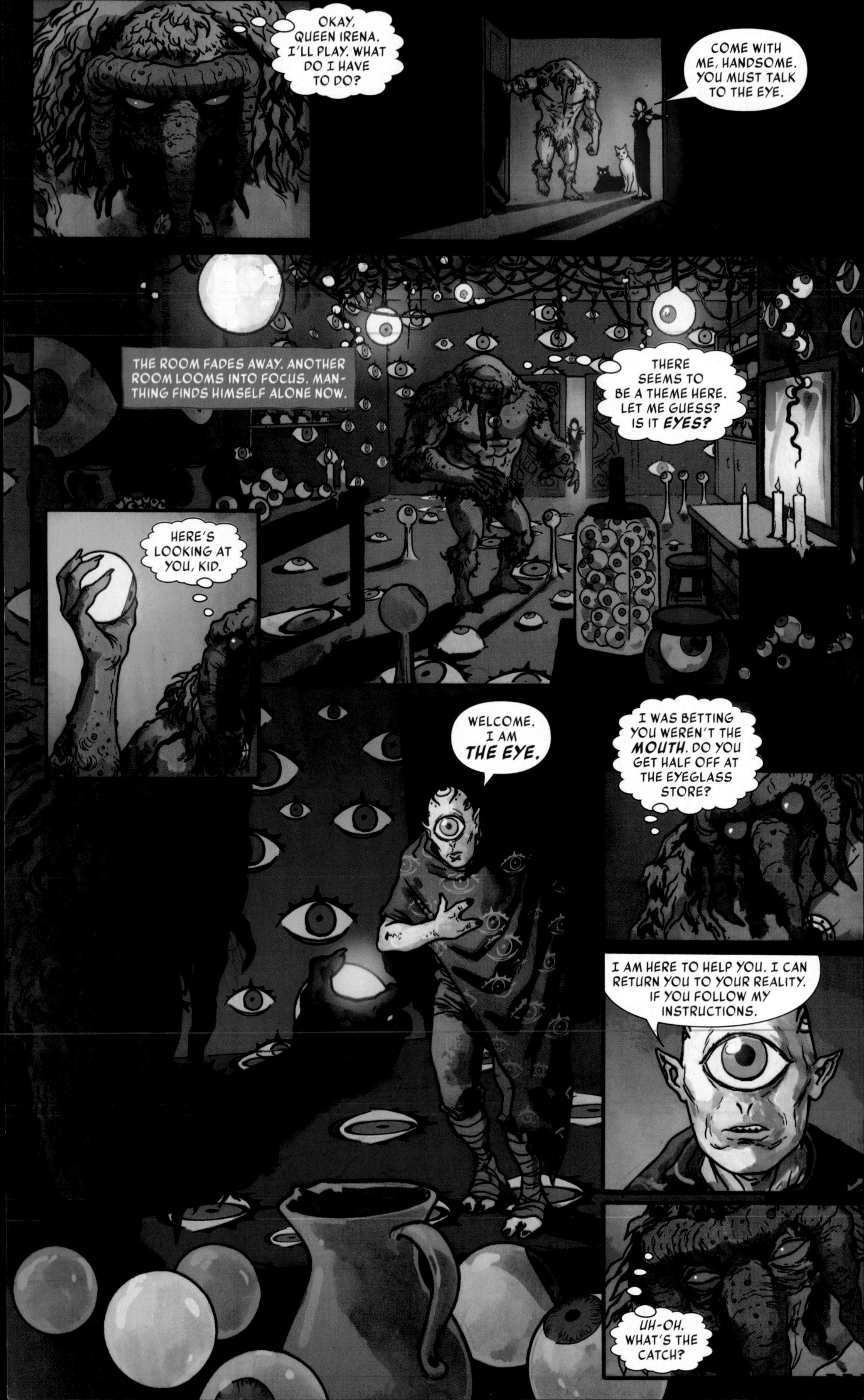
OKAY, QUEEN IRENA. I'LL PLAY. WHAT DO I HAVE TO DO?
COME WITH ME, HANDSOME. YOU MUST TALK TO THE EYE.
THE ROOM FADES AWAY. ANOTHER ROOM LOOMS INTO FOCUS. MAN-THING FINDS HIMSELF ALONE NOW.
THERE SEEMS TO BE A THEME HERE. LET ME GUESS? IS IT EYES?
HERE'S LOOKING AT YOU, KID.
WELCOME. I AM THE EYE.
I WAS BETTING YOU WEREN'T THE MOUTH. DO YOU GET HALF OFF AT THE EYEGLASS STORE?
I AM HERE TO HELP YOU. I CAN RETURN YOU TO YOUR REALITY. IF YOU FOLLOW MY INSTRUCTIONS.
UH-OH. WHAT'S THE CATCH?

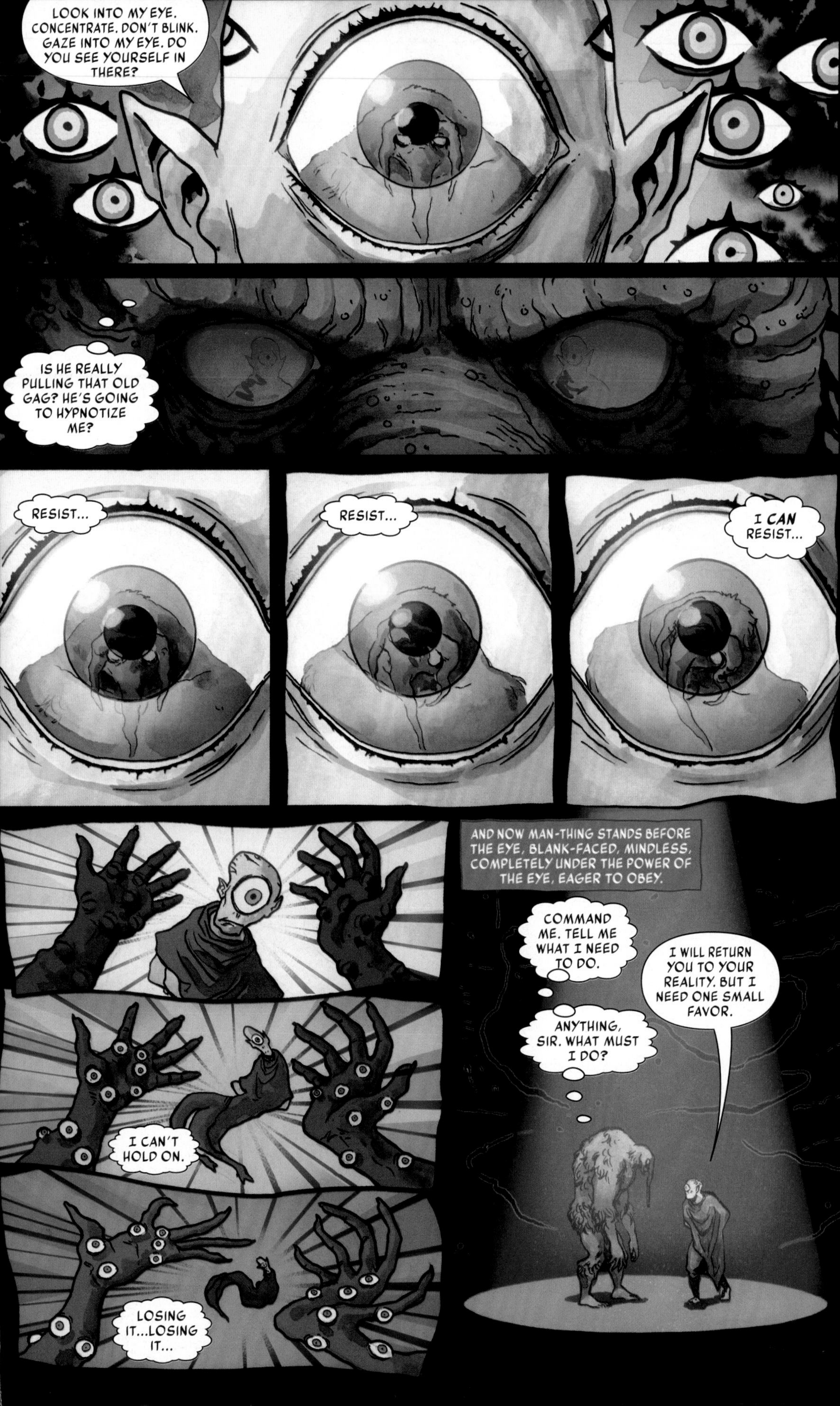
LOOK INTO MY EYE. CONCENTRATE. DON'T BLINK. GAZE INTO MY EYE. DO YOU SEE YOURSELF IN THERE?
IS HE REALLY PULLING THAT OLD GAG? HE'S GOING TO HYPNOTIZE ME?
RESIST...
RESIST...
I *CAN* RESIST...
I CAN'T HOLD ON.
LOSING IT...LOSING IT...
AND NOW MAN-THING STANDS BEFORE THE EYE, BLANK-FACED, MINDLESS, COMPLETELY UNDER THE POWER OF THE EYE, EAGER TO OBEY.
COMMAND ME. TELL ME WHAT I NEED TO DO.
I WILL RETURN YOU TO YOUR REALITY. BUT I NEED ONE SMALL FAVOR.
ANYTHING, SIR. WHAT MUST I DO?

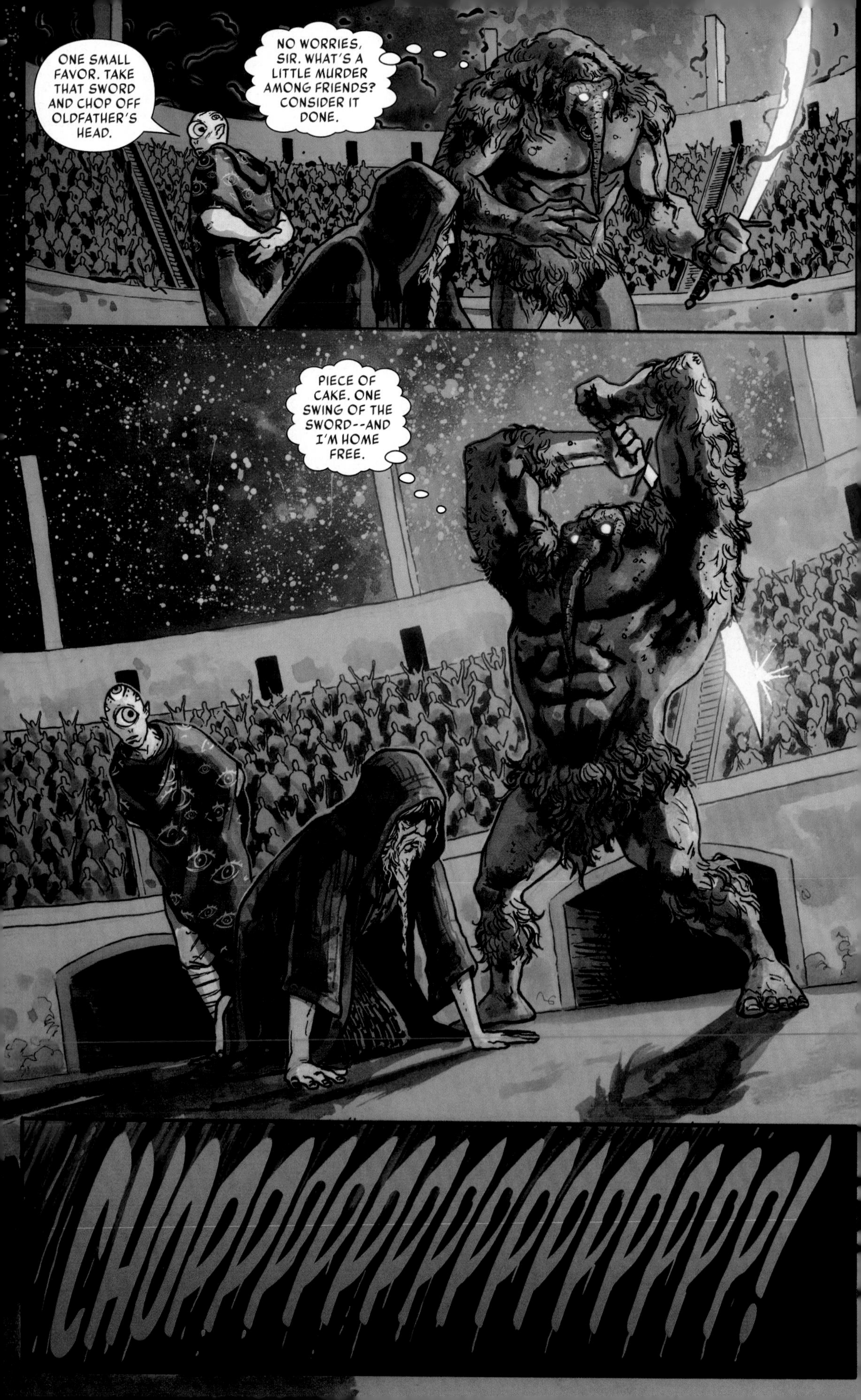
ONE SMALL FAVOR. TAKE THAT SWORD AND CHOP OFF OLDFATHER'S HEAD.
NO WORRIES, SIR. WHAT'S A LITTLE MURDER AMONG FRIENDS? CONSIDER IT DONE.
PIECE OF CAKE. ONE SWING OF THE SWORD--AND I'M HOME FREE.
CHOPPPPPPPPPPPPPPP?!

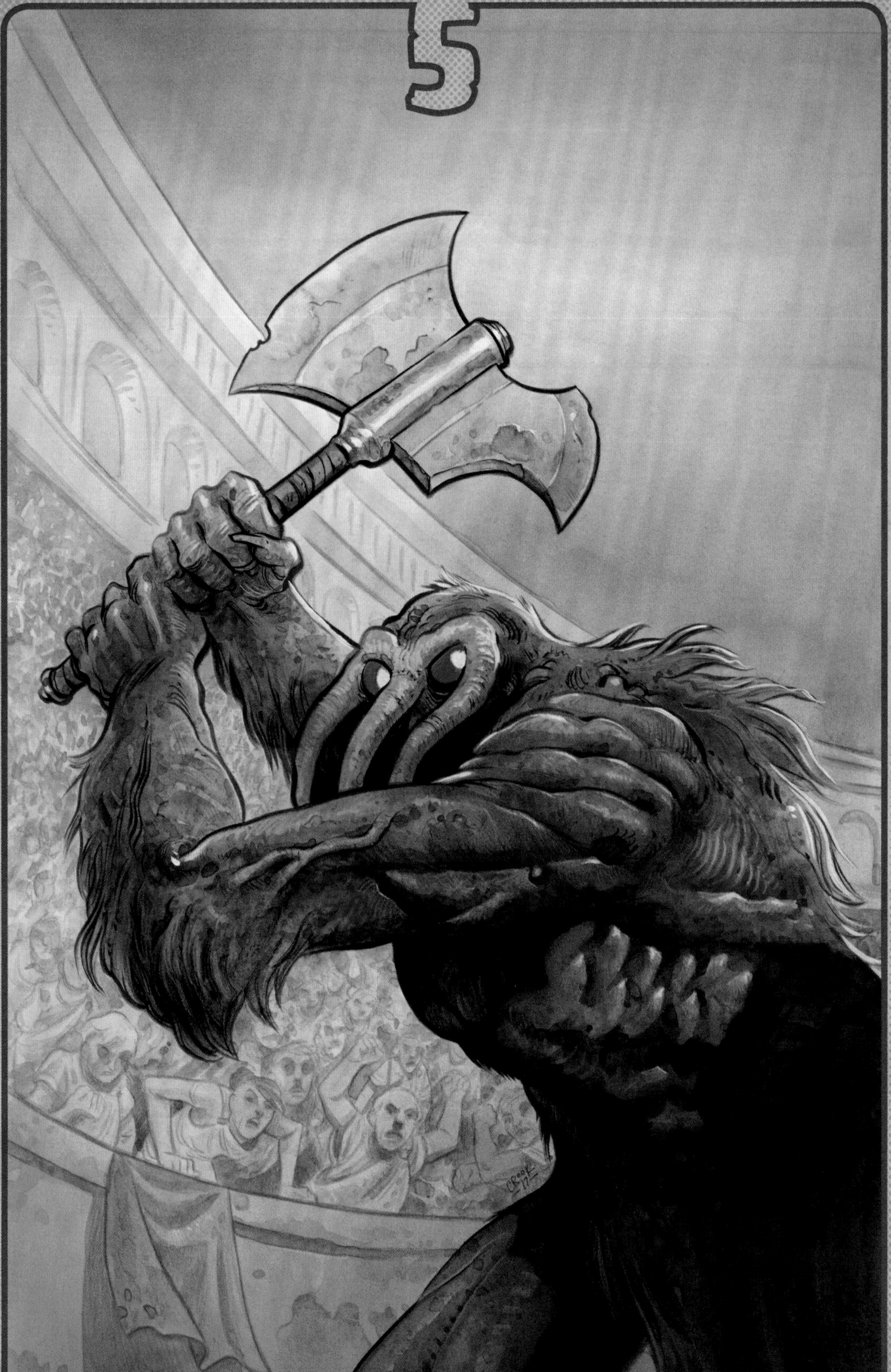
5

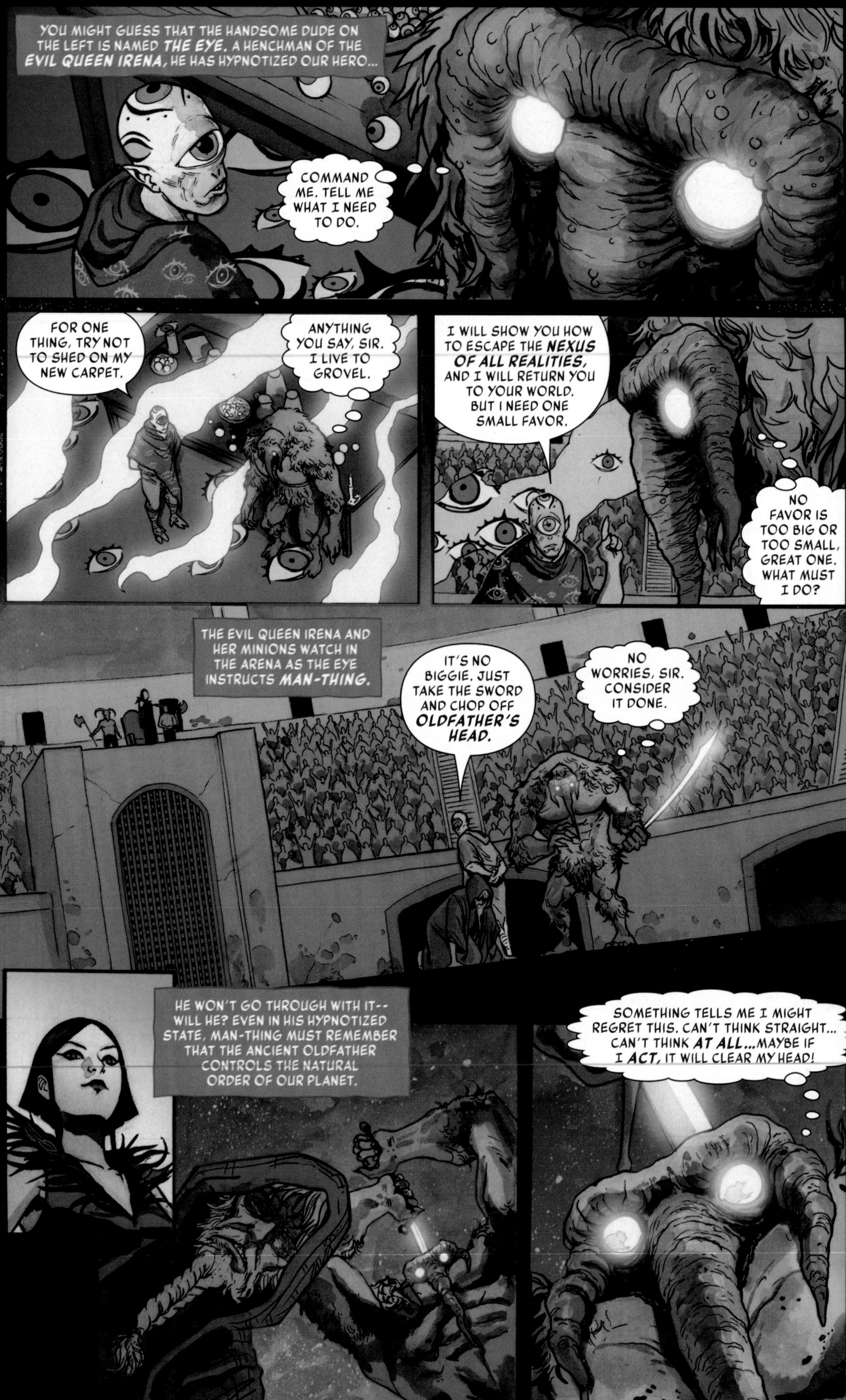
YOU MIGHT GUESS THAT THE HANDSOME DUDE ON THE LEFT IS NAMED THE EYE. A HENCHMAN OF THE EVIL QUEEN IRENA, HE HAS HYPNOTIZED OUR HERO...
COMMAND ME. TELL ME WHAT I NEED TO DO.
FOR ONE THING, TRY NOT TO SHED ON MY NEW CARPET.
ANYTHING YOU SAY, SIR. I LIVE TO GROVEL.
I WILL SHOW YOU HOW TO ESCAPE THE NEXUS OF ALL REALITIES, AND I WILL RETURN YOU TO YOUR WORLD. BUT I NEED ONE SMALL FAVOR.
NO FAVOR IS TOO BIG OR TOO SMALL, GREAT ONE. WHAT MUST I DO?
THE EVIL QUEEN IRENA AND HER MINIONS WATCH IN THE ARENA AS THE EYE INSTRUCTS MAN-THING.
IT'S NO BIGGIE. JUST TAKE THE SWORD AND CHOP OFF OLDFATHER'S HEAD.
NO WORRIES, SIR. CONSIDER IT DONE.
HE WON'T GO THROUGH WITH IT-- WILL HE? EVEN IN HIS HYPNOTIZED STATE, MAN-THING MUST REMEMBER THAT THE ANCIENT OLDFATHER CONTROLS THE NATURAL ORDER OF OUR PLANET.
SOMETHING TELLS ME I MIGHT REGRET THIS. CAN'T THINK STRAIGHT... CAN'T THINK AT ALL...MAYBE IF I ACT, IT WILL CLEAR MY HEAD!

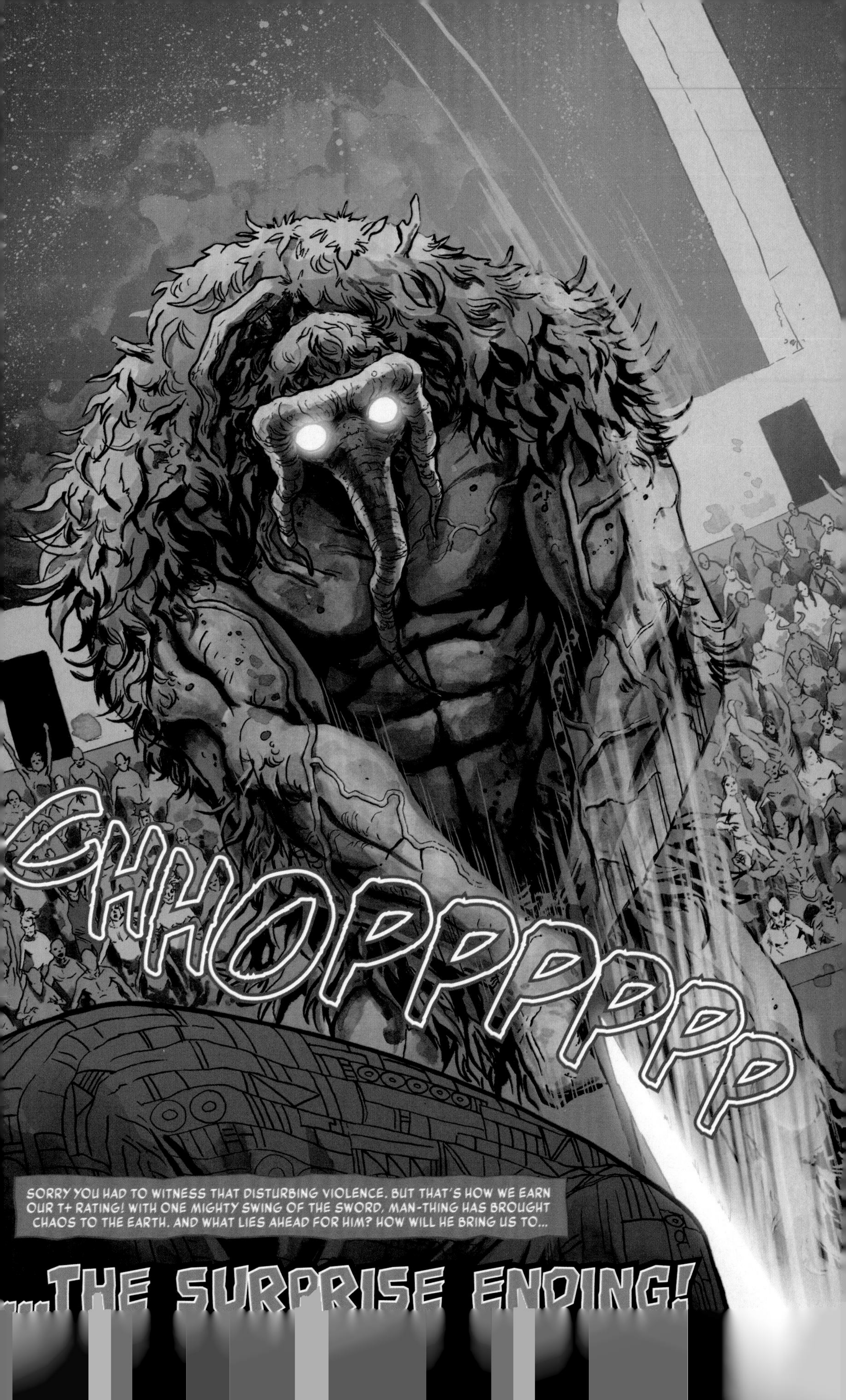
CHHOPPPPPPP
SORRY YOU HAD TO WITNESS THAT DISTURBING VIOLENCE. BUT THAT'S HOW WE EARN OUR T+ RATING! WITH ONE MIGHTY SWING OF THE SWORD, MAN-THING HAS BROUGHT CHAOS TO THE EARTH. AND WHAT LIES AHEAD FOR HIM? HOW WILL HE BRING US TO...
...THE SURPRISE ENDING!

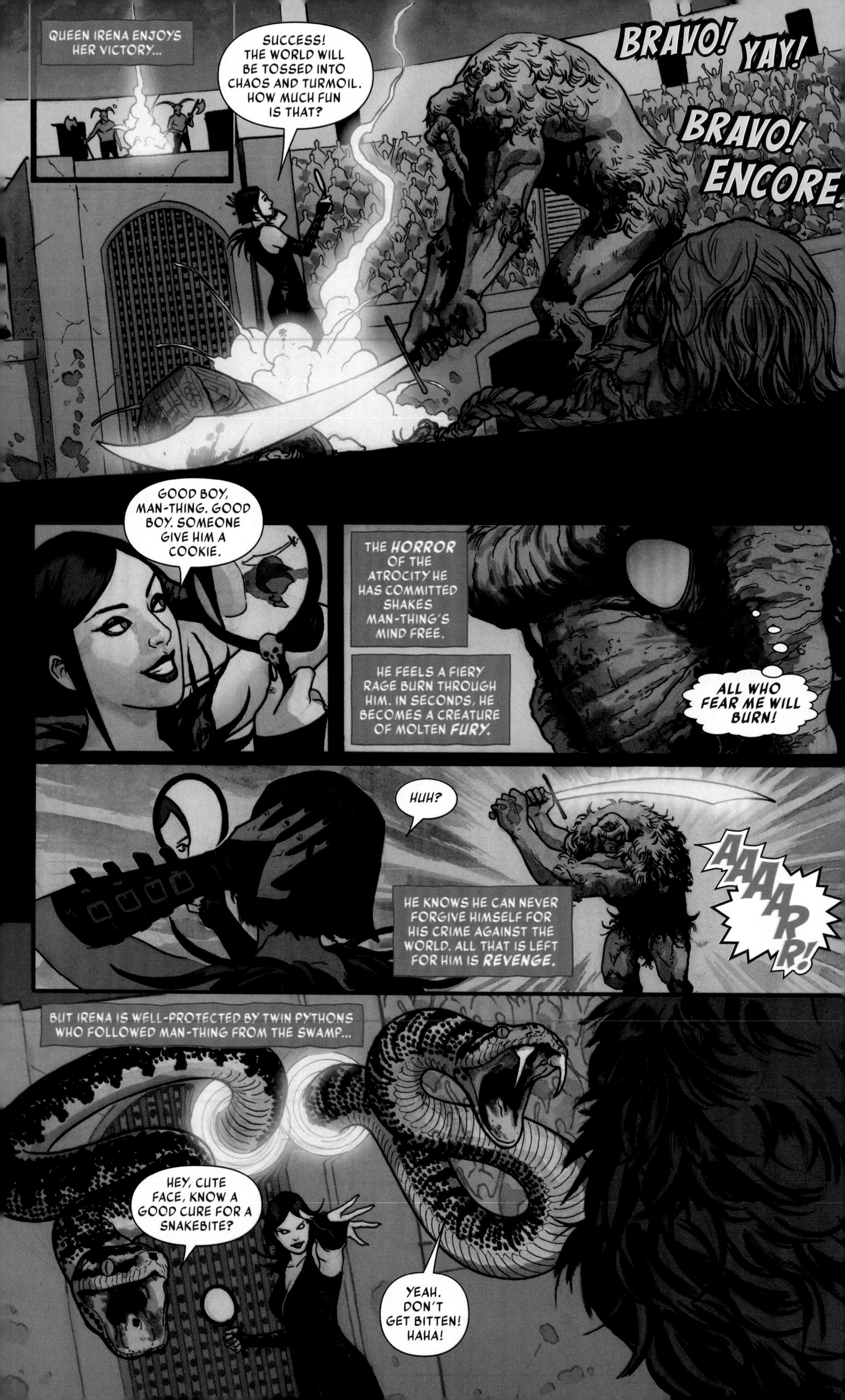
QUEEN IRENA ENJOYS HER VICTORY...
SUCCESS! THE WORLD WILL BE TOSSED INTO CHAOS AND TURMOIL. HOW MUCH FUN IS THAT?
BRAVO! YAY!
BRAVO! ENCORE!
GOOD BOY, MAN-THING. GOOD BOY. SOMEONE GIVE HIM A COOKIE.
THE HORROR OF THE ATROCITY HE HAS COMMITTED SHAKES MAN-THING'S MIND FREE.
HE FEELS A FIERY RAGE BURN THROUGH HIM. IN SECONDS, HE BECOMES A CREATURE OF MOLTEN FURY.
ALL WHO FEAR ME WILL BURN!
HUH?
HE KNOWS HE CAN NEVER FORGIVE HIMSELF FOR HIS CRIME AGAINST THE WORLD. ALL THAT IS LEFT FOR HIM IS REVENGE.
AAAARR!
BUT IRENA IS WELL-PROTECTED BY TWIN PYTHONS WHO FOLLOWED MAN-THING FROM THE SWAMP...
HEY, CUTE FACE, KNOW A GOOD CURE FOR A SNAKEBITE?
YEAH. DON'T GET BITTEN! HAHA!

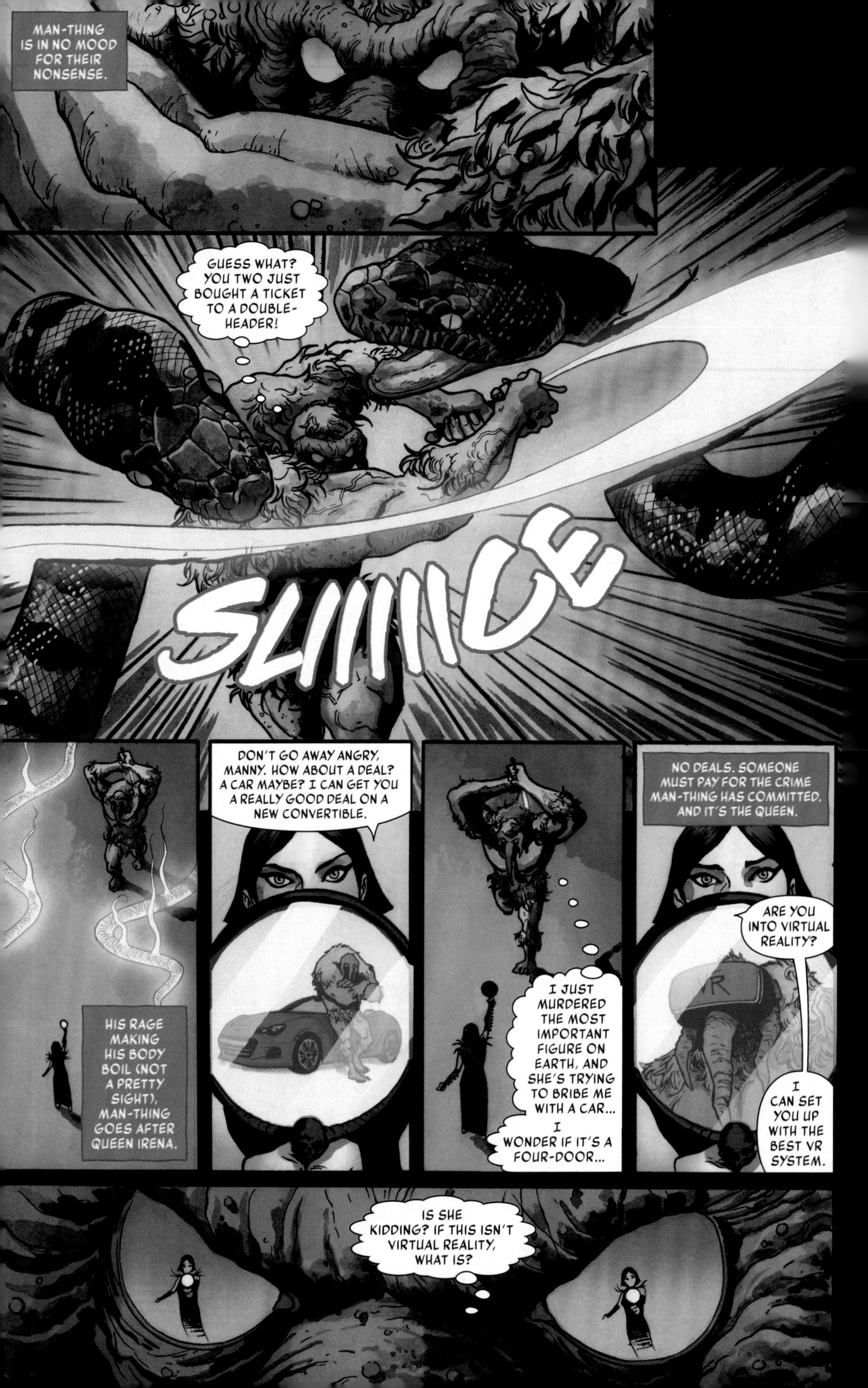
MAN-THING IS IN NO MOOD FOR THEIR NONSENSE.
GUESS WHAT? YOU TWO JUST BOUGHT A TICKET TO A DOUBLE-HEADER!
SLIIIICE
HIS RAGE MAKING HIS BODY BOIL (NOT A PRETTY SIGHT), MAN-THING GOES AFTER QUEEN IRENA.
DON'T GO AWAY ANGRY, MANNY. HOW ABOUT A DEAL? A CAR MAYBE? I CAN GET YOU A REALLY GOOD DEAL ON A NEW CONVERTIBLE.
I JUST MURDERED THE MOST IMPORTANT FIGURE ON EARTH, AND SHE'S TRYING TO BRIBE ME WITH A CAR...
I WONDER IF IT'S A FOUR-DOOR...
NO DEALS. SOMEONE MUST PAY FOR THE CRIME MAN-THING HAS COMMITTED. AND IT'S THE QUEEN.
ARE YOU INTO VIRTUAL REALITY?
I CAN SET YOU UP WITH THE BEST VR SYSTEM.
IS SHE KIDDING? IF THIS ISN'T VIRTUAL REALITY, WHAT IS?

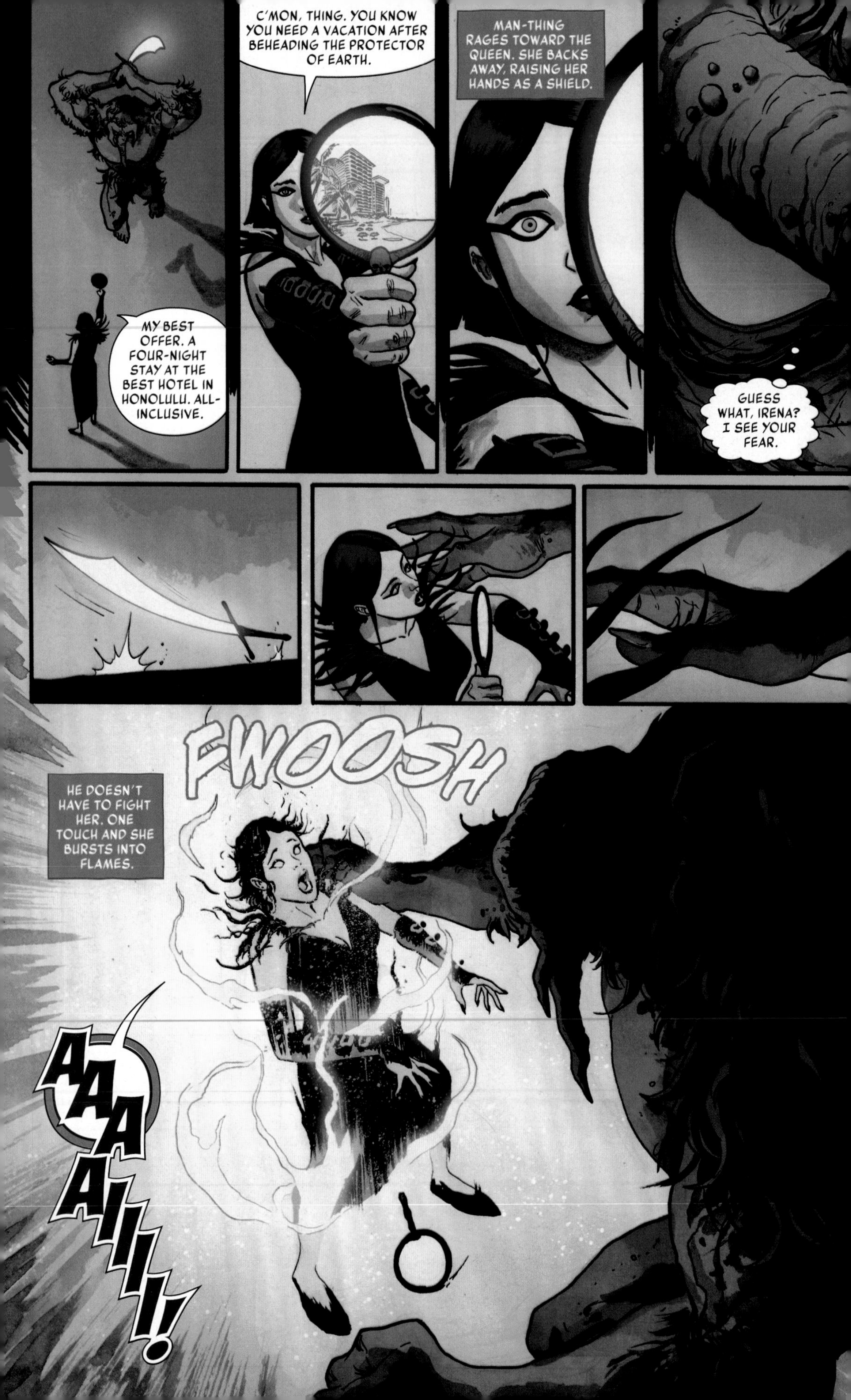
MY BEST OFFER. A FOUR-NIGHT STAY AT THE BEST HOTEL IN HONOLULU. ALL-INCLUSIVE.
C'MON, THING. YOU KNOW YOU NEED A VACATION AFTER BEHEADING THE PROTECTOR OF EARTH.
MAN-THING RAGES TOWARD THE QUEEN. SHE BACKS AWAY, RAISING HER HANDS AS A SHIELD.
GUESS WHAT, IRENA? I SEE YOUR FEAR.
FWOOSH
HE DOESN'T HAVE TO FIGHT HER. ONE TOUCH AND SHE BURSTS INTO FLAMES.
AAAAIIII!

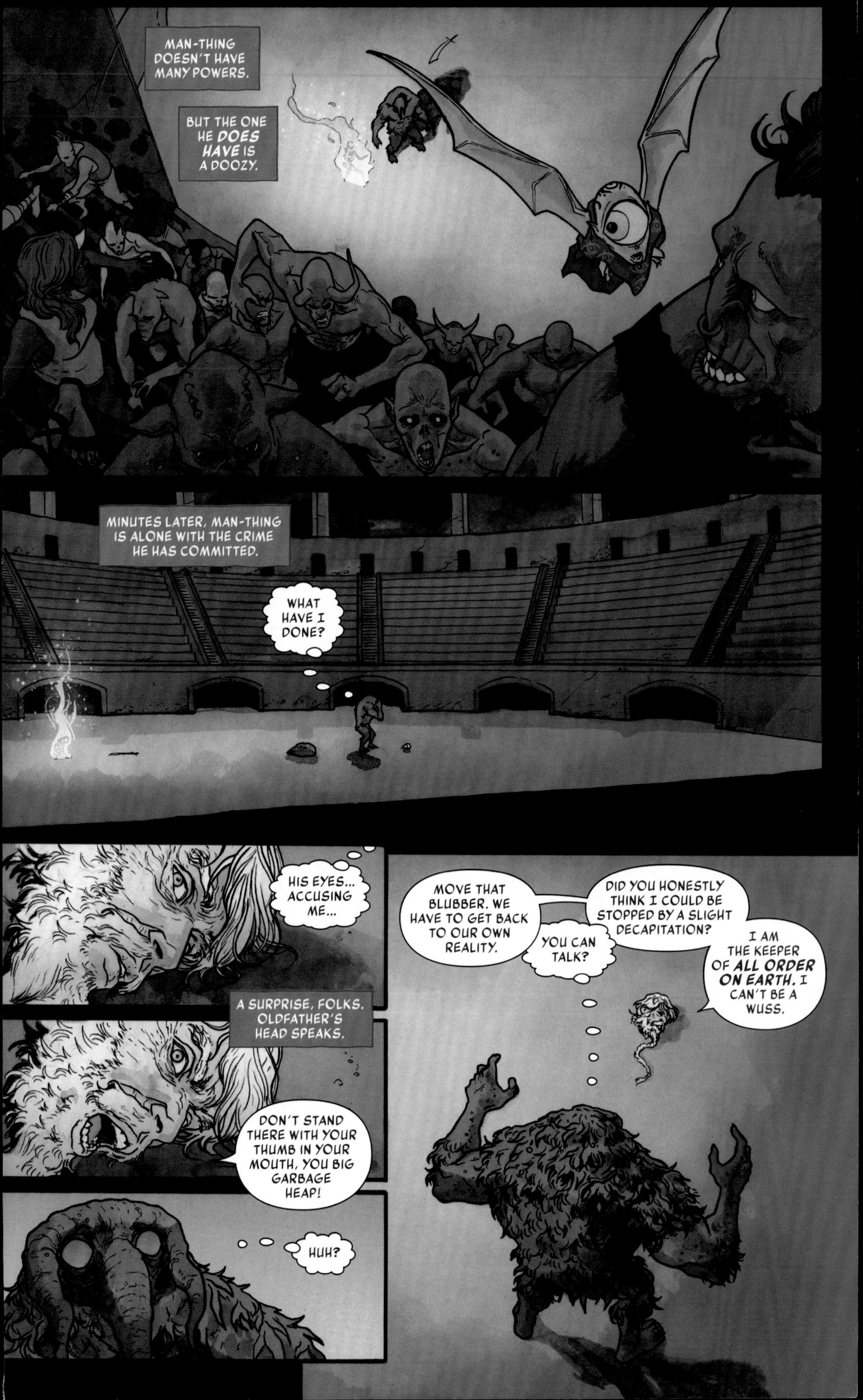
MAN-THING DOESN'T HAVE MANY POWERS.
BUT THE ONE HE *DOES HAVE* IS A DOOZY.
MINUTES LATER, MAN-THING IS ALONE WITH THE CRIME HE HAS COMMITTED.
WHAT HAVE I DONE?
HIS EYES... ACCUSING ME...
A SURPRISE, FOLKS. OLDFATHER'S HEAD SPEAKS.
DON'T STAND THERE WITH YOUR THUMB IN YOUR MOUTH, YOU BIG GARBAGE HEAP!
HUH?
MOVE THAT BLUBBER. WE HAVE TO GET BACK TO OUR OWN REALITY.
YOU CAN TALK?
DID YOU HONESTLY THINK I COULD BE STOPPED BY A SLIGHT DECAPITATION?
I AM THE KEEPER OF *ALL ORDER ON EARTH.* I CAN'T BE A WUSS.

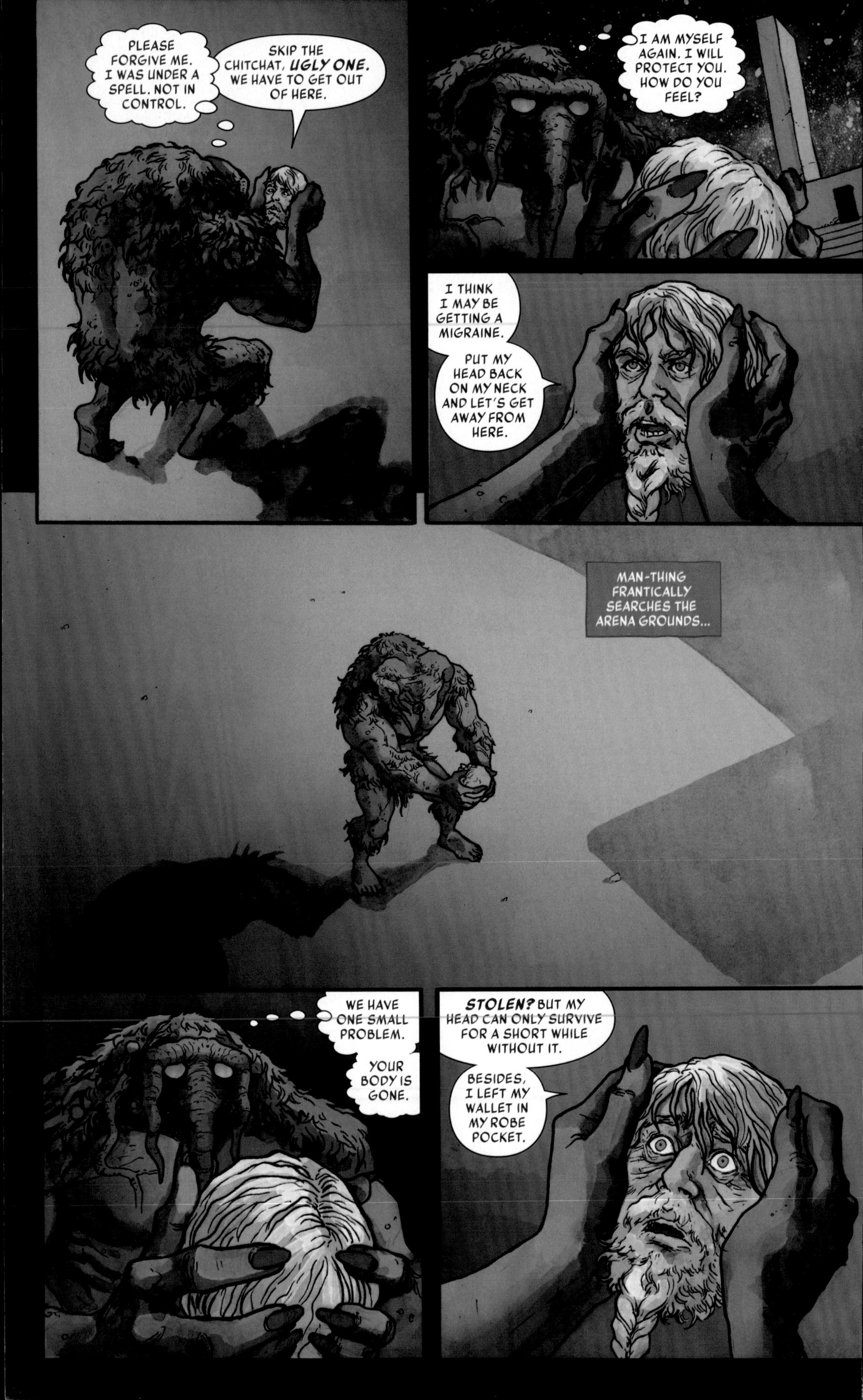
PLEASE FORGIVE ME. I WAS UNDER A SPELL. NOT IN CONTROL.
SKIP THE CHITCHAT, UGLY ONE. WE HAVE TO GET OUT OF HERE.
I AM MYSELF AGAIN. I WILL PROTECT YOU. HOW DO YOU FEEL?
I THINK I MAY BE GETTING A MIGRAINE.
PUT MY HEAD BACK ON MY NECK AND LET'S GET AWAY FROM HERE.
MAN-THING FRANTICALLY SEARCHES THE ARENA GROUNDS...
WE HAVE ONE SMALL PROBLEM.
YOUR BODY IS GONE.
STOLEN? BUT MY HEAD CAN ONLY SURVIVE FOR A SHORT WHILE WITHOUT IT.
BESIDES, I LEFT MY WALLET IN MY ROBE POCKET.

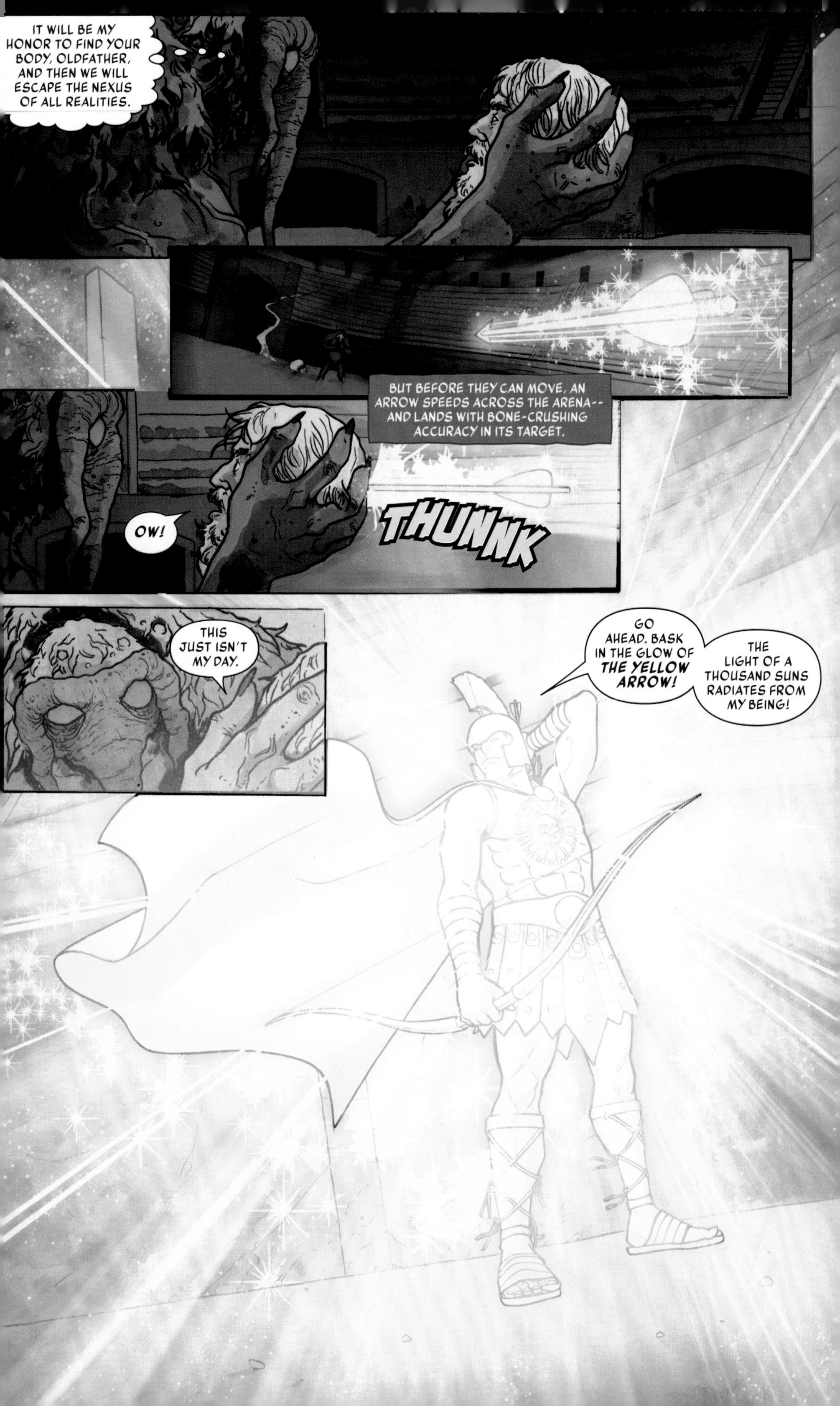
IT WILL BE MY HONOR TO FIND YOUR BODY, OLDFATHER, AND THEN WE WILL ESCAPE THE NEXUS OF ALL REALITIES.
BUT BEFORE THEY CAN MOVE, AN ARROW SPEEDS ACROSS THE ARENA--AND LANDS WITH BONE-CRUSHING ACCURACY IN ITS TARGET.
OW!
THUNNK
THIS JUST ISN'T MY DAY.
GO AHEAD. BASK IN THE GLOW OF THE YELLOW ARROW!
THE LIGHT OF A THOUSAND SUNS RADIATES FROM MY BEING!

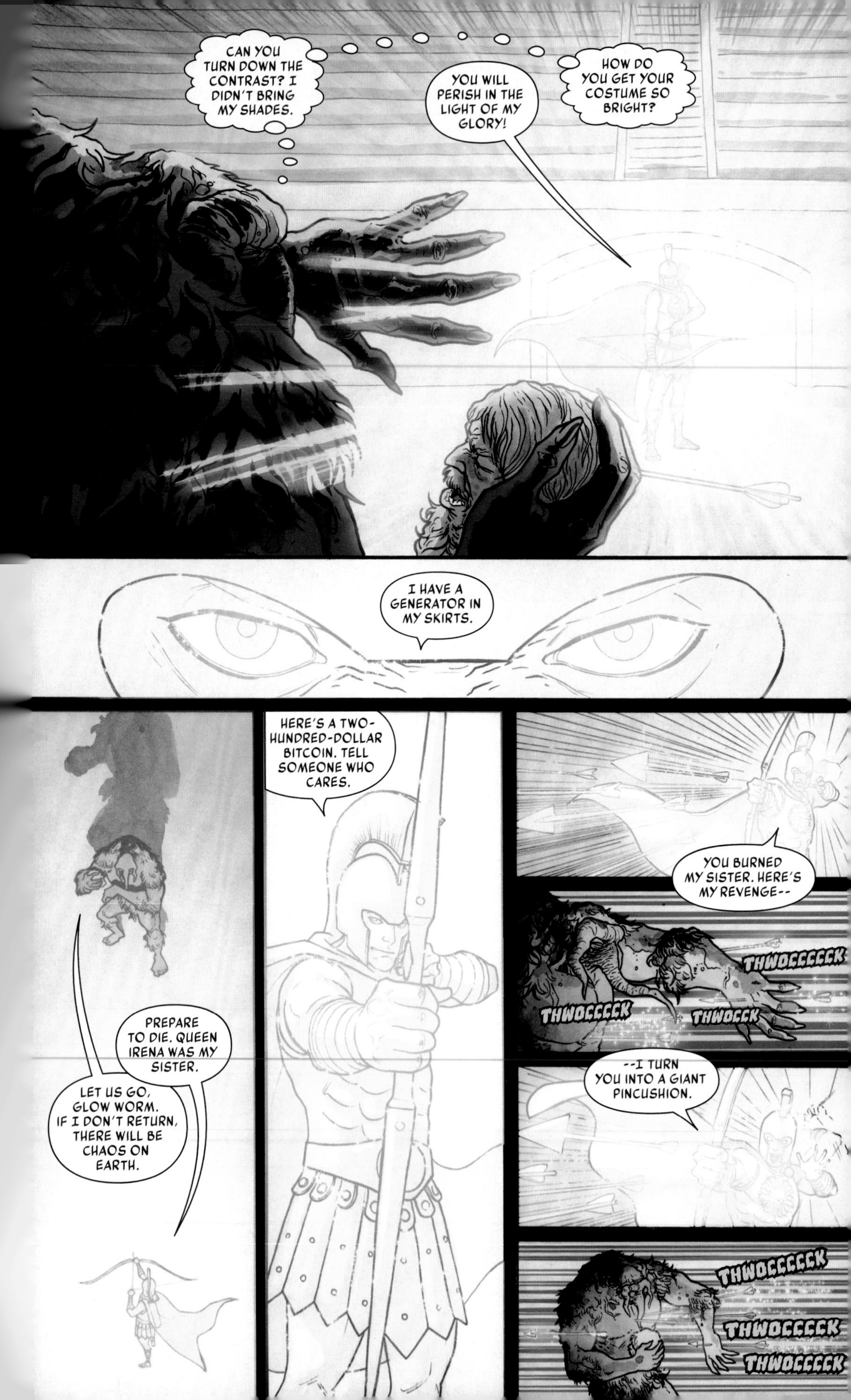
CAN YOU TURN DOWN THE CONTRAST? I DIDN'T BRING MY SHADES.
YOU WILL PERISH IN THE LIGHT OF MY GLORY!
HOW DO YOU GET YOUR COSTUME SO BRIGHT?
I HAVE A GENERATOR IN MY SKIRTS.
LET US GO, GLOW WORM. IF I DON'T RETURN, THERE WILL BE CHAOS ON EARTH.
PREPARE TO DIE. QUEEN IRENA WAS MY SISTER.
HERE'S A TWO-HUNDRED-DOLLAR BITCOIN. TELL SOMEONE WHO CARES.
YOU BURNED MY SISTER. HERE'S MY REVENGE--
THWOCCCCCK
THWOCCCCK
THWOCCK
--I TURN YOU INTO A GIANT PINCUSHION.
THWOCCCCCK
THWOCCCCK
THWOCCCCK

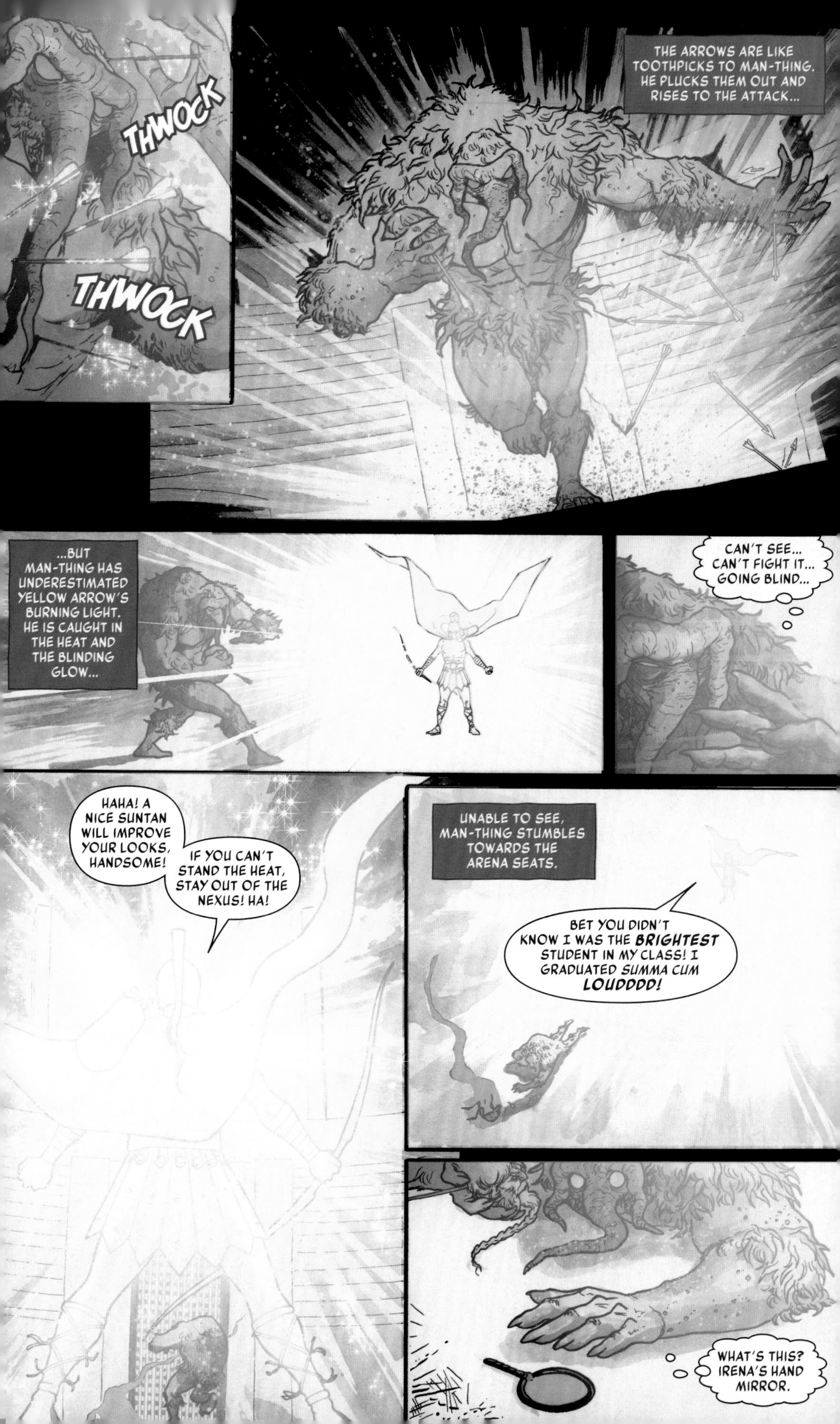
THWOCK
THWOCK
THE ARROWS ARE LIKE TOOTHPICKS TO MAN-THING. HE PLUCKS THEM OUT AND RISES TO THE ATTACK...
...BUT MAN-THING HAS UNDERESTIMATED YELLOW ARROW'S BURNING LIGHT. HE IS CAUGHT IN THE HEAT AND THE BLINDING GLOW...
CAN'T SEE... CAN'T FIGHT IT... GOING BLIND...
HAHA! A NICE SUNTAN WILL IMPROVE YOUR LOOKS, HANDSOME!
IF YOU CAN'T STAND THE HEAT, STAY OUT OF THE NEXUS! HA!
UNABLE TO SEE, MAN-THING STUMBLES TOWARDS THE ARENA SEATS.
BET YOU DIDN'T KNOW I WAS THE BRIGHTEST STUDENT IN MY CLASS! I GRADUATED SUMMA CUM LOUDDDD!
WHAT'S THIS? IRENA'S HAND MIRROR.

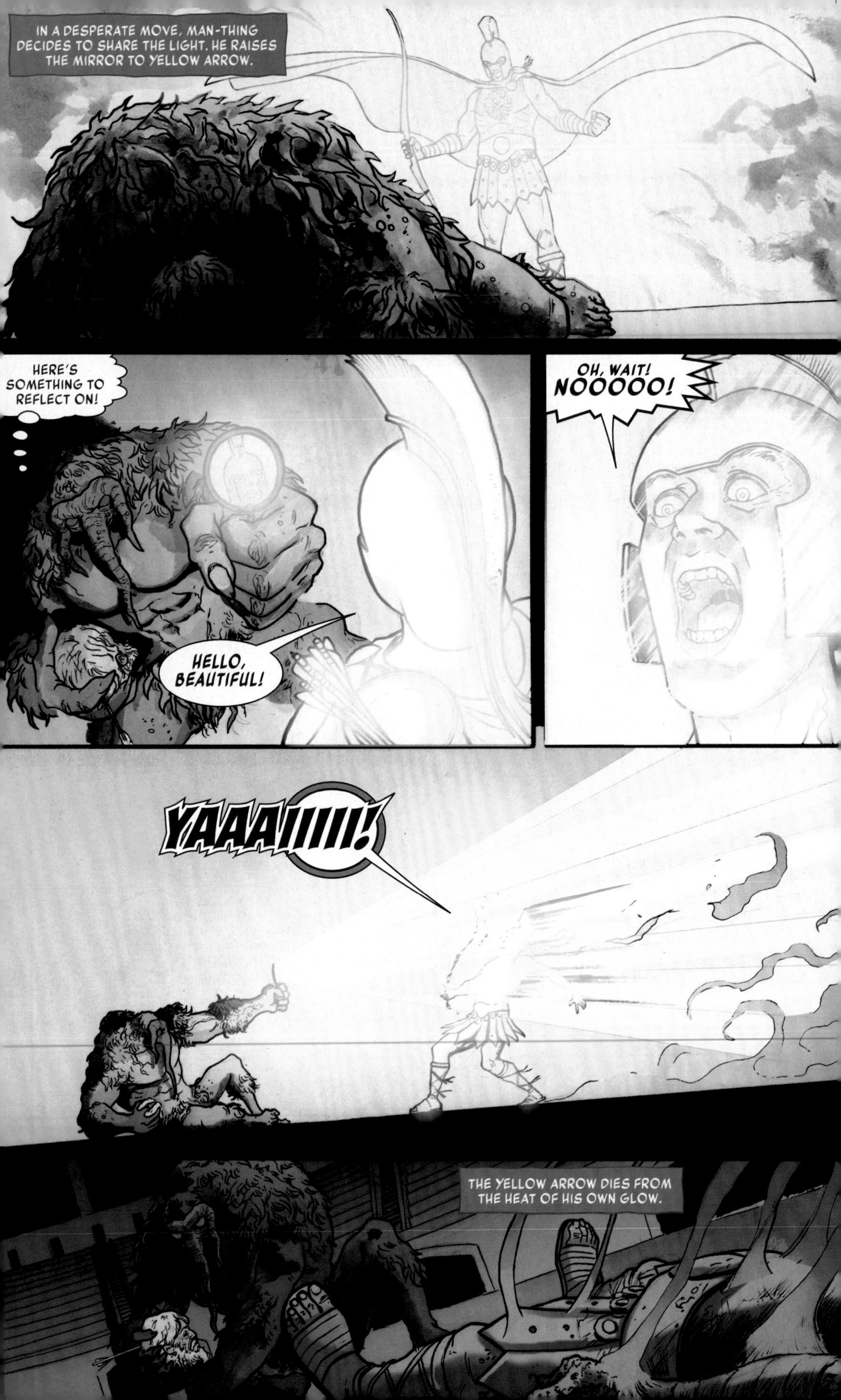

IN A DESPERATE MOVE, MAN-THING DECIDES TO SHARE THE LIGHT. HE RAISES THE MIRROR TO YELLOW ARROW.
HERE'S SOMETHING TO REFLECT ON!
HELLO, BEAUTIFUL!
OH, WAIT! NOOOOO!
YAAAIIIII!
THE YELLOW ARROW DIES FROM THE HEAT OF HIS OWN GLOW.

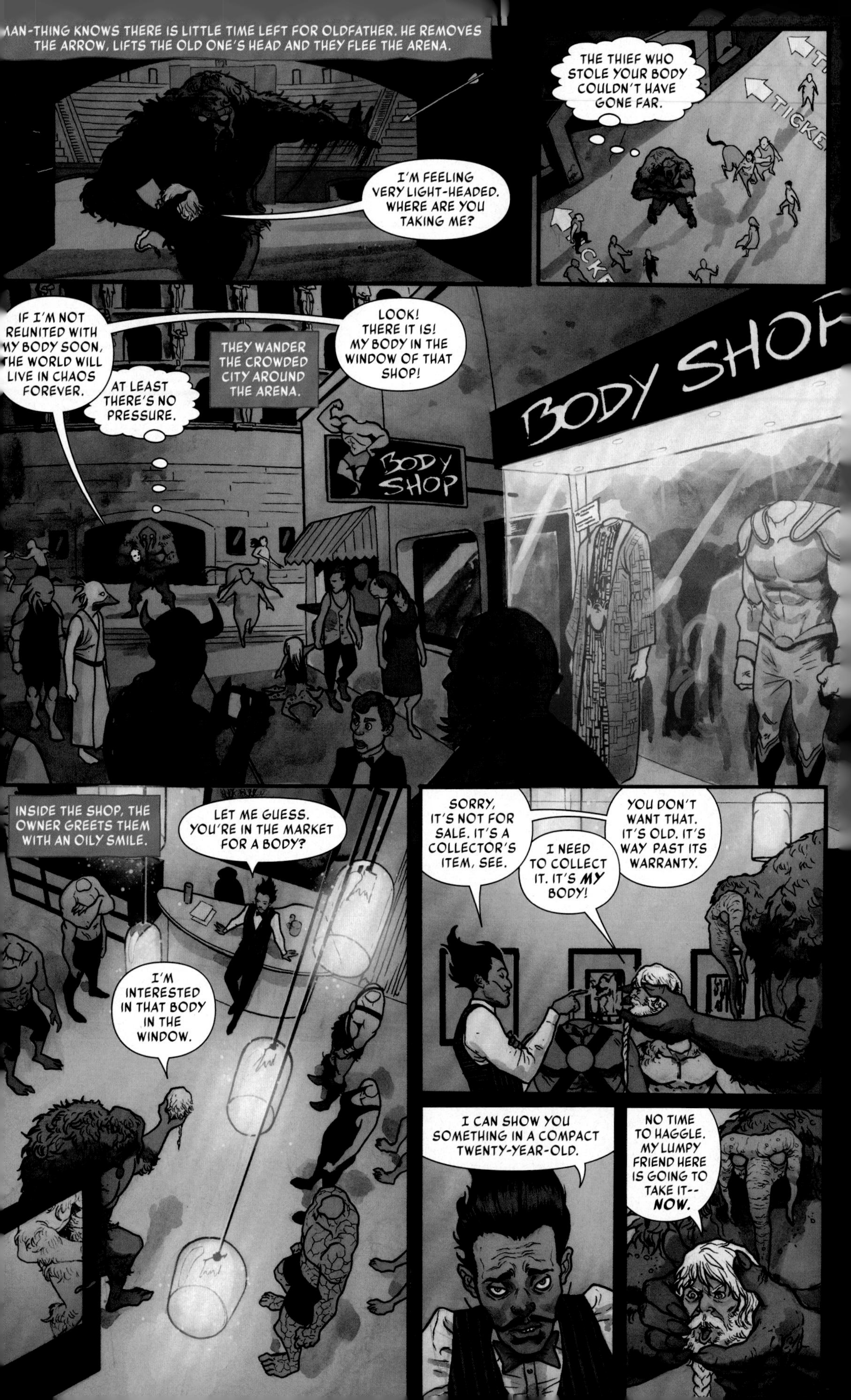
MAN-THING KNOWS THERE IS LITTLE TIME LEFT FOR OLDFATHER. HE REMOVES THE ARROW, LIFTS THE OLD ONE'S HEAD AND THEY FLEE THE ARENA.
I'M FEELING VERY LIGHT-HEADED. WHERE ARE YOU TAKING ME?
THE THIEF WHO STOLE YOUR BODY COULDN'T HAVE GONE FAR.
TICKE
IF I'M NOT REUNITED WITH MY BODY SOON, THE WORLD WILL LIVE IN CHAOS FOREVER.
AT LEAST THERE'S NO PRESSURE.
THEY WANDER THE CROWDED CITY AROUND THE ARENA.
LOOK! THERE IT IS! MY BODY IN THE WINDOW OF THAT SHOP!
BODY SHOP
BODY SHOP
INSIDE THE SHOP, THE OWNER GREETS THEM WITH AN OILY SMILE.
LET ME GUESS. YOU'RE IN THE MARKET FOR A BODY?
I'M INTERESTED IN THAT BODY IN THE WINDOW.
SORRY, IT'S NOT FOR SALE. IT'S A COLLECTOR'S ITEM, SEE.
I NEED TO COLLECT IT. IT'S *MY* BODY!
YOU DON'T WANT THAT. IT'S OLD. IT'S WAY PAST ITS WARRANTY.
I CAN SHOW YOU SOMETHING IN A COMPACT TWENTY-YEAR-OLD.
NO TIME TO HAGGLE. MY LUMPY FRIEND HERE IS GOING TO TAKE IT-- **NOW.**

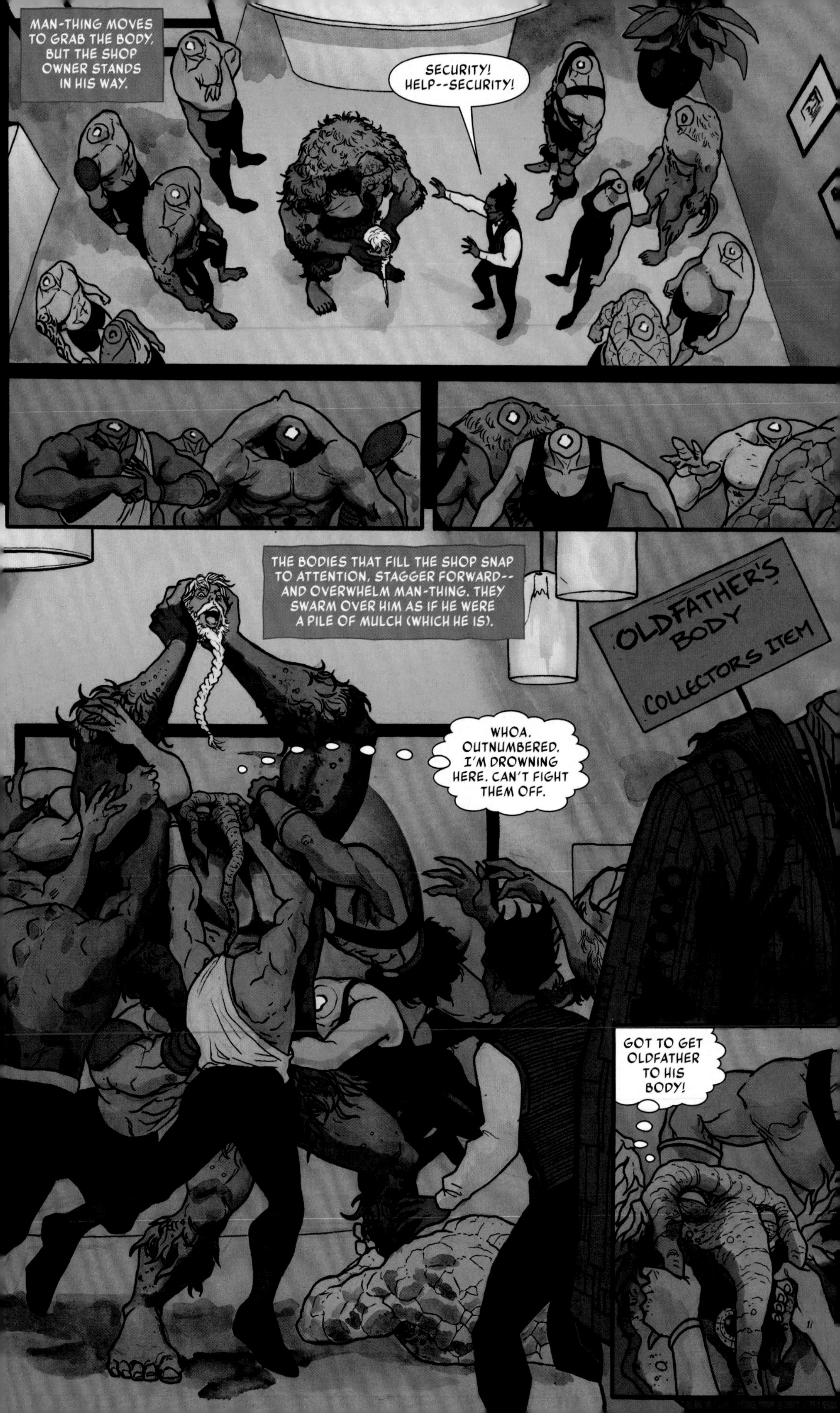
MAN-THING MOVES TO GRAB THE BODY, BUT THE SHOP OWNER STANDS IN HIS WAY.
SECURITY! HELP--SECURITY!
THE BODIES THAT FILL THE SHOP SNAP TO ATTENTION, STAGGER FORWARD-- AND OVERWHELM MAN-THING. THEY SWARM OVER HIM AS IF HE WERE A PILE OF MULCH (WHICH HE IS).
OLDFATHER'S BODY COLLECTORS ITEM
WHOA. OUTNUMBERED. I'M DROWNING HERE. CAN'T FIGHT THEM OFF.
GOT TO GET OLDFATHER TO HIS BODY!

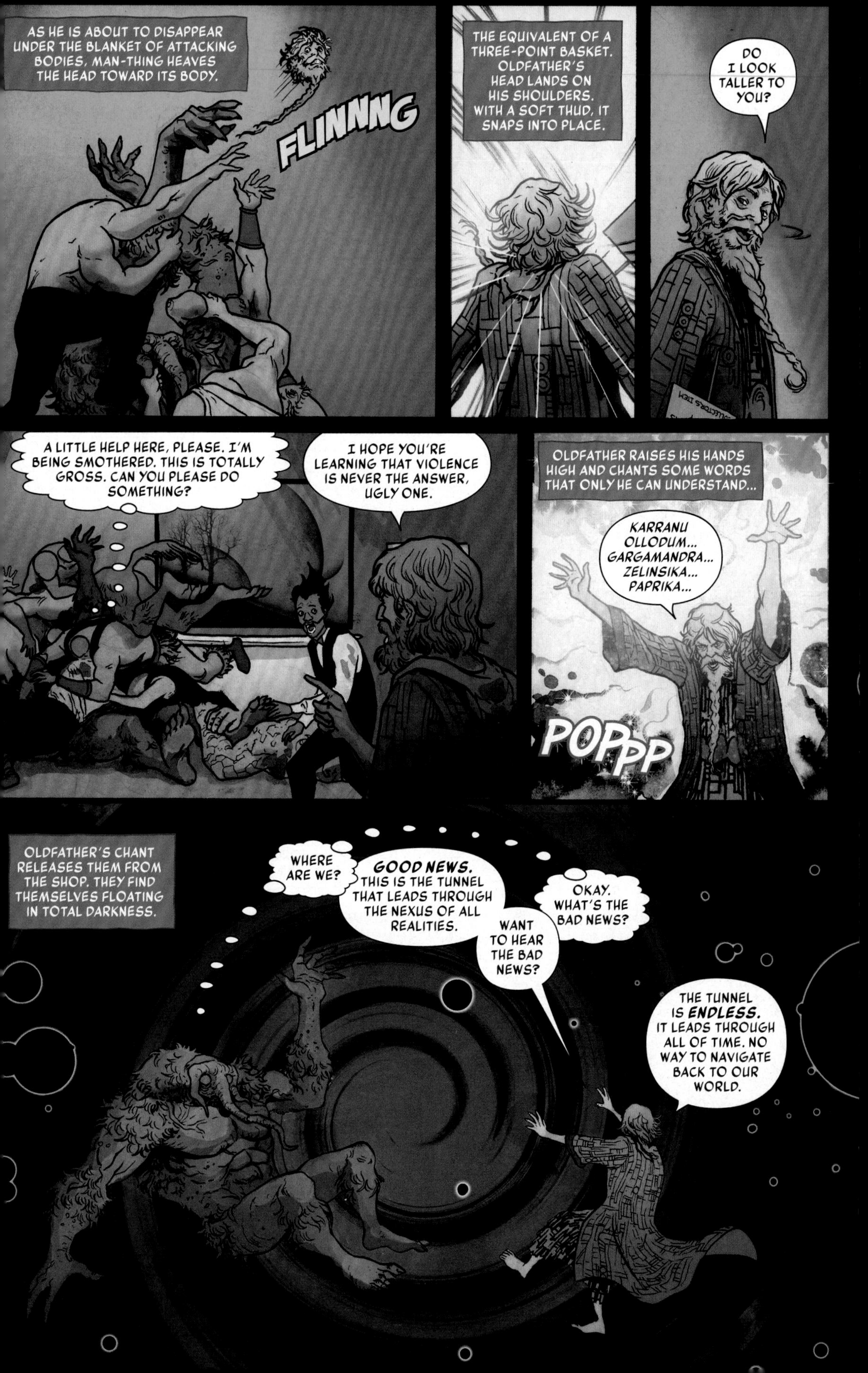
AS HE IS ABOUT TO DISAPPEAR UNDER THE BLANKET OF ATTACKING BODIES, MAN-THING HEAVES THE HEAD TOWARD ITS BODY.
FLINNNG
THE EQUIVALENT OF A THREE-POINT BASKET. OLDFATHER'S HEAD LANDS ON HIS SHOULDERS. WITH A SOFT THUD, IT SNAPS INTO PLACE.
DO I LOOK TALLER TO YOU?
A LITTLE HELP HERE, PLEASE. I'M BEING SMOTHERED. THIS IS TOTALLY GROSS. CAN YOU PLEASE DO SOMETHING?
I HOPE YOU'RE LEARNING THAT VIOLENCE IS NEVER THE ANSWER, UGLY ONE.
OLDFATHER RAISES HIS HANDS HIGH AND CHANTS SOME WORDS THAT ONLY HE CAN UNDERSTAND...
KARRANU OLLODUM... GARGAMANDRA... ZELINSIKA... PAPRIKA...
POPPP
OLDFATHER'S CHANT RELEASES THEM FROM THE SHOP. THEY FIND THEMSELVES FLOATING IN TOTAL DARKNESS.
WHERE ARE WE?
GOOD NEWS. THIS IS THE TUNNEL THAT LEADS THROUGH THE NEXUS OF ALL REALITIES.
WANT TO HEAR THE BAD NEWS?
OKAY. WHAT'S THE BAD NEWS?
THE TUNNEL IS ENDLESS. IT LEADS THROUGH ALL OF TIME. NO WAY TO NAVIGATE BACK TO OUR WORLD.

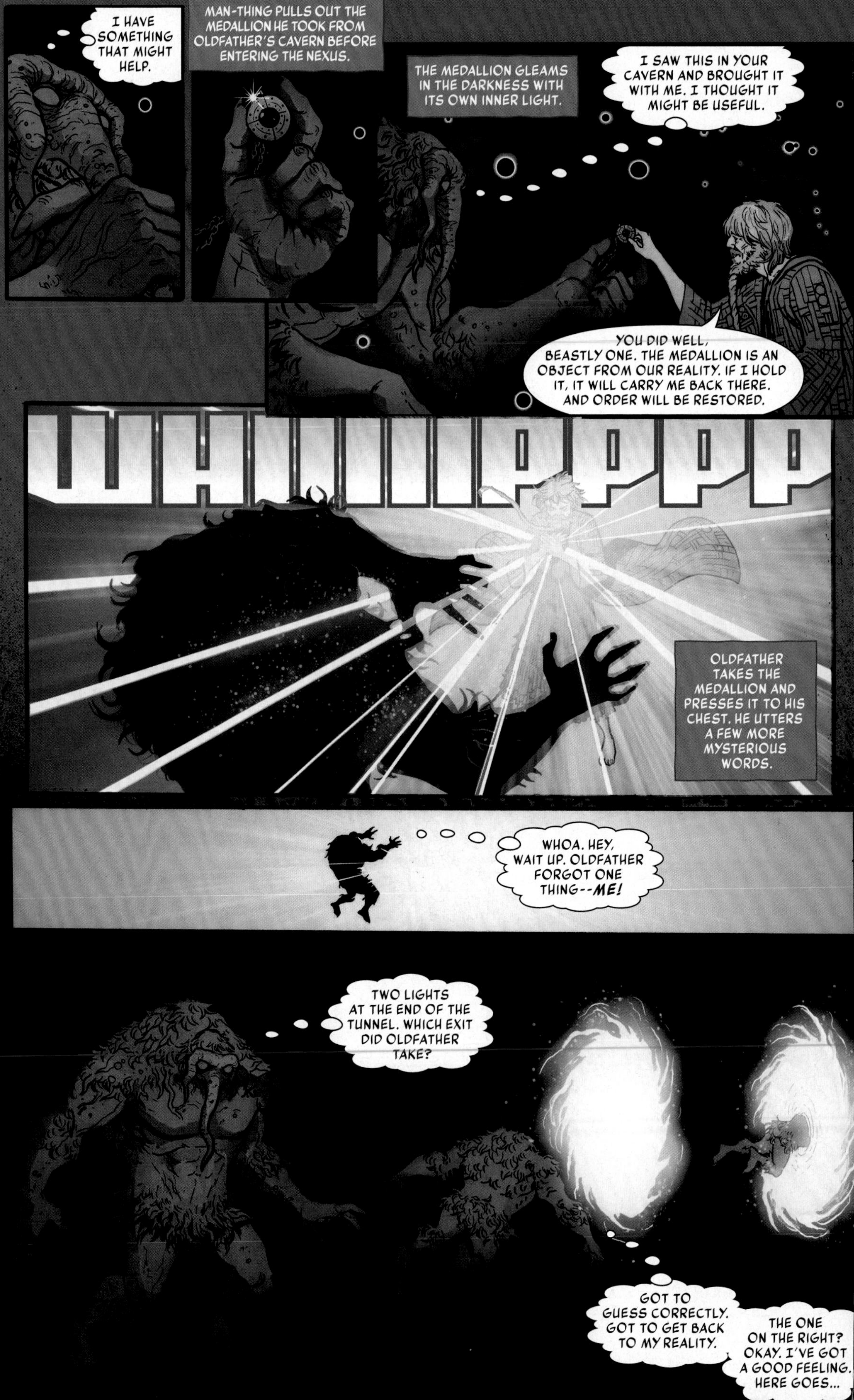
I HAVE SOMETHING THAT MIGHT HELP.
MAN-THING PULLS OUT THE MEDALLION HE TOOK FROM OLDFATHER'S CAVERN BEFORE ENTERING THE NEXUS.
THE MEDALLION GLEAMS IN THE DARKNESS WITH ITS OWN INNER LIGHT.
I SAW THIS IN YOUR CAVERN AND BROUGHT IT WITH ME. I THOUGHT IT MIGHT BE USEFUL.
YOU DID WELL, BEASTLY ONE. THE MEDALLION IS AN OBJECT FROM OUR REALITY. IF I HOLD IT, IT WILL CARRY ME BACK THERE. AND ORDER WILL BE RESTORED.
WHHHHPPPP
OLDFATHER TAKES THE MEDALLION AND PRESSES IT TO HIS CHEST. HE UTTERS A FEW MORE MYSTERIOUS WORDS.
WHOA. HEY, WAIT UP. OLDFATHER FORGOT ONE THING--*ME!*
TWO LIGHTS AT THE END OF THE TUNNEL. WHICH EXIT DID OLDFATHER TAKE?
GOT TO GUESS CORRECTLY. GOT TO GET BACK TO MY REALITY.
THE ONE ON THE RIGHT? OKAY. I'VE GOT A GOOD FEELING. HERE GOES...

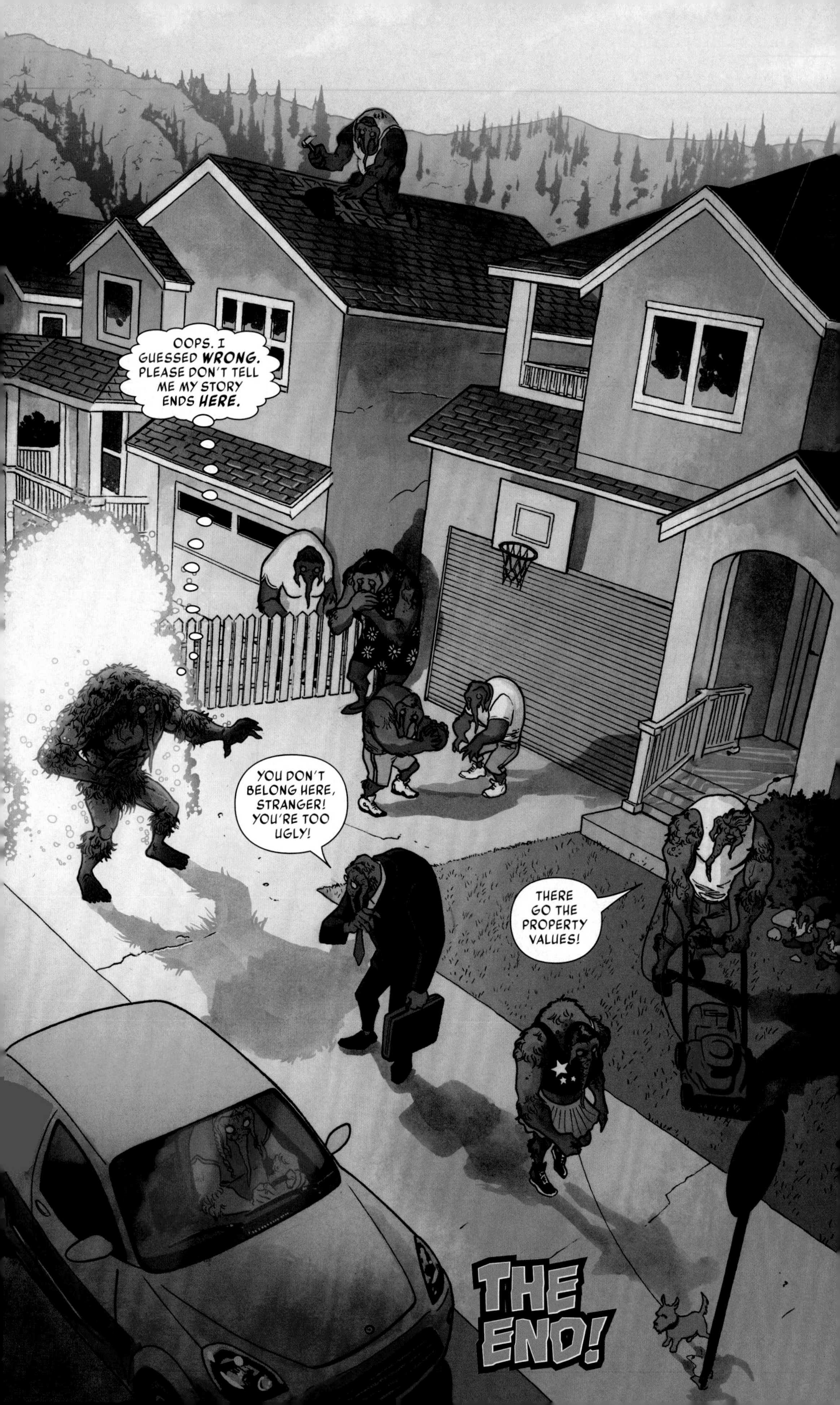

OOPS. I GUESSED **WRONG.** PLEASE DON'T TELL ME MY STORY ENDS **HERE.**
YOU DON'T BELONG HERE, STRANGER! YOU'RE TOO UGLY!
THERE GO THE PROPERTY VALUES!
THE END!

THIS YACHT SAILS OVER CALM WATERS. BUT WILL THERE BE CALM ON BOARD AS WELL?

ASHLI, YOUR EYES ARE THE COLOR OF THE OCEAN TODAY, ONLY MORE BEAUTIFUL.

YOU'RE SWEET, DANIEL. I'M SO LUCKY...

DANIEL, YOU PLAY SO BEAUTIFULLY. YOUR FINGERS ARE LIKE *MAGIC!*

I MIGHT MAKE MY LIVING AS A PIANIST, BUT I PLAY ONLY FOR YOU, DEAR. ONLY FOR YOU.

TELL ME AGAIN. YOU'RE NOT MARRYING ME FOR MY MONEY, ARE YOU?

MONEY MEANS NOTHING TO ME. WHEN I'M WITH YOU, I CAN ONLY THINK ABOUT HOW MUCH I CARE ABOUT YOU.

AND THAT RING. THAT MAGICAL RING WILL SOON BE MINE!

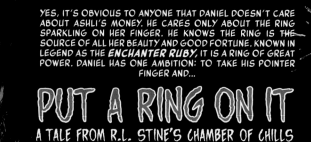

YES, IT'S OBVIOUS TO ANYONE THAT DANIEL DOESN'T CARE ABOUT ASHLI'S MONEY. HE CARES ONLY ABOUT THE RING SPARKLING ON HER FINGER. HE KNOWS THE RING IS THE SOURCE OF ALL HER BEAUTY AND GOOD FORTUNE. KNOWN IN LEGEND AS THE *ENCHANTER RUBY,* IT IS A RING OF GREAT POWER. DANIEL HAS ONE AMBITION: TO TAKE HIS POINTER FINGER AND...

PUT A RING ON IT
A TALE FROM R.L. STINE'S CHAMBER OF CHILLS

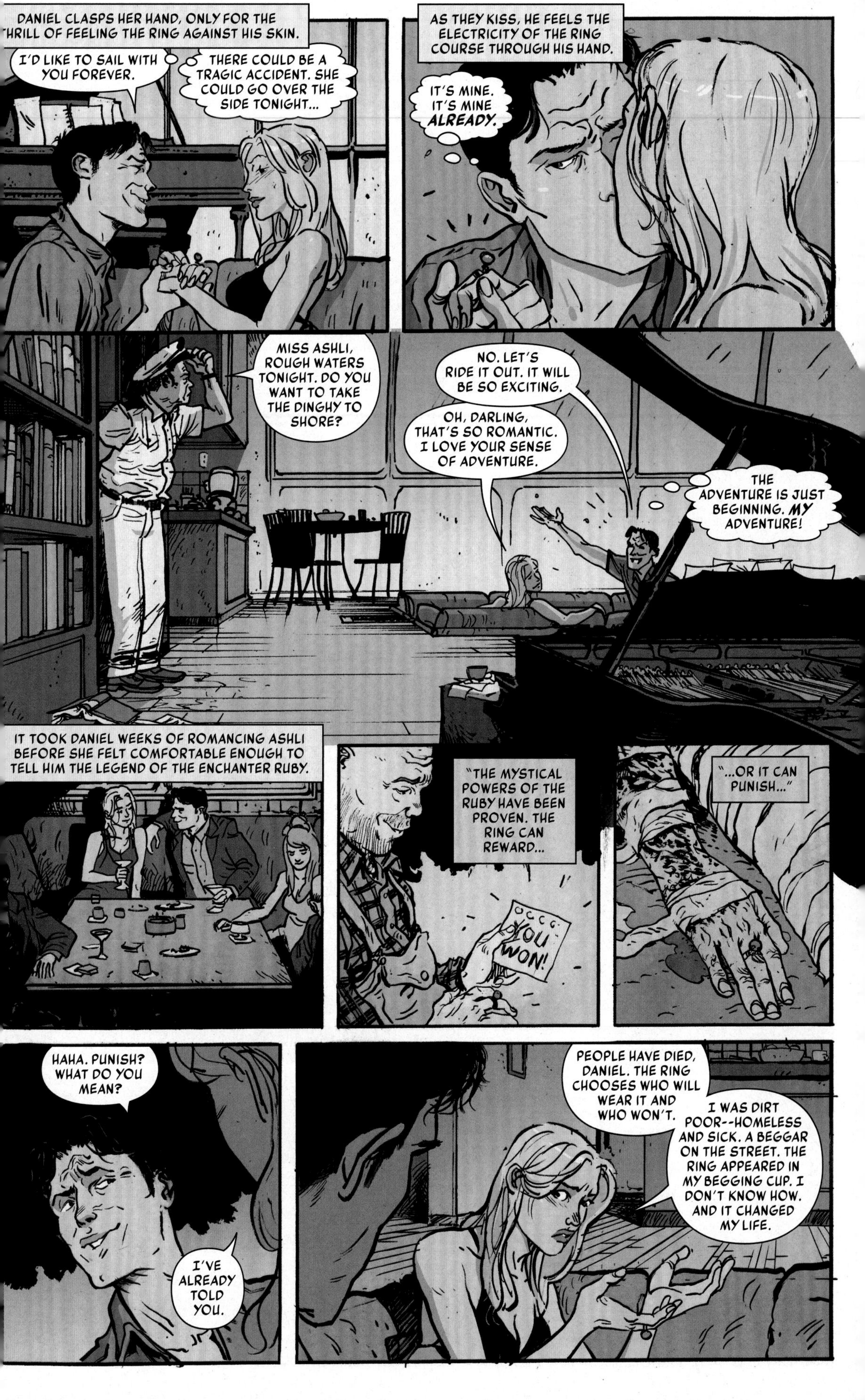

DANIEL CLASPS HER HAND, ONLY FOR THE THRILL OF FEELING THE RING AGAINST HIS SKIN.
I'D LIKE TO SAIL WITH YOU FOREVER.
THERE COULD BE A TRAGIC ACCIDENT. SHE COULD GO OVER THE SIDE TONIGHT...
AS THEY KISS, HE FEELS THE ELECTRICITY OF THE RING COURSE THROUGH HIS HAND.
IT'S MINE. IT'S MINE ALREADY.
MISS ASHLI, ROUGH WATERS TONIGHT. DO YOU WANT TO TAKE THE DINGHY TO SHORE?
NO. LET'S RIDE IT OUT. IT WILL BE SO EXCITING.
OH, DARLING, THAT'S SO ROMANTIC. I LOVE YOUR SENSE OF ADVENTURE.
THE ADVENTURE IS JUST BEGINNING. MY ADVENTURE!
IT TOOK DANIEL WEEKS OF ROMANCING ASHLI BEFORE SHE FELT COMFORTABLE ENOUGH TO TELL HIM THE LEGEND OF THE ENCHANTER RUBY.
"THE MYSTICAL POWERS OF THE RUBY HAVE BEEN PROVEN. THE RING CAN REWARD...
YOU WON!
"...OR IT CAN PUNISH..."
HAHA. PUNISH? WHAT DO YOU MEAN?
I'VE ALREADY TOLD YOU.
PEOPLE HAVE DIED, DANIEL. THE RING CHOOSES WHO WILL WEAR IT AND WHO WON'T.
I WAS DIRT POOR--HOMELESS AND SICK. A BEGGAR ON THE STREET. THE RING APPEARED IN MY BEGGING CUP. I DON'T KNOW HOW. AND IT CHANGED MY LIFE.

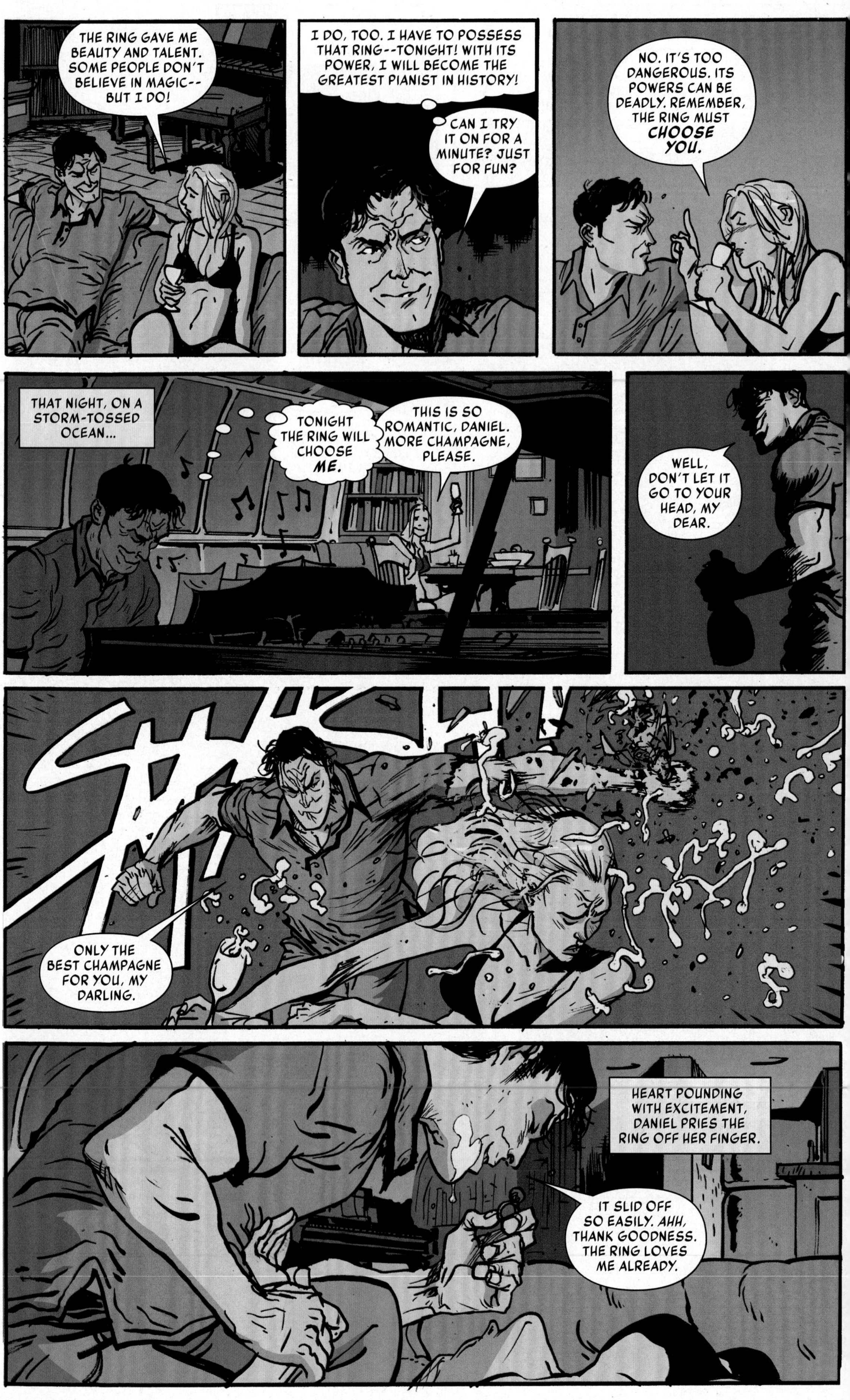
THE RING GAVE ME BEAUTY AND TALENT. SOME PEOPLE DON'T BELIEVE IN MAGIC--BUT I DO!
I DO, TOO. I HAVE TO POSSESS THAT RING--TONIGHT! WITH ITS POWER, I WILL BECOME THE GREATEST PIANIST IN HISTORY!
CAN I TRY IT ON FOR A MINUTE? JUST FOR FUN?
NO. IT'S TOO DANGEROUS. ITS POWERS CAN BE DEADLY. REMEMBER, THE RING MUST CHOOSE YOU.
THAT NIGHT, ON A STORM-TOSSED OCEAN...
TONIGHT THE RING WILL CHOOSE ME.
THIS IS SO ROMANTIC, DANIEL. MORE CHAMPAGNE, PLEASE.
WELL, DON'T LET IT GO TO YOUR HEAD, MY DEAR.
ONLY THE BEST CHAMPAGNE FOR YOU, MY DARLING.
HEART POUNDING WITH EXCITEMENT, DANIEL PRIES THE RING OFF HER FINGER.
IT SLID OFF SO EASILY. AHH, THANK GOODNESS. THE RING LOVES ME ALREADY.

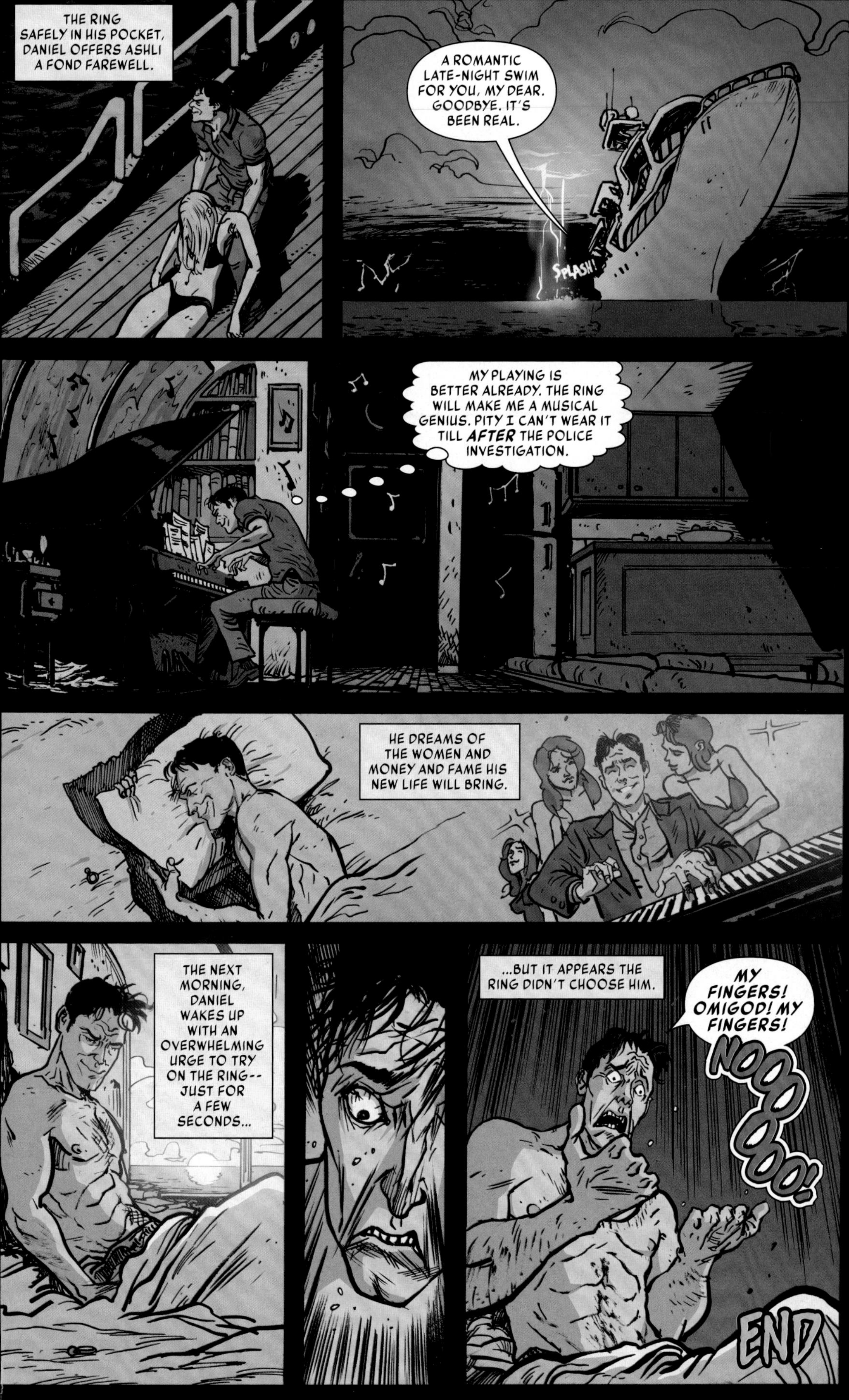
THE RING SAFELY IN HIS POCKET, DANIEL OFFERS ASHLI A FOND FAREWELL.
A ROMANTIC LATE-NIGHT SWIM FOR YOU, MY DEAR. GOODBYE. IT'S BEEN REAL.
SPLASH!
MY PLAYING IS BETTER ALREADY. THE RING WILL MAKE ME A MUSICAL GENIUS. PITY I CAN'T WEAR IT TILL AFTER THE POLICE INVESTIGATION.
HE DREAMS OF THE WOMEN AND MONEY AND FAME HIS NEW LIFE WILL BRING.
THE NEXT MORNING, DANIEL WAKES UP WITH AN OVERWHELMING URGE TO TRY ON THE RING--JUST FOR A FEW SECONDS...
...BUT IT APPEARS THE RING DIDN'T CHOOSE HIM.
MY FINGERS! OMIGOD! MY FINGERS!
NOOOOOO!
END

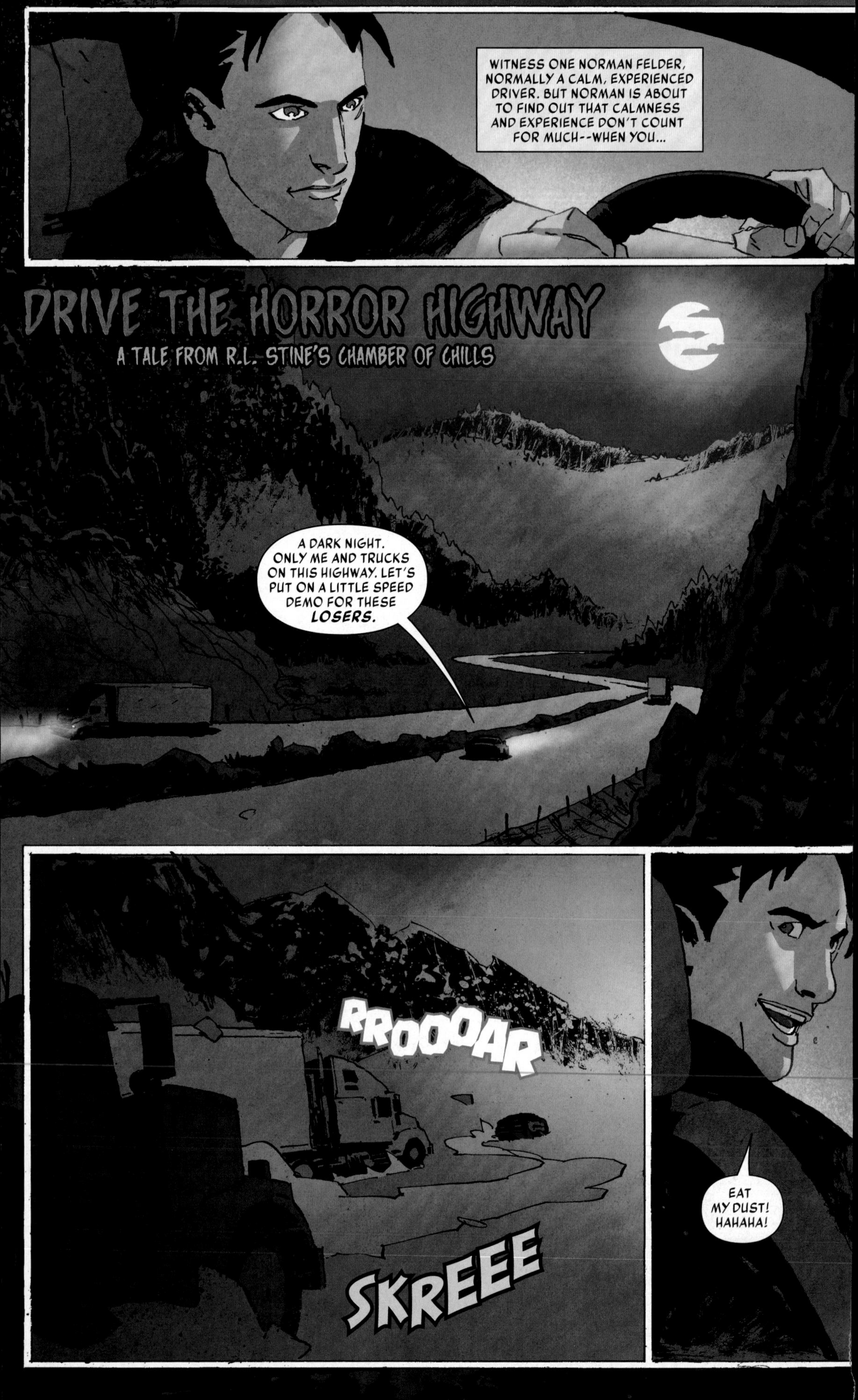
WITNESS ONE NORMAN FELDER, NORMALLY A CALM, EXPERIENCED DRIVER. BUT NORMAN IS ABOUT TO FIND OUT THAT CALMNESS AND EXPERIENCE DON'T COUNT FOR MUCH--WHEN YOU...
DRIVE THE HORROR HIGHWAY
A TALE FROM R.L. STINE'S CHAMBER OF CHILLS
A DARK NIGHT. ONLY ME AND TRUCKS ON THIS HIGHWAY. LET'S PUT ON A LITTLE SPEED DEMO FOR THESE LOSERS.
RROOOAR
SKREEE
EAT MY DUST! HAHAHA!

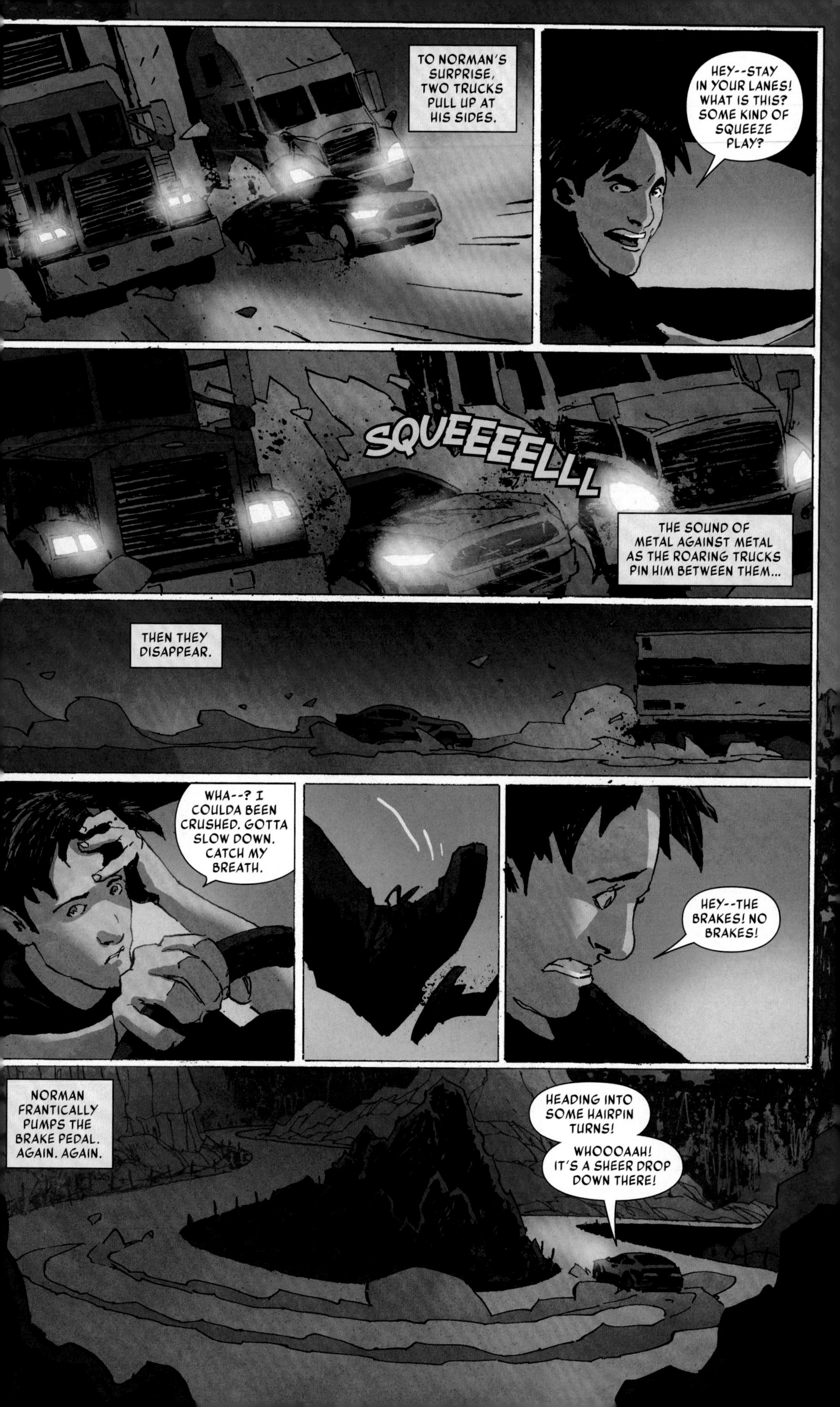
TO NORMAN'S SURPRISE, TWO TRUCKS PULL UP AT HIS SIDES.
HEY--STAY IN YOUR LANES! WHAT IS THIS? SOME KIND OF SQUEEZE PLAY?
SQUEEEEELLL
THE SOUND OF METAL AGAINST METAL AS THE ROARING TRUCKS PIN HIM BETWEEN THEM...
THEN THEY DISAPPEAR.
WHA--? I COULDA BEEN CRUSHED. GOTTA SLOW DOWN. CATCH MY BREATH.
HEY--THE BRAKES! NO BRAKES!
NORMAN FRANTICALLY PUMPS THE BRAKE PEDAL. AGAIN. AGAIN.
HEADING INTO SOME HAIRPIN TURNS!
WHOOOAAH! IT'S A SHEER DROP DOWN THERE!

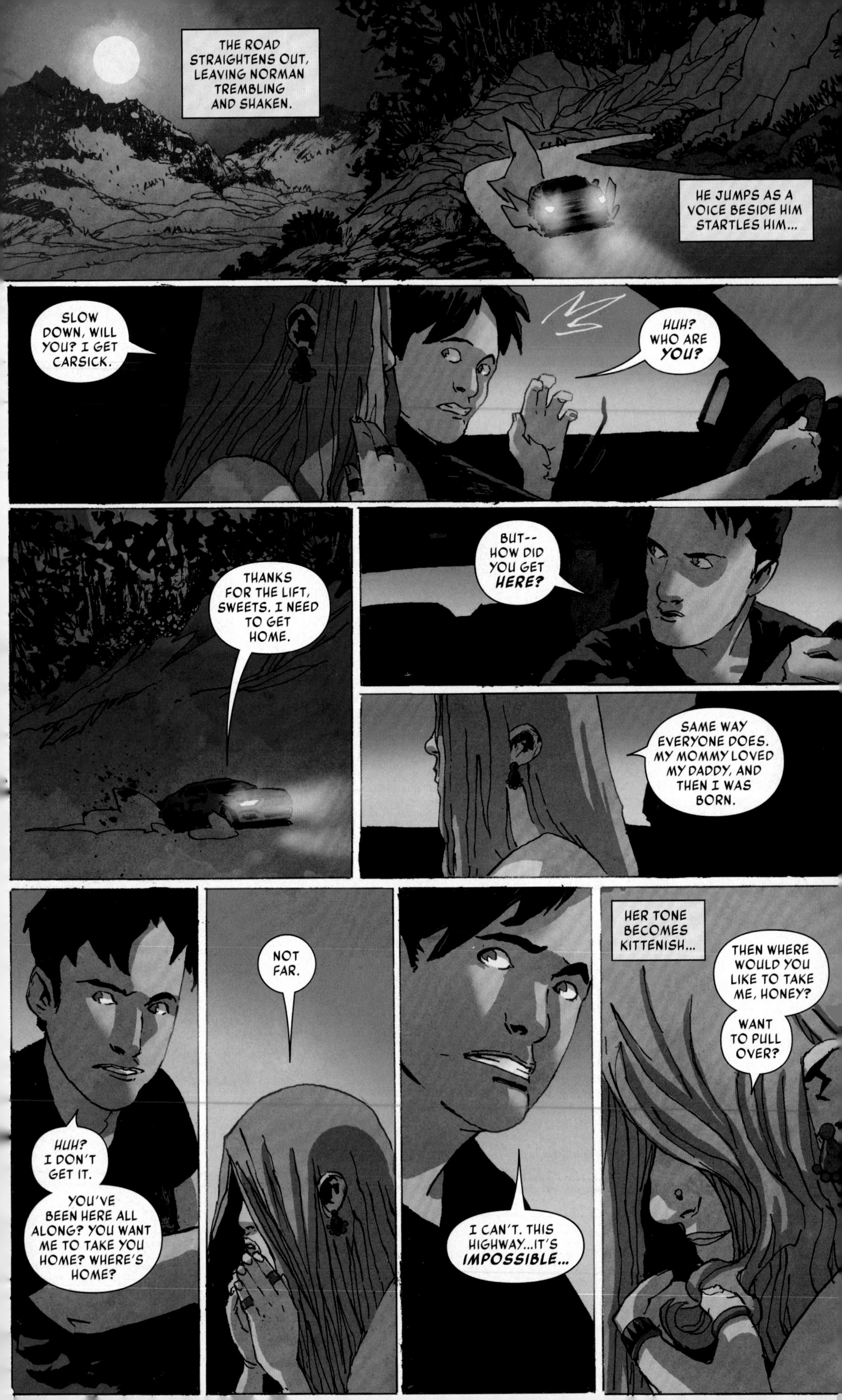
THE ROAD STRAIGHTENS OUT, LEAVING NORMAN TREMBLING AND SHAKEN.
HE JUMPS AS A VOICE BESIDE HIM STARTLES HIM...
SLOW DOWN, WILL YOU? I GET CARSICK.
HUH? WHO ARE YOU?
THANKS FOR THE LIFT, SWEETS. I NEED TO GET HOME.
BUT-- HOW DID YOU GET HERE?
SAME WAY EVERYONE DOES. MY MOMMY LOVED MY DADDY, AND THEN I WAS BORN.
HUH? I DON'T GET IT.
YOU'VE BEEN HERE ALL ALONG? YOU WANT ME TO TAKE YOU HOME? WHERE'S HOME?
NOT FAR.
I CAN'T. THIS HIGHWAY...IT'S IMPOSSIBLE...
HER TONE BECOMES KITTENISH...
THEN WHERE WOULD YOU LIKE TO TAKE ME, HONEY?
WANT TO PULL OVER?

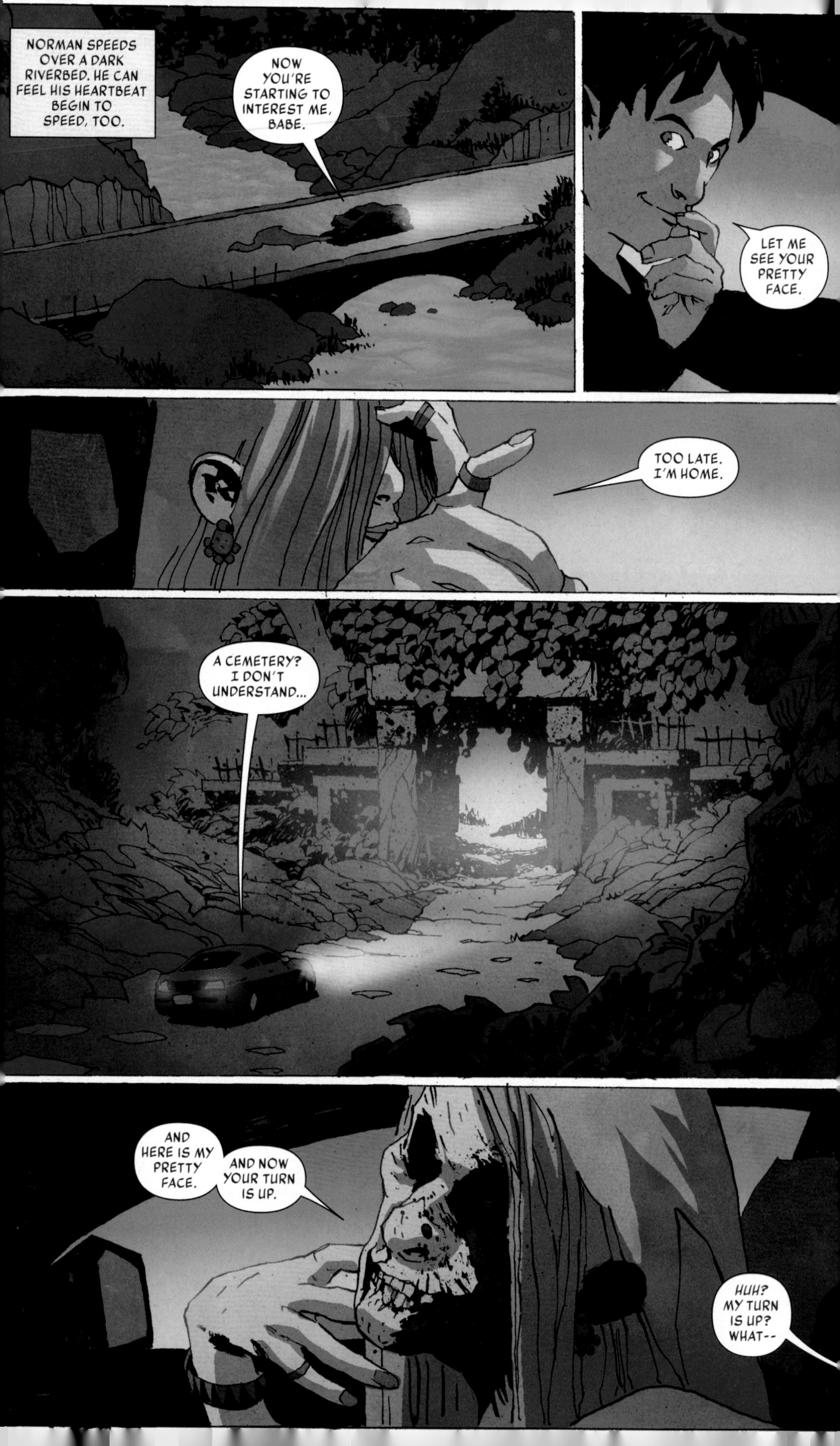
NORMAN SPEEDS OVER A DARK RIVERBED. HE CAN FEEL HIS HEARTBEAT BEGIN TO SPEED, TOO.
NOW YOU'RE STARTING TO INTEREST ME, BABE.
LET ME SEE YOUR PRETTY FACE.
TOO LATE. I'M HOME.
A CEMETERY? I DON'T UNDERSTAND...
AND HERE IS MY PRETTY FACE.
AND NOW YOUR TURN IS UP.
HUH? MY TURN IS UP? WHAT--

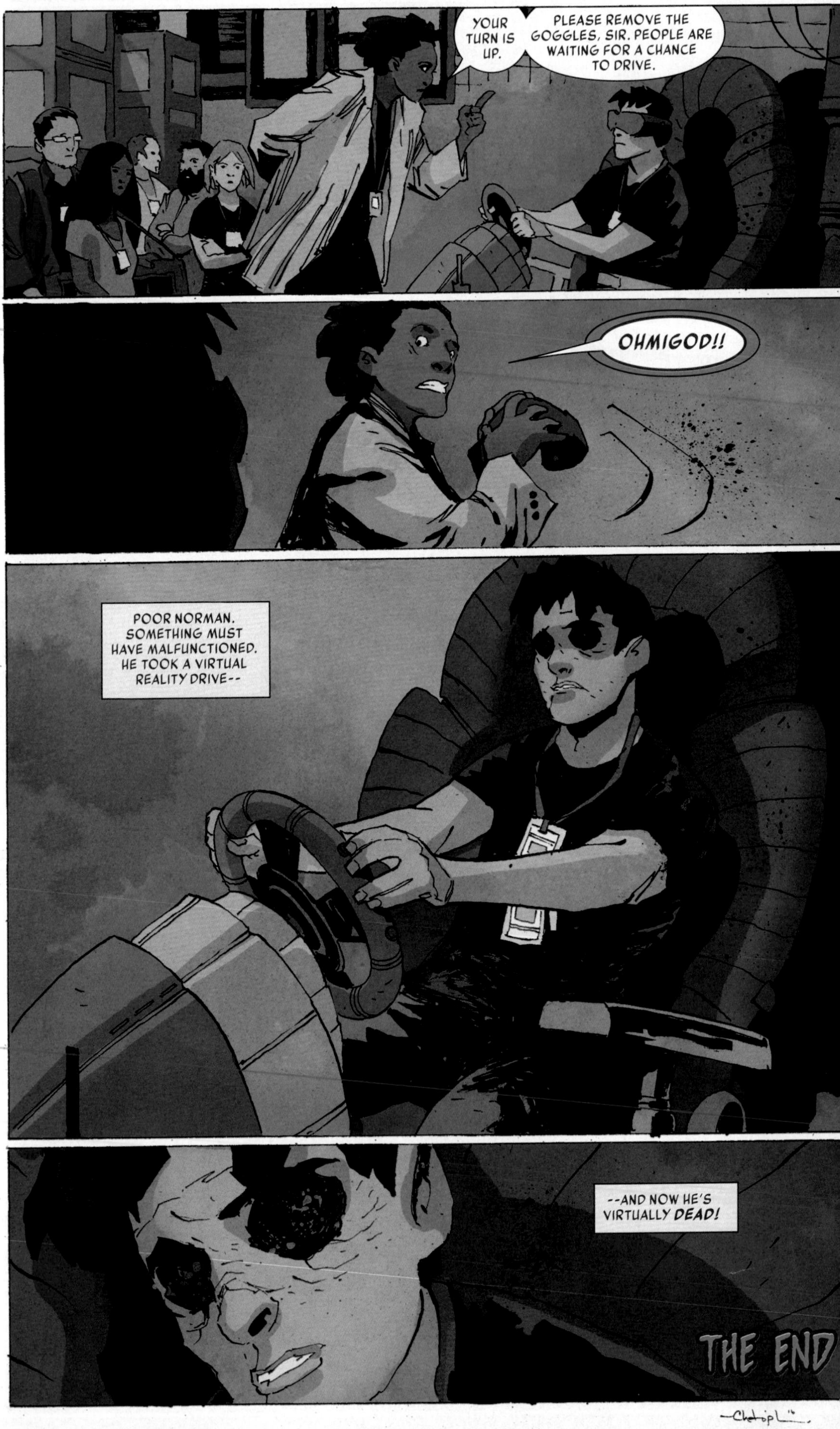

YOUR TURN IS UP.
PLEASE REMOVE THE GOGGLES, SIR. PEOPLE ARE WAITING FOR A CHANCE TO DRIVE.
OHMIGOD!!
POOR NORMAN. SOMETHING MUST HAVE MALFUNCTIONED. HE TOOK A VIRTUAL REALITY DRIVE--
--AND NOW HE'S VIRTUALLY *DEAD!*
THE END

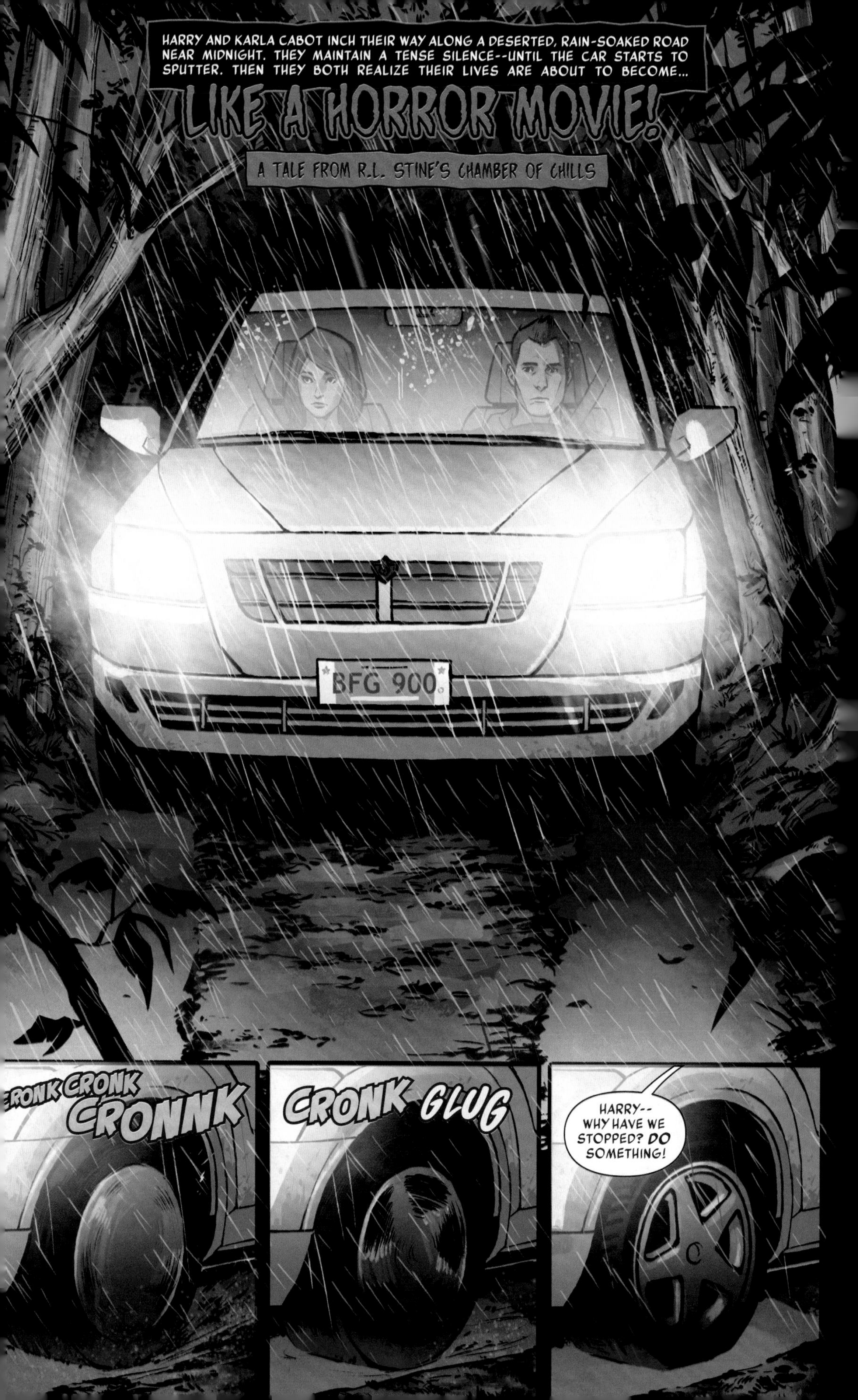

HARRY AND KARLA CABOT INCH THEIR WAY ALONG A DESERTED, RAIN-SOAKED ROAD NEAR MIDNIGHT. THEY MAINTAIN A TENSE SILENCE--UNTIL THE CAR STARTS TO SPUTTER. THEN THEY BOTH REALIZE THEIR LIVES ARE ABOUT TO BECOME...
LIKE A HORROR MOVIE!
A TALE FROM R.L. STINE'S CHAMBER OF CHILLS
BFG 900
CRONK CRONK CRONNK
CRONK GLUG
HARRY-- WHY HAVE WE STOPPED? DO SOMETHING!

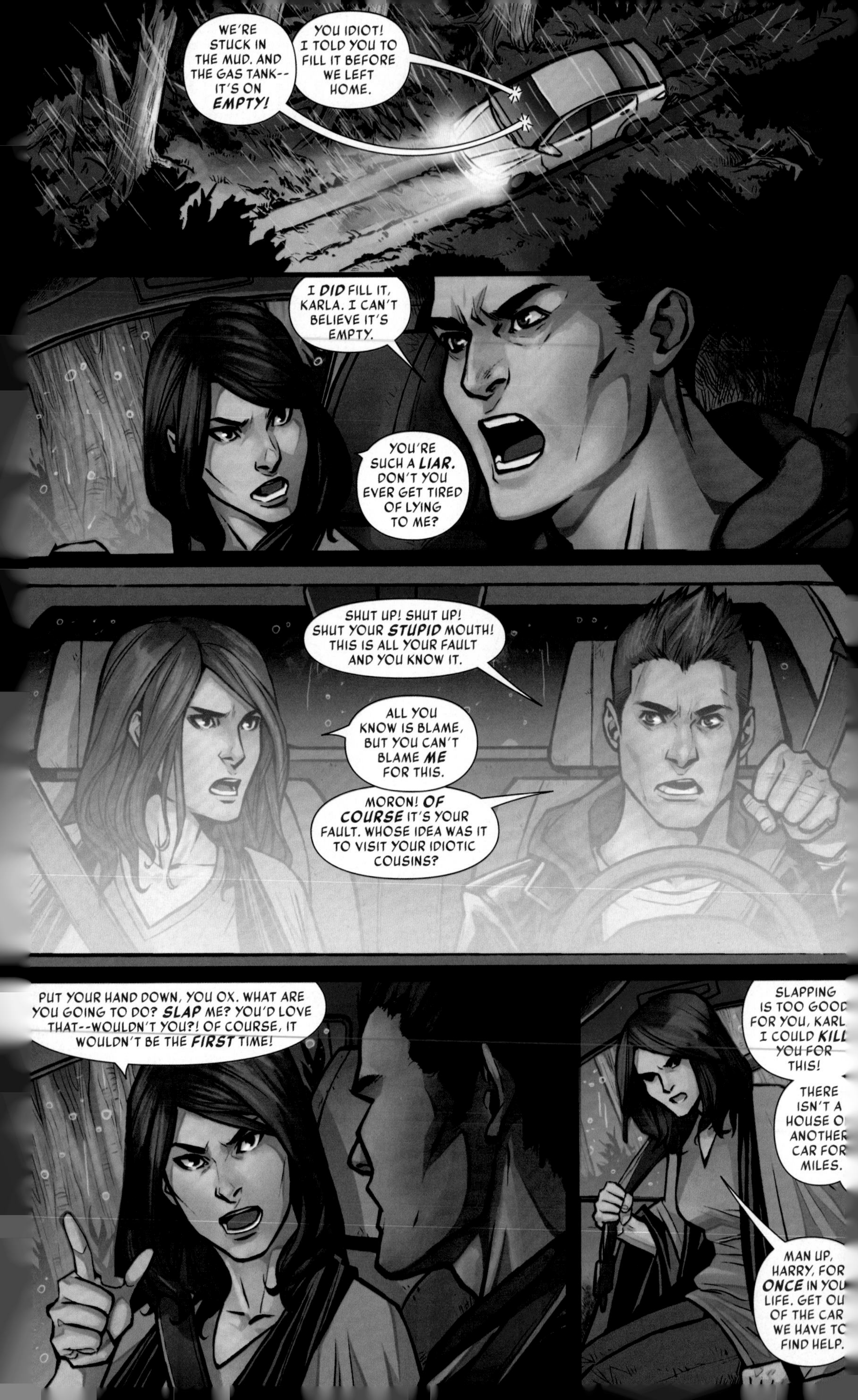

WE'RE STUCK IN THE MUD. AND THE GAS TANK-- IT'S ON EMPTY!
YOU IDIOT! I TOLD YOU TO FILL IT BEFORE WE LEFT HOME.
I DID FILL IT, KARLA. I CAN'T BELIEVE IT'S EMPTY.
YOU'RE SUCH A LIAR. DON'T YOU EVER GET TIRED OF LYING TO ME?
SHUT UP! SHUT UP! SHUT YOUR STUPID MOUTH! THIS IS ALL YOUR FAULT AND YOU KNOW IT.
ALL YOU KNOW IS BLAME, BUT YOU CAN'T BLAME ME FOR THIS.
MORON! OF COURSE IT'S YOUR FAULT. WHOSE IDEA WAS IT TO VISIT YOUR IDIOTIC COUSINS?
PUT YOUR HAND DOWN, YOU OX. WHAT ARE YOU GOING TO DO? SLAP ME? YOU'D LOVE THAT--WOULDN'T YOU?! OF COURSE, IT WOULDN'T BE THE FIRST TIME!
SLAPPING IS TOO GOOD FOR YOU, KARL I COULD KILL YOU FOR THIS!
THERE ISN'T A HOUSE O ANOTHER CAR FOR MILES.
MAN UP, HARRY, FOR ONCE IN YOU LIFE. GET OU OF THE CAR WE HAVE TO FIND HELP.

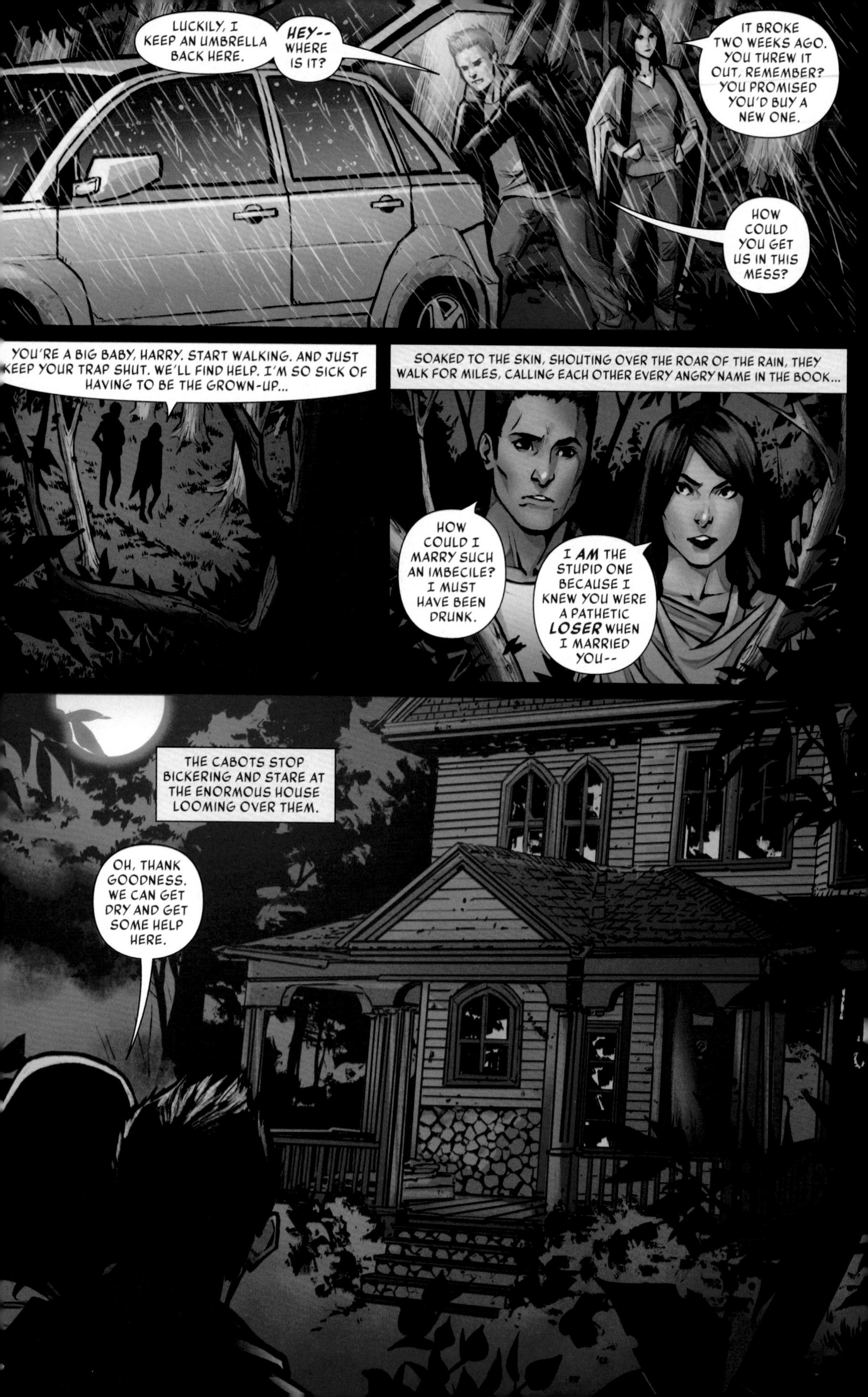
LUCKILY, I KEEP AN UMBRELLA BACK HERE.
HEY-- WHERE IS IT?
IT BROKE TWO WEEKS AGO. YOU THREW IT OUT, REMEMBER? YOU PROMISED YOU'D BUY A NEW ONE.
HOW COULD YOU GET US IN THIS MESS?
YOU'RE A BIG BABY, HARRY. START WALKING. AND JUST KEEP YOUR TRAP SHUT. WE'LL FIND HELP. I'M SO SICK OF HAVING TO BE THE GROWN-UP...
SOAKED TO THE SKIN, SHOUTING OVER THE ROAR OF THE RAIN, THEY WALK FOR MILES, CALLING EACH OTHER EVERY ANGRY NAME IN THE BOOK...
HOW COULD I MARRY SUCH AN IMBECILE? I MUST HAVE BEEN DRUNK.
I AM THE STUPID ONE BECAUSE I KNEW YOU WERE A PATHETIC LOSER WHEN I MARRIED YOU--
THE CABOTS STOP BICKERING AND STARE AT THE ENORMOUS HOUSE LOOMING OVER THEM.
OH, THANK GOODNESS. WE CAN GET DRY AND GET SOME HELP HERE.

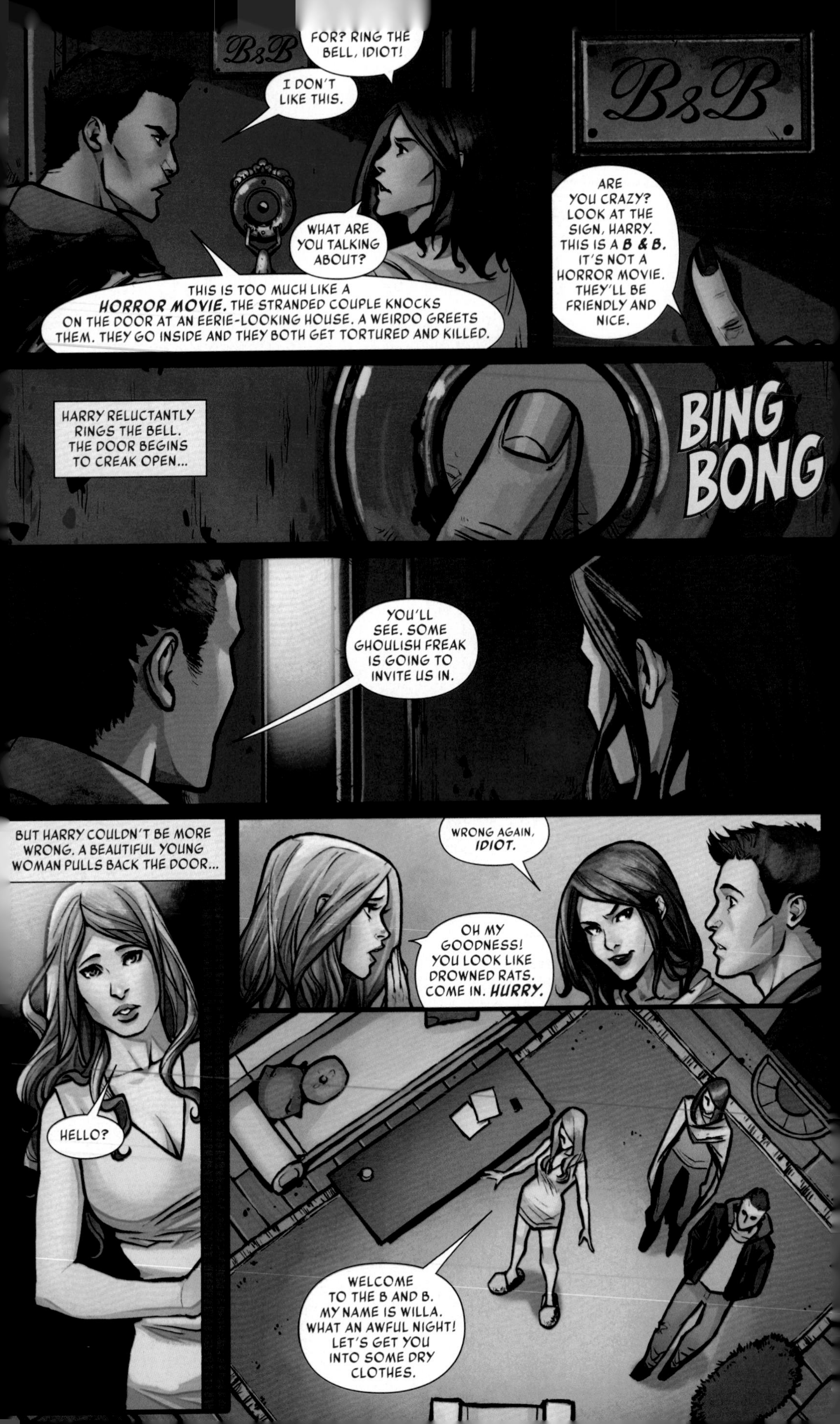
B&B
FOR? RING THE BELL, IDIOT!
I DON'T LIKE THIS.
WHAT ARE YOU TALKING ABOUT?
THIS IS TOO MUCH LIKE A HORROR MOVIE. THE STRANDED COUPLE KNOCKS ON THE DOOR AT AN EERIE-LOOKING HOUSE. A WEIRDO GREETS THEM. THEY GO INSIDE AND THEY BOTH GET TORTURED AND KILLED.
B&B
ARE YOU CRAZY? LOOK AT THE SIGN, HARRY. THIS IS A B & B. IT'S NOT A HORROR MOVIE. THEY'LL BE FRIENDLY AND NICE.
HARRY RELUCTANTLY RINGS THE BELL. THE DOOR BEGINS TO CREAK OPEN...
BING BONG
YOU'LL SEE. SOME GHOULISH FREAK IS GOING TO INVITE US IN.
BUT HARRY COULDN'T BE MORE WRONG. A BEAUTIFUL YOUNG WOMAN PULLS BACK THE DOOR...
HELLO?
WRONG AGAIN, IDIOT.
OH MY GOODNESS! YOU LOOK LIKE DROWNED RATS. COME IN. HURRY.
WELCOME TO THE B AND B. MY NAME IS WILLA. WHAT AN AWFUL NIGHT! LET'S GET YOU INTO SOME DRY CLOTHES.

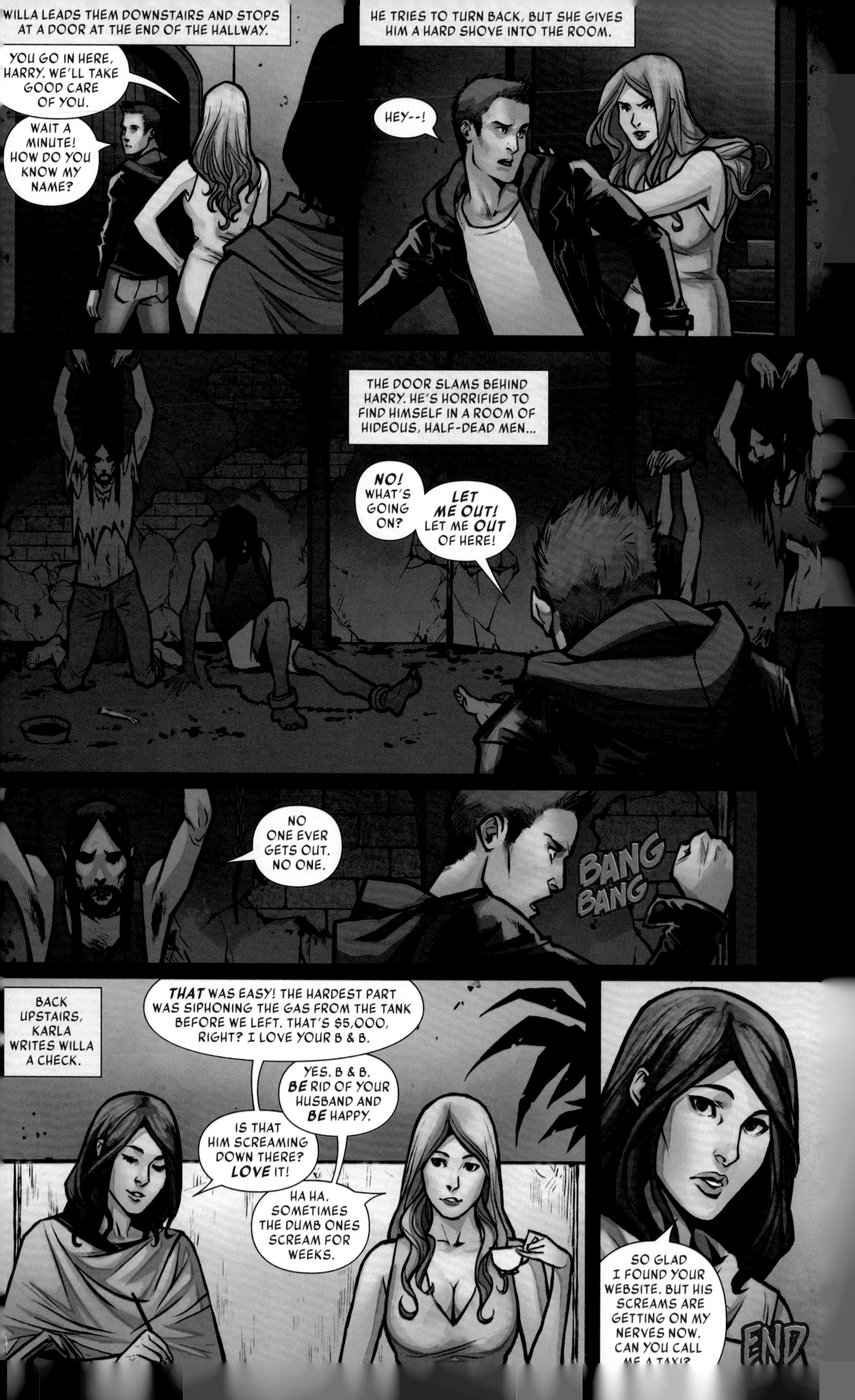

WILLA LEADS THEM DOWNSTAIRS AND STOPS AT A DOOR AT THE END OF THE HALLWAY.
YOU GO IN HERE, HARRY. WE'LL TAKE GOOD CARE OF YOU.
WAIT A MINUTE! HOW DO YOU KNOW MY NAME?
HE TRIES TO TURN BACK, BUT SHE GIVES HIM A HARD SHOVE INTO THE ROOM.
HEY--!
THE DOOR SLAMS BEHIND HARRY. HE'S HORRIFIED TO FIND HIMSELF IN A ROOM OF HIDEOUS, HALF-DEAD MEN...
NO! WHAT'S GOING ON?
LET ME OUT! LET ME OUT OF HERE!
NO ONE EVER GETS OUT. NO ONE.
BANG BANG
BACK UPSTAIRS, KARLA WRITES WILLA A CHECK.
THAT WAS EASY! THE HARDEST PART WAS SIPHONING THE GAS FROM THE TANK BEFORE WE LEFT. THAT'S $5,000, RIGHT? I LOVE YOUR B & B.
YES. B & B. BE RID OF YOUR HUSBAND AND BE HAPPY.
IS THAT HIM SCREAMING DOWN THERE? LOVE IT!
HA HA. SOMETIMES THE DUMB ONES SCREAM FOR WEEKS.
SO GLAD I FOUND YOUR WEBSITE. BUT HIS SCREAMS ARE GETTING ON MY NERVES NOW. CAN YOU CALL
END

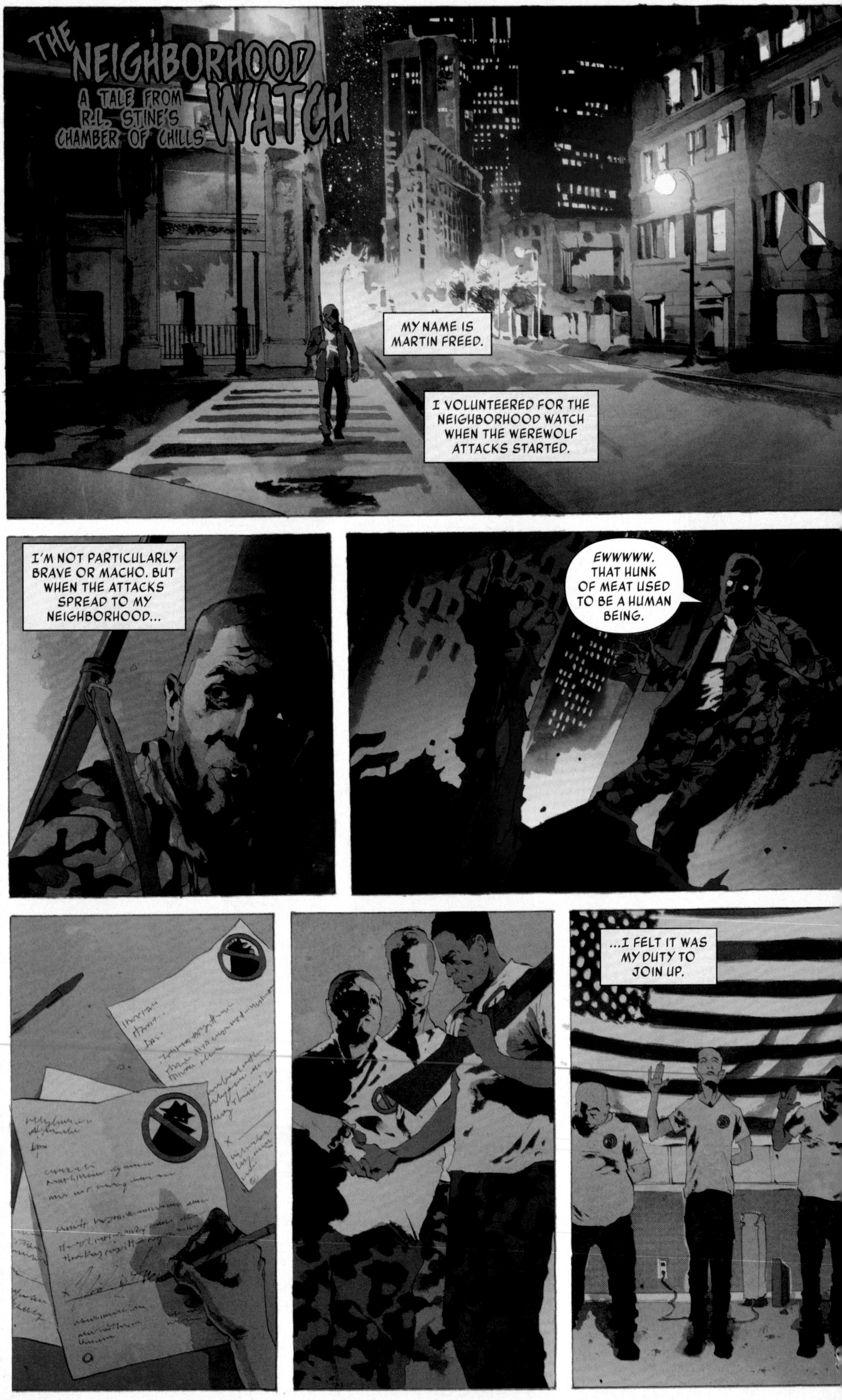
THE NEIGHBORHOOD WATCH
A TALE FROM R.L. STINE'S CHAMBER OF CHILLS
MY NAME IS MARTIN FREED.
I VOLUNTEERED FOR THE NEIGHBORHOOD WATCH WHEN THE WEREWOLF ATTACKS STARTED.
I'M NOT PARTICULARLY BRAVE OR MACHO. BUT WHEN THE ATTACKS SPREAD TO MY NEIGHBORHOOD...
EWWWWW. THAT HUNK OF MEAT USED TO BE A HUMAN BEING.
...I FELT IT WAS MY DUTY TO JOIN UP.

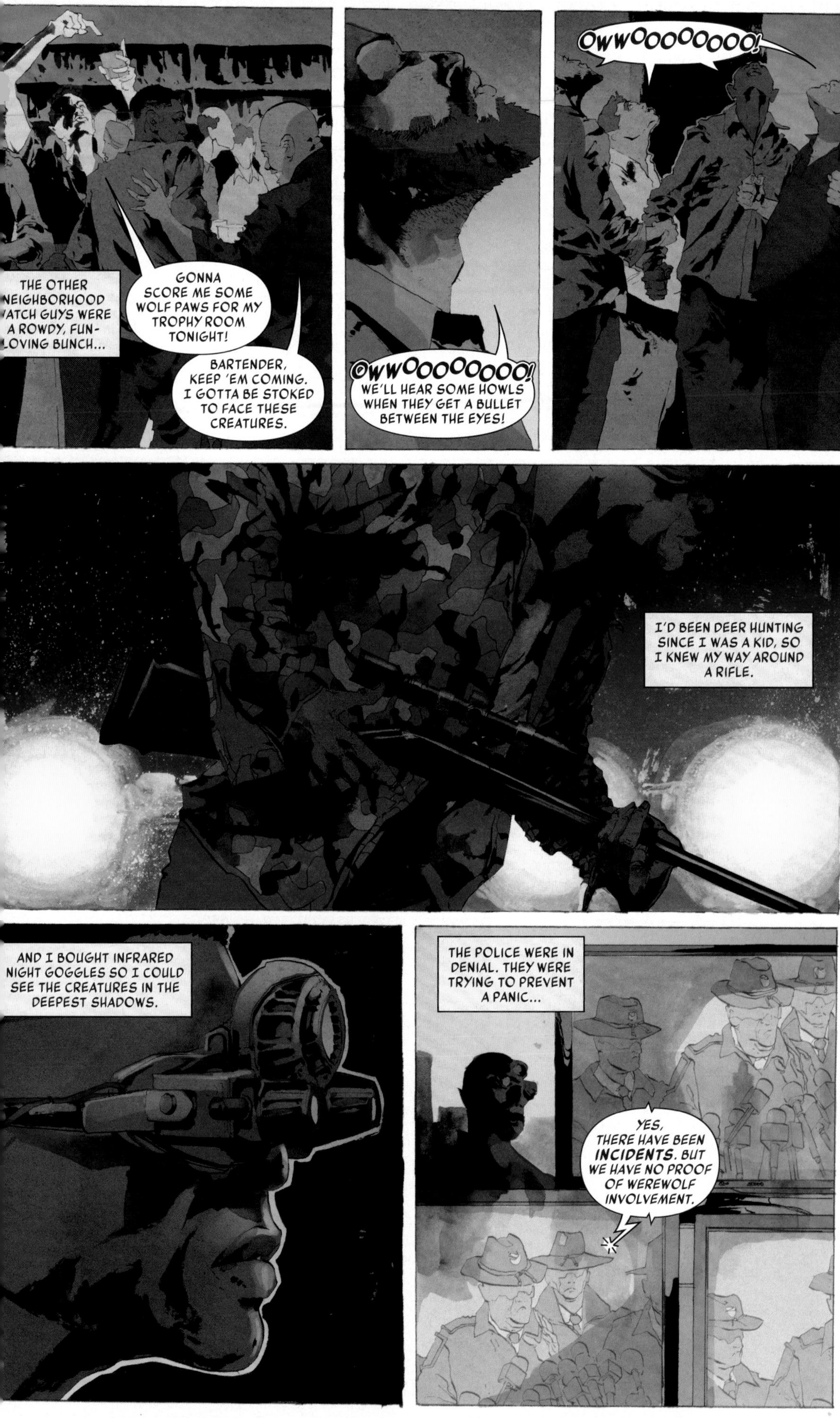
THE OTHER NEIGHBORHOOD WATCH GUYS WERE A ROWDY, FUN-LOVING BUNCH...
GONNA SCORE ME SOME WOLF PAWS FOR MY TROPHY ROOM TONIGHT!
BARTENDER, KEEP 'EM COMING. I GOTTA BE STOKED TO FACE THESE CREATURES.
OWWOOOOOOOO! WE'LL HEAR SOME HOWLS WHEN THEY GET A BULLET BETWEEN THE EYES!
OWWOOOOOOOO!
I'D BEEN DEER HUNTING SINCE I WAS A KID, SO I KNEW MY WAY AROUND A RIFLE.
AND I BOUGHT INFRARED NIGHT GOGGLES SO I COULD SEE THE CREATURES IN THE DEEPEST SHADOWS.
THE POLICE WERE IN DENIAL. THEY WERE TRYING TO PREVENT A PANIC...
YES, THERE HAVE BEEN **INCIDENTS**. BUT WE HAVE NO PROOF OF WEREWOLF INVOLVEMENT.

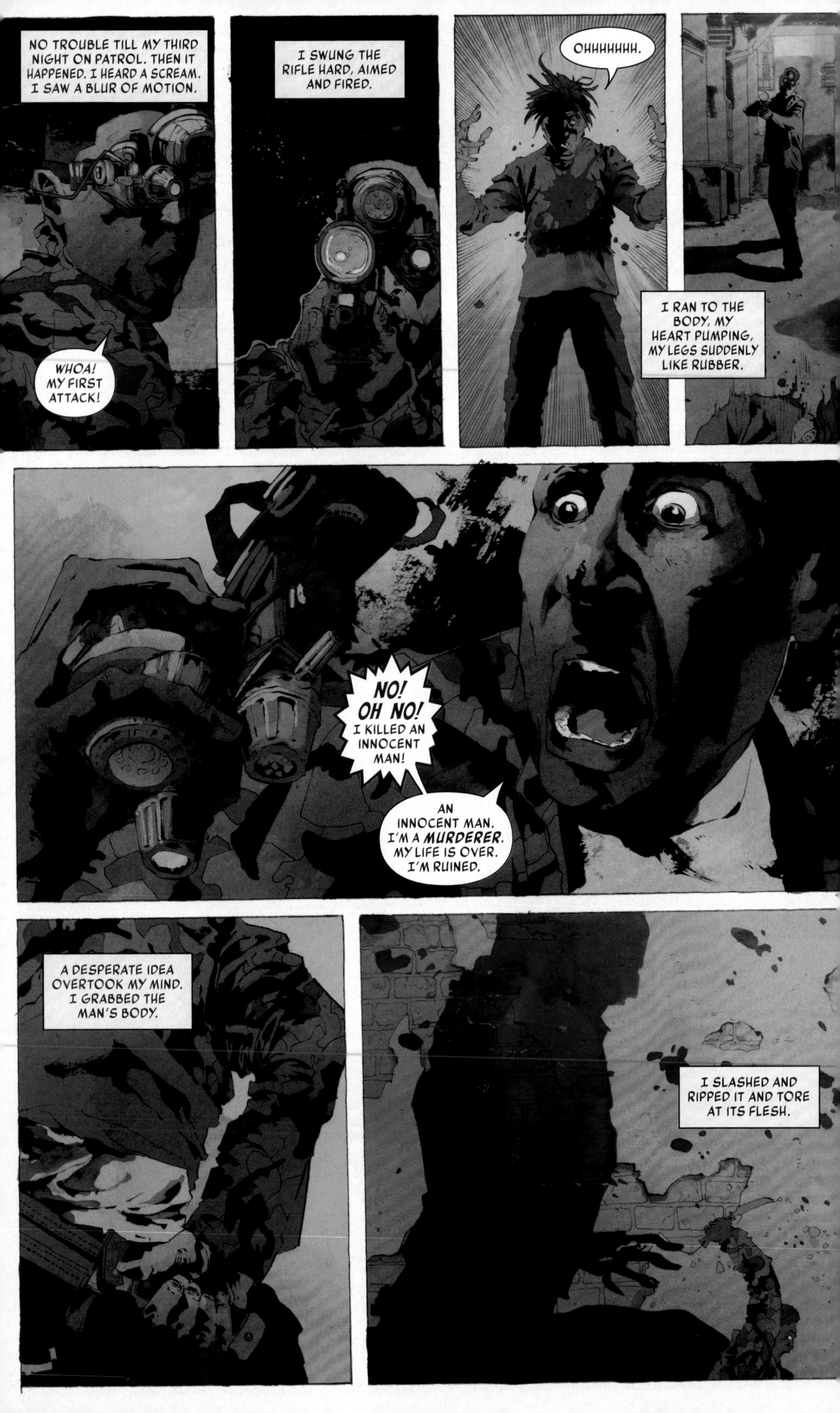

NO TROUBLE TILL MY THIRD NIGHT ON PATROL. THEN IT HAPPENED. I HEARD A SCREAM. I SAW A BLUR OF MOTION.
WHOA! MY FIRST ATTACK!
I SWUNG THE RIFLE HARD, AIMED AND FIRED.
OHHHHHHH.
I RAN TO THE BODY, MY HEART PUMPING, MY LEGS SUDDENLY LIKE RUBBER.
NO! OH NO! I KILLED AN INNOCENT MAN!
AN INNOCENT MAN. I'M A MURDERER. MY LIFE IS OVER. I'M RUINED.
A DESPERATE IDEA OVERTOOK MY MIND. I GRABBED THE MAN'S BODY.
I SLASHED AND RIPPED IT AND TORE AT ITS FLESH.

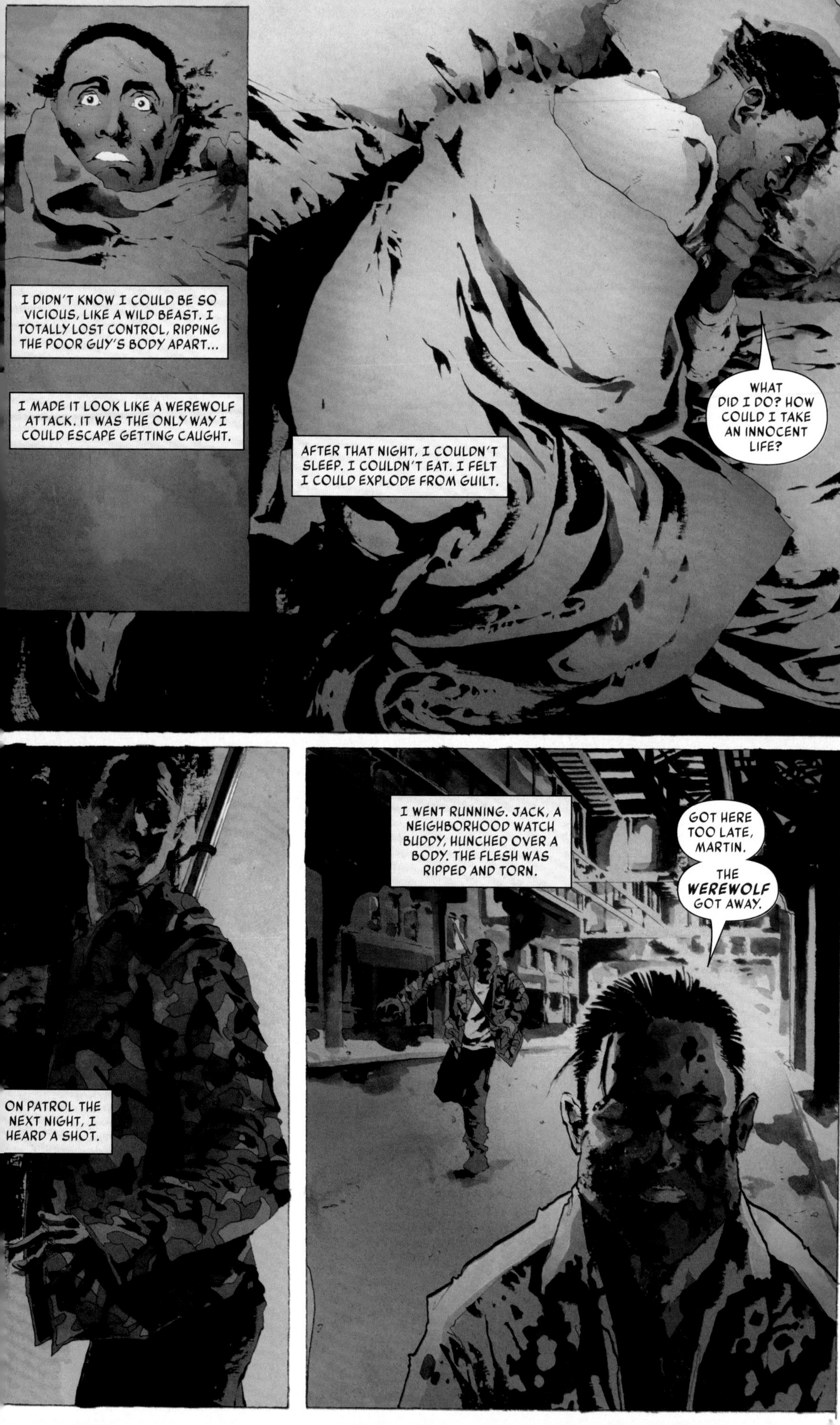
I DIDN'T KNOW I COULD BE SO VICIOUS, LIKE A WILD BEAST. I TOTALLY LOST CONTROL, RIPPING THE POOR GUY'S BODY APART...
I MADE IT LOOK LIKE A WEREWOLF ATTACK. IT WAS THE ONLY WAY I COULD ESCAPE GETTING CAUGHT.
AFTER THAT NIGHT, I COULDN'T SLEEP. I COULDN'T EAT. I FELT I COULD EXPLODE FROM GUILT.
WHAT DID I DO? HOW COULD I TAKE AN INNOCENT LIFE?
ON PATROL THE NEXT NIGHT, I HEARD A SHOT.
I WENT RUNNING. JACK, A NEIGHBORHOOD WATCH BUDDY, HUNCHED OVER A BODY. THE FLESH WAS RIPPED AND TORN.
GOT HERE TOO LATE, MARTIN.
THE ***WEREWOLF*** GOT AWAY.

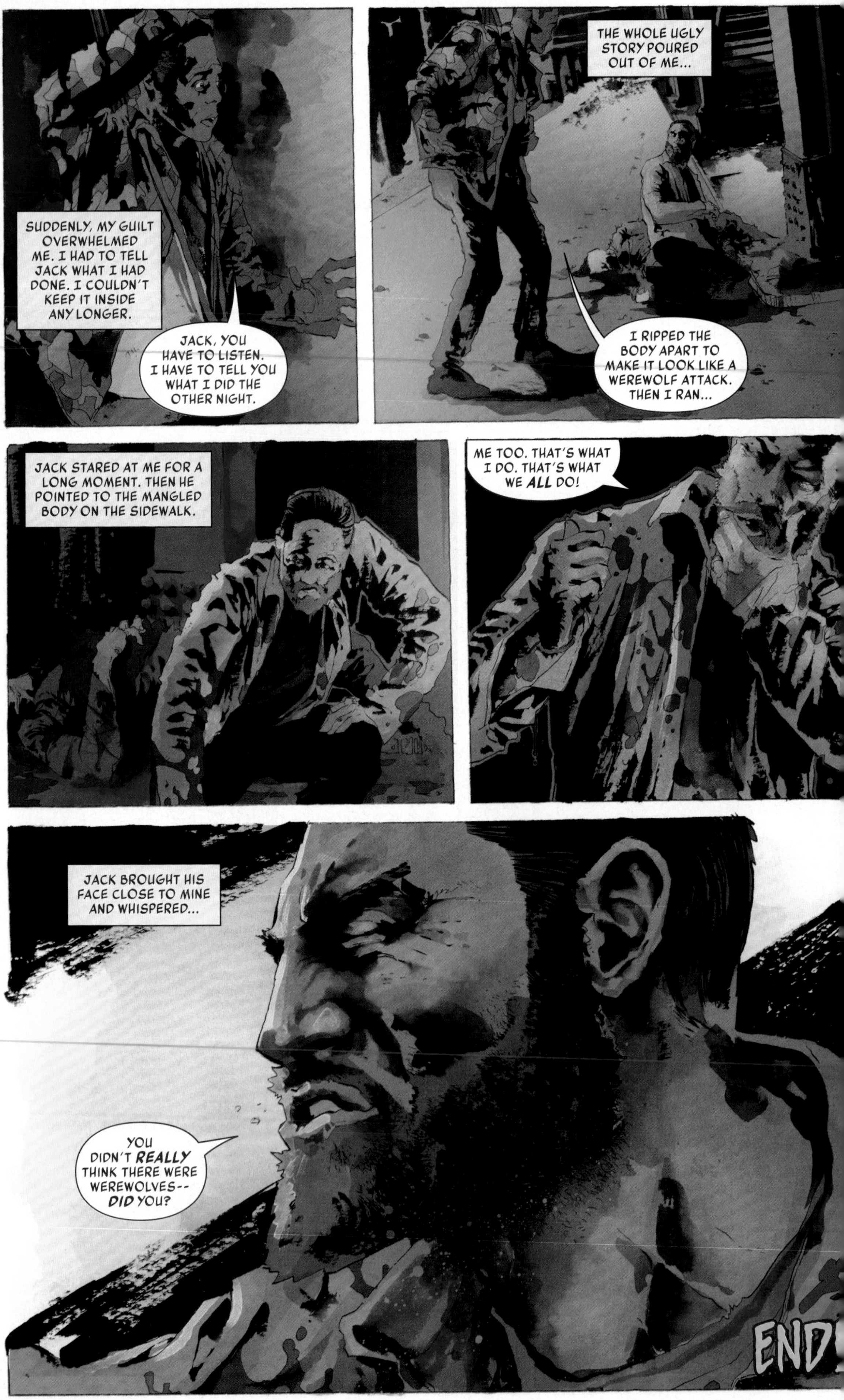
SUDDENLY, MY GUILT OVERWHELMED ME. I HAD TO TELL JACK WHAT I HAD DONE. I COULDN'T KEEP IT INSIDE ANY LONGER.
JACK, YOU HAVE TO LISTEN. I HAVE TO TELL YOU WHAT I DID THE OTHER NIGHT.
THE WHOLE UGLY STORY POURED OUT OF ME...
I RIPPED THE BODY APART TO MAKE IT LOOK LIKE A WEREWOLF ATTACK. THEN I RAN...
JACK STARED AT ME FOR A LONG MOMENT. THEN HE POINTED TO THE MANGLED BODY ON THE SIDEWALK.
ME TOO. THAT'S WHAT I DO. THAT'S WHAT WE ALL DO!
JACK BROUGHT HIS FACE CLOSE TO MINE AND WHISPERED...
YOU DIDN'T REALLY THINK THERE WERE WEREWOLVES-- DID YOU?
END

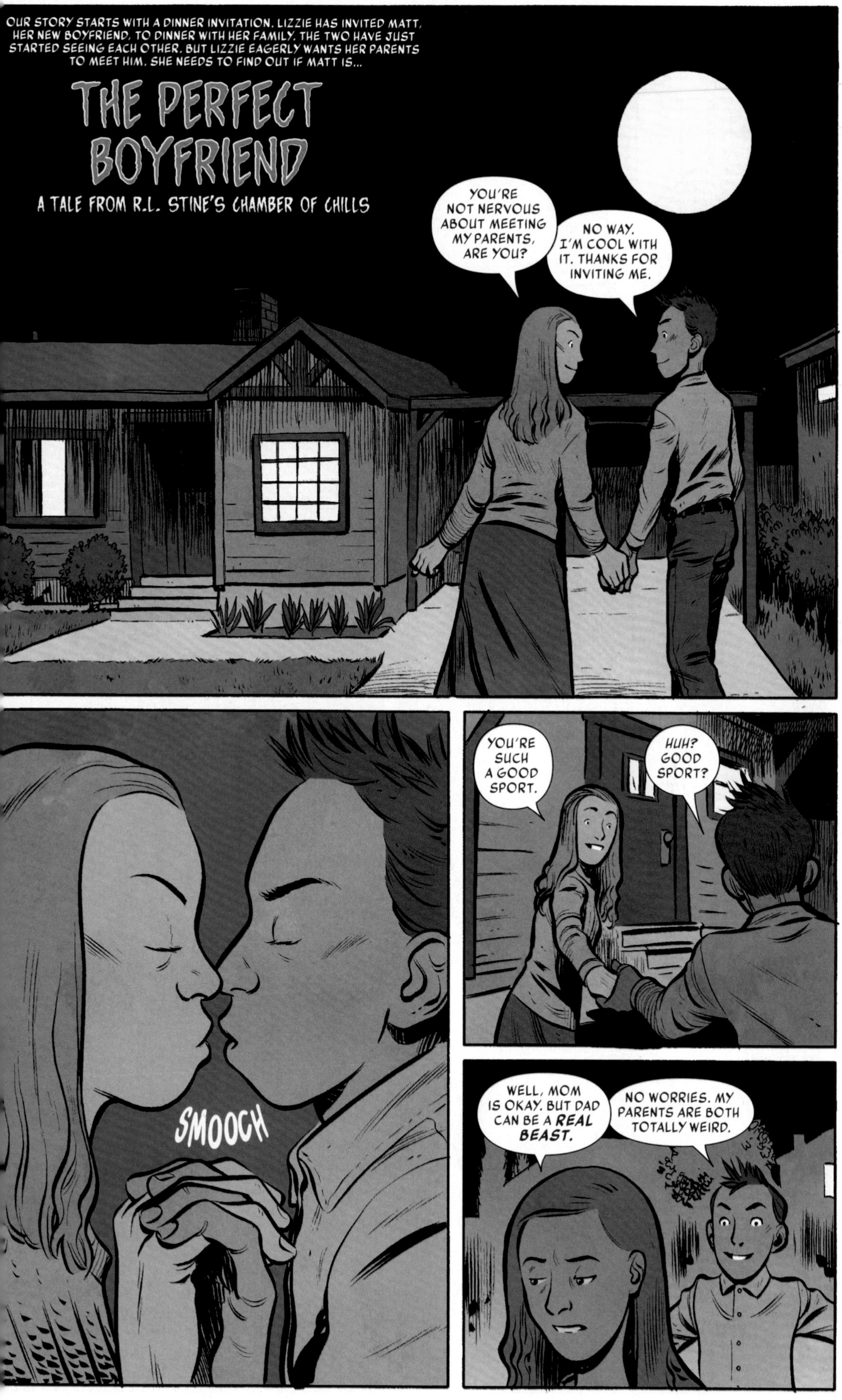
OUR STORY STARTS WITH A DINNER INVITATION. LIZZIE HAS INVITED MATT, HER NEW BOYFRIEND, TO DINNER WITH HER FAMILY. THE TWO HAVE JUST STARTED SEEING EACH OTHER, BUT LIZZIE EAGERLY WANTS HER PARENTS TO MEET HIM. SHE NEEDS TO FIND OUT IF MATT IS...
THE PERFECT BOYFRIEND
A TALE FROM R.L. STINE'S CHAMBER OF CHILLS
YOU'RE NOT NERVOUS ABOUT MEETING MY PARENTS, ARE YOU?
NO WAY. I'M COOL WITH IT. THANKS FOR INVITING ME.
SMOOCH
YOU'RE SUCH A GOOD SPORT.
HUH? GOOD SPORT?
WELL, MOM IS OKAY. BUT DAD CAN BE A REAL BEAST.
NO WORRIES. MY PARENTS ARE BOTH TOTALLY WEIRD.

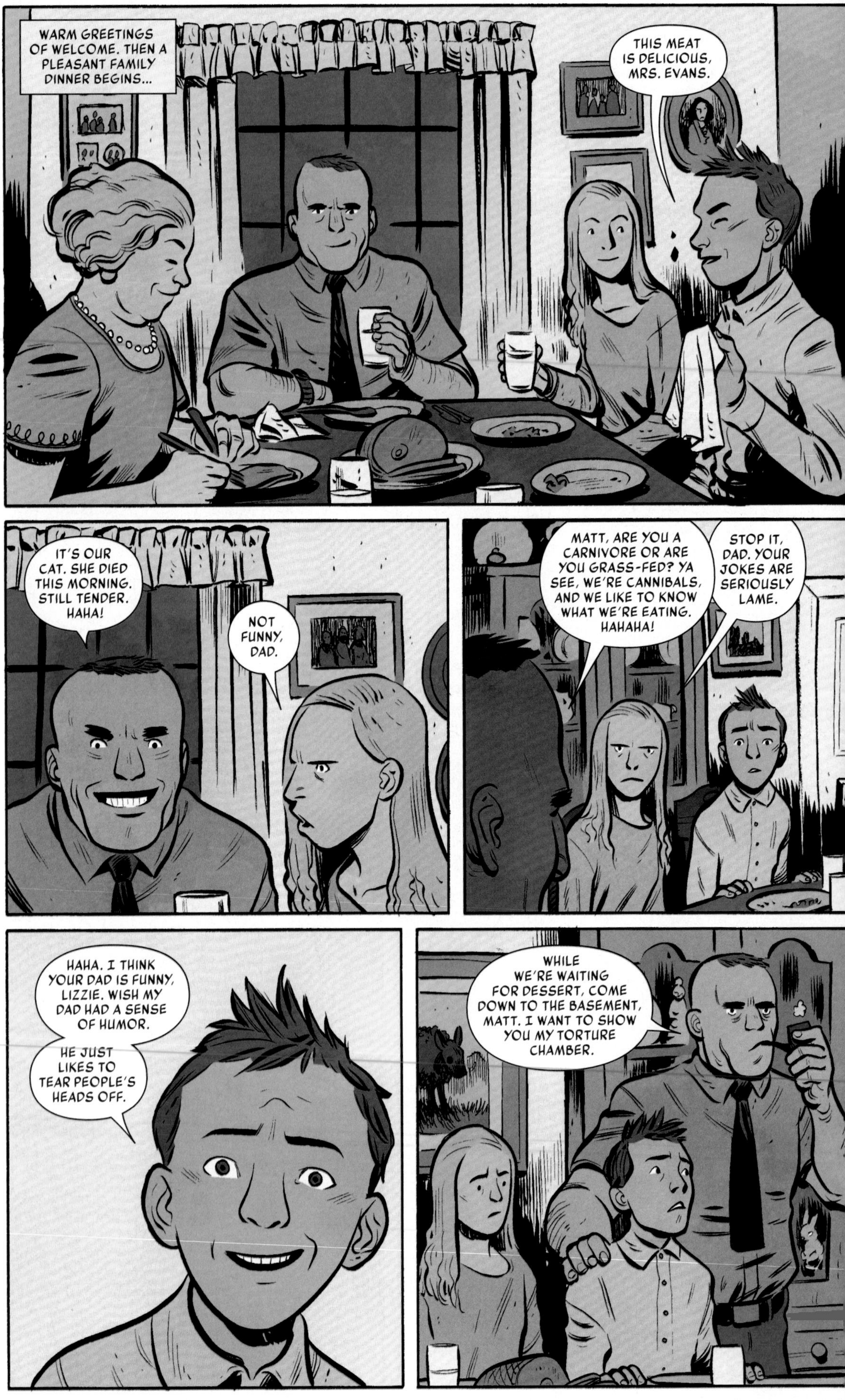
WARM GREETINGS OF WELCOME. THEN A PLEASANT FAMILY DINNER BEGINS...
THIS MEAT IS DELICIOUS, MRS. EVANS.
IT'S OUR CAT. SHE DIED THIS MORNING. STILL TENDER. HAHA!
NOT FUNNY, DAD.
MATT, ARE YOU A CARNIVORE OR ARE YOU GRASS-FED? YA SEE, WE'RE CANNIBALS, AND WE LIKE TO KNOW WHAT WE'RE EATING. HAHAHA!
STOP IT, DAD. YOUR JOKES ARE SERIOUSLY LAME.
HAHA. I THINK YOUR DAD IS FUNNY, LIZZIE. WISH MY DAD HAD A SENSE OF HUMOR.
HE JUST LIKES TO TEAR PEOPLE'S HEADS OFF.
WHILE WE'RE WAITING FOR DESSERT, COME DOWN TO THE BASEMENT, MATT. I WANT TO SHOW YOU MY TORTURE CHAMBER.

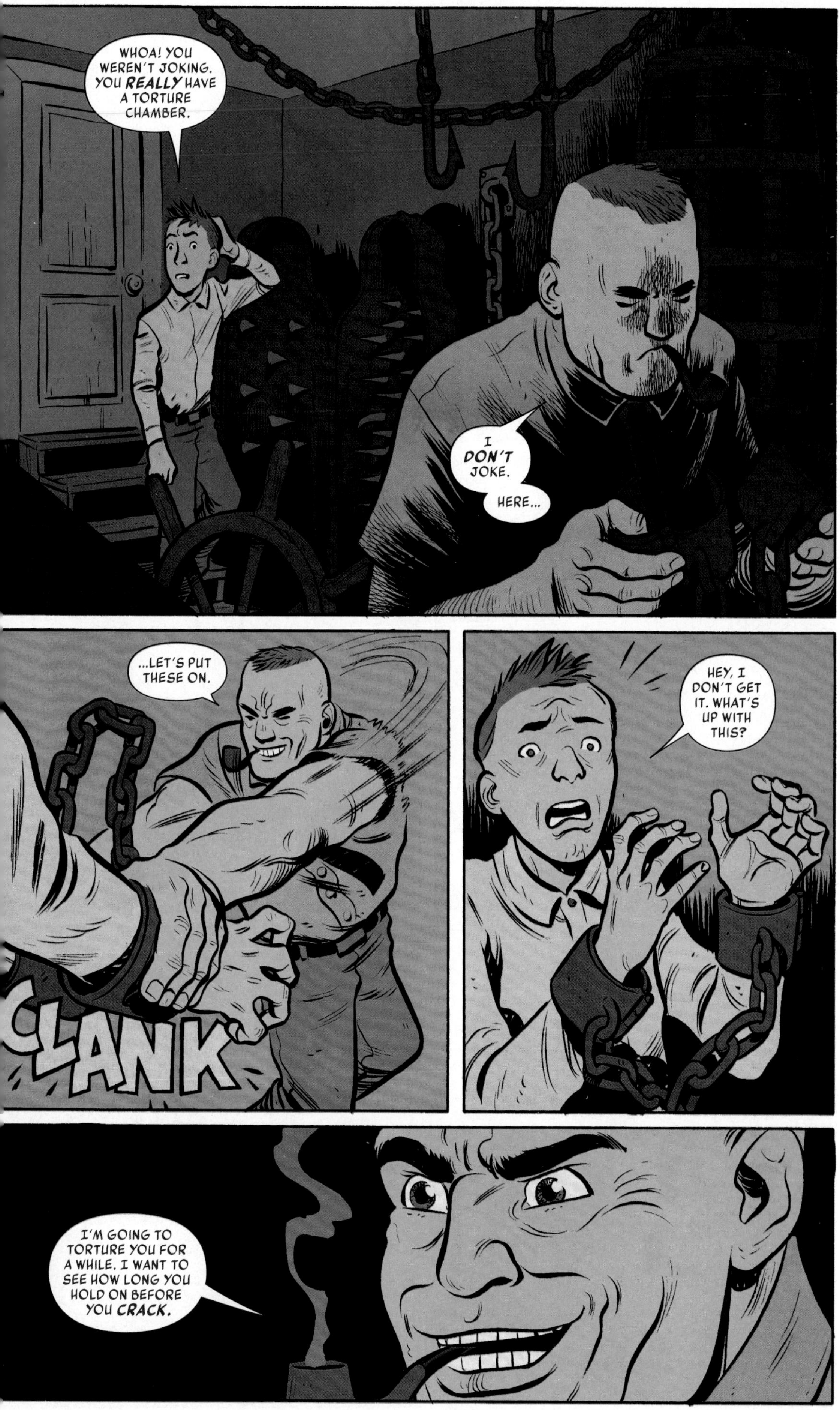
WHOA! YOU WEREN'T JOKING. YOU REALLY HAVE A TORTURE CHAMBER.
I DON'T JOKE.
HERE...
...LET'S PUT THESE ON.
CLANK
HEY, I DON'T GET IT. WHAT'S UP WITH THIS?
I'M GOING TO TORTURE YOU FOR A WHILE. I WANT TO SEE HOW LONG YOU HOLD ON BEFORE YOU CRACK.

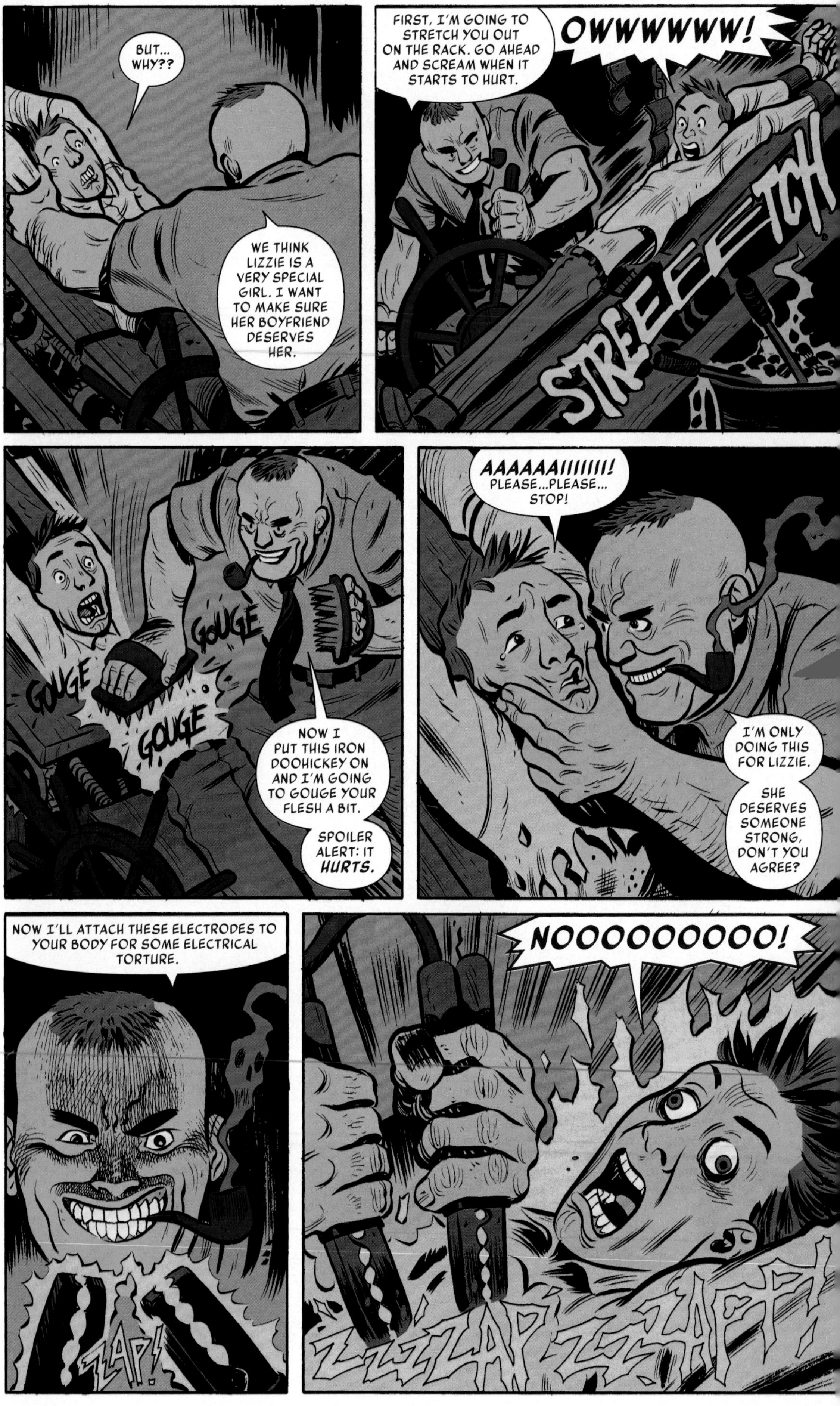
BUT... WHY??
WE THINK LIZZIE IS A VERY SPECIAL GIRL. I WANT TO MAKE SURE HER BOYFRIEND DESERVES HER.
FIRST, I'M GOING TO STRETCH YOU OUT ON THE RACK. GO AHEAD AND SCREAM WHEN IT STARTS TO HURT.
OWWWWWW!
STREEEETCH
GOUGE
GOUGE
GOUGE
NOW I PUT THIS IRON DOOHICKEY ON AND I'M GOING TO GOUGE YOUR FLESH A BIT.
SPOILER ALERT: IT HURTS.
AAAAAAIIIIIII! PLEASE...PLEASE... STOP!
I'M ONLY DOING THIS FOR LIZZIE.
SHE DESERVES SOMEONE STRONG, DON'T YOU AGREE?
NOW I'LL ATTACH THESE ELECTRODES TO YOUR BODY FOR SOME ELECTRICAL TORTURE.
ZAP!
NOOOOOOOOO!
ZZZZAP! ZZZAPP!

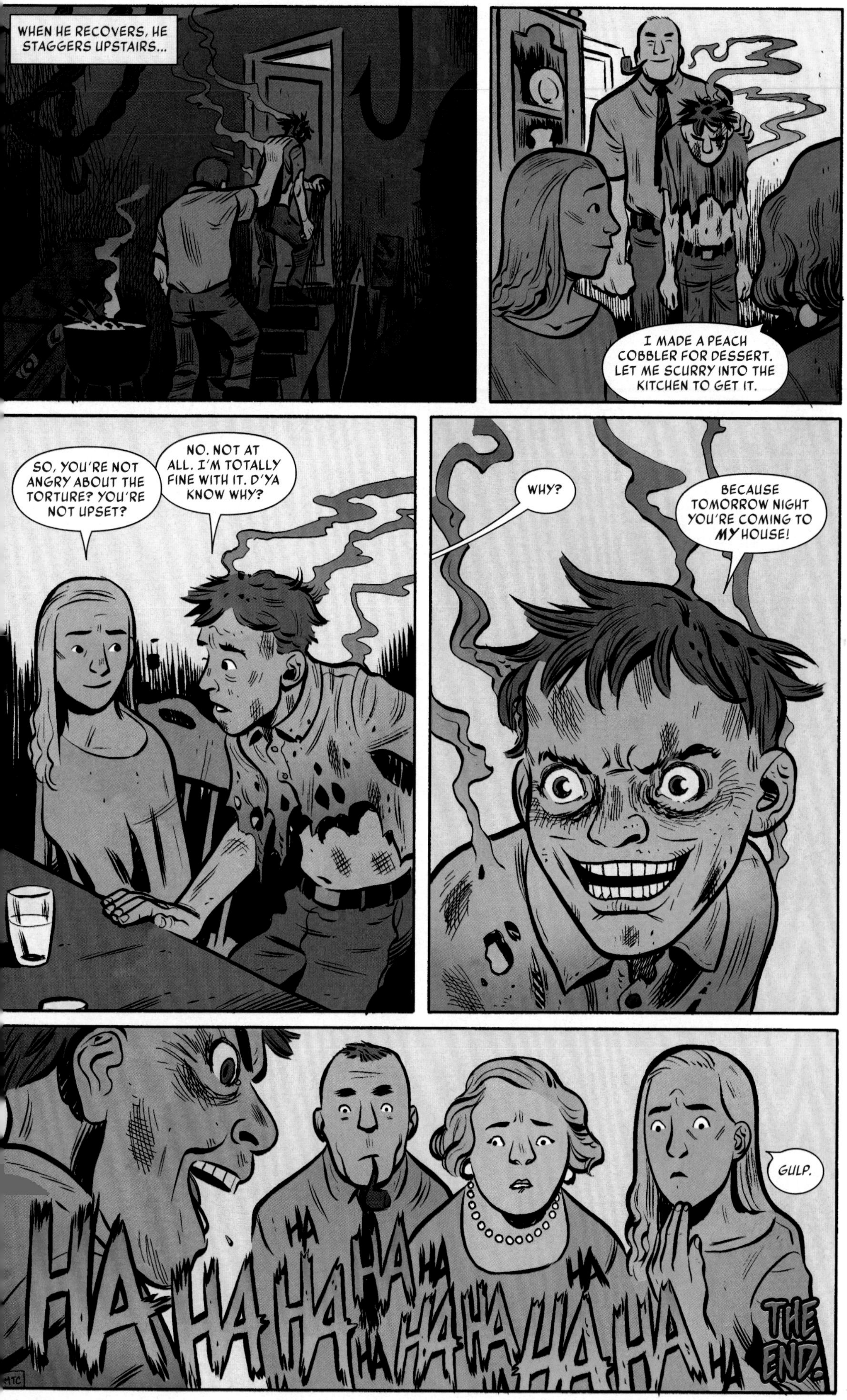
WHEN HE RECOVERS, HE STAGGERS UPSTAIRS...
I MADE A PEACH COBBLER FOR DESSERT. LET ME SCURRY INTO THE KITCHEN TO GET IT.
SO, YOU'RE NOT ANGRY ABOUT THE TORTURE? YOU'RE NOT UPSET?
NO. NOT AT ALL. I'M TOTALLY FINE WITH IT. D'YA KNOW WHY?
WHY?
BECAUSE TOMORROW NIGHT YOU'RE COMING TO MY HOUSE!
GULP.
HA HA HA HA HA HA HA HA HA HA HA HA HA HA HA HA HA HA
THE END.
MTC

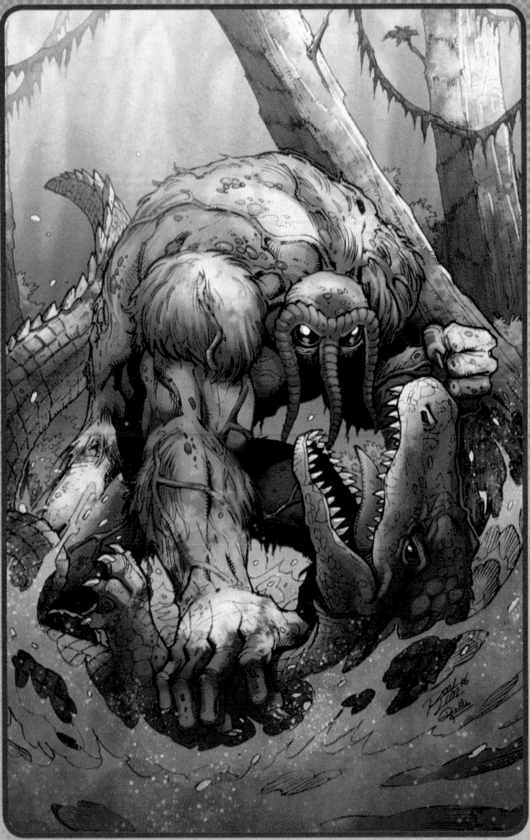

#1 variant by
RON LIM & RACHELLE ROSENBERG

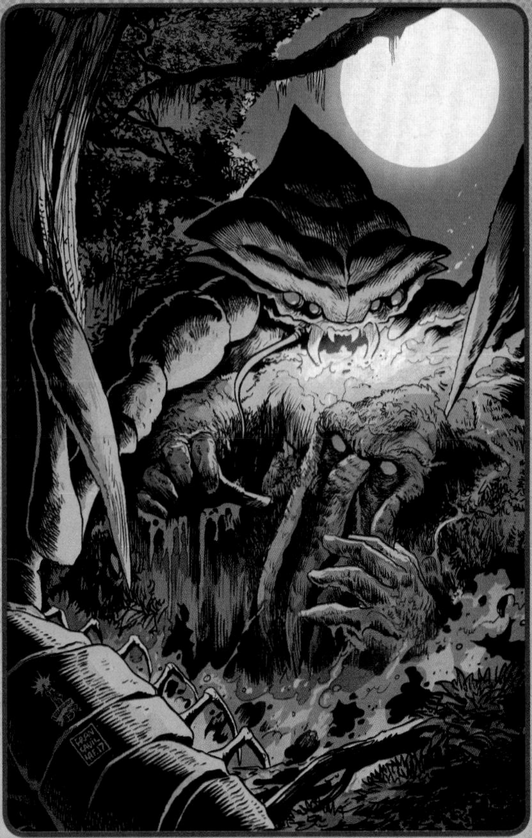

#1 variant by
FRANCESCO FRANCAVILLA

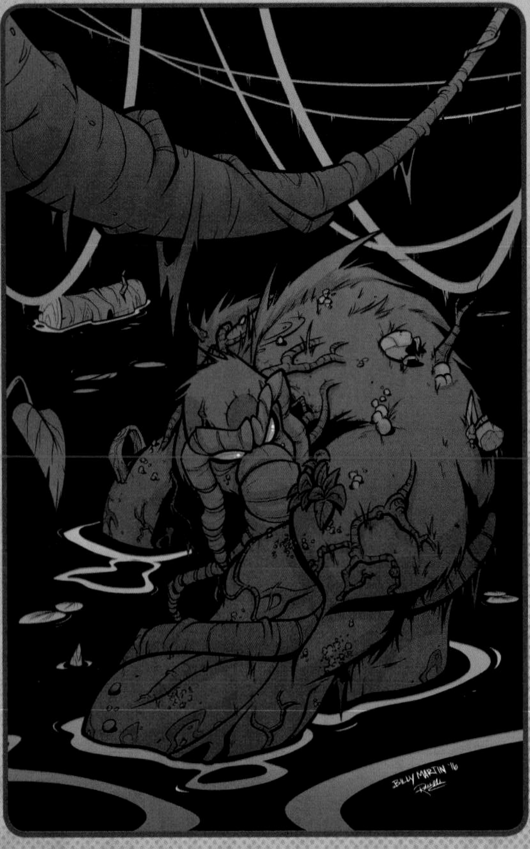

#1 variant by
BILLY MARTIN & RACHELLE ROSENBERG

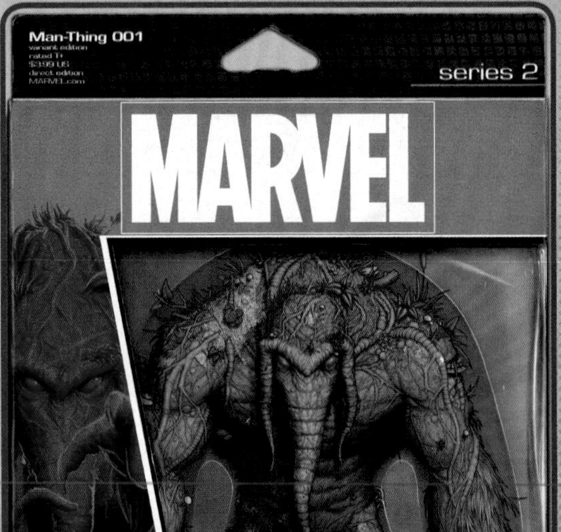
Man-Thing 001
variant edition
rated T+
$3.99 US
direct edition
MARVEL.com
series 2
MARVEL
MAN-THING
MAN-THING
nexus guardian

#1 action figure variant by
JOHN TYLER CHRISTOPHER

THOSE WHO KNOW FEAR... BURN!!

#1 Venomized variant by
BILLY MARTIN & RACHELLE ROSENBERG

#1 variant by
KALMAN ANDRASOFSZKY

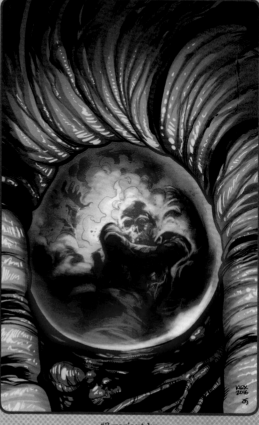

#2 variant by
MIKE DEODATO JR. & FRANK MARTIN

#3 variant by
LEONARD KIRK & FRANK MARTIN

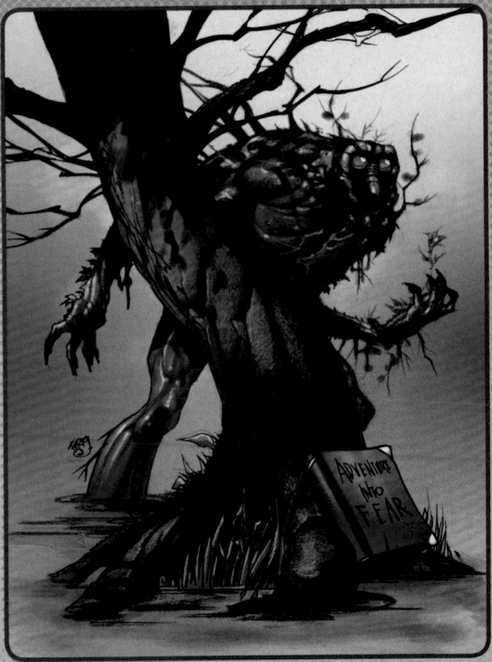
ADVENTURE INTO FEAR

#4 variant by
PASQUAL FERRY & CHRIS SOTOMAYOR

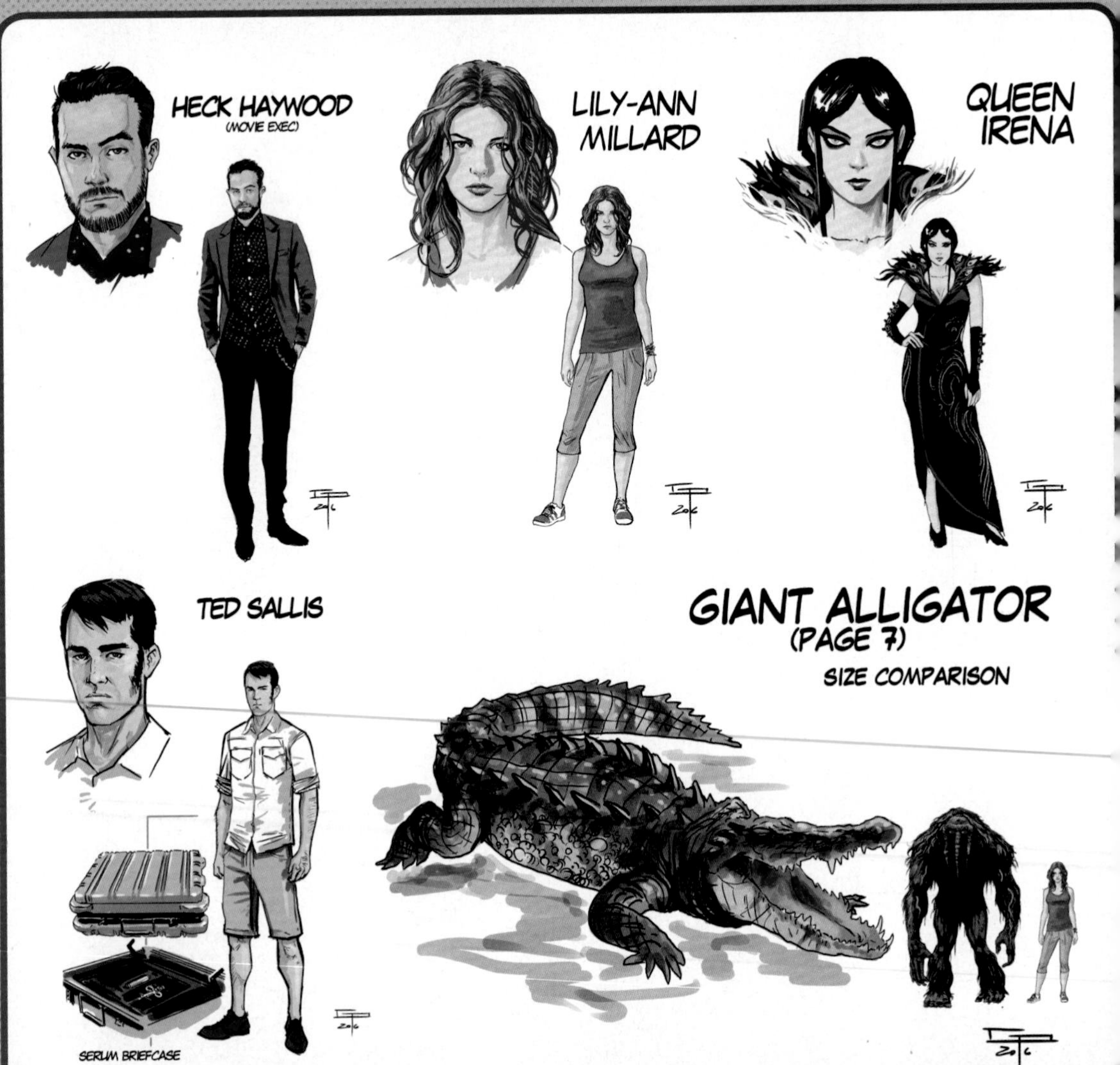
HECK HAYWOOD
(MOVIE EXEC)
LILY-ANN MILLARD
QUEEN IRENA
TED SALLIS
SERUM BRIEFCASE
GIANT ALLIGATOR
(PAGE 7)
SIZE COMPARISON

character designs by **GERMÁN PERALTA**